Building Blocks

4TH EDITION

for Teaching Young Children in Inclusive Settings

by

Susan R. Sandall, Ph.D.
University of Washington
Seattle

Ariane N. Gauvreau, Ph.D., BCBA-D
University of Washington
Seattle

Gail E. Joseph, Ph.D.
University of Washington
Seattle

and

Ilene S. Schwartz, Ph.D., BCBA-D
University of Washington
Seattle

PAUL·H·
BROOKES
PUBLISHING CO. ®

Baltimore • London • Sydney

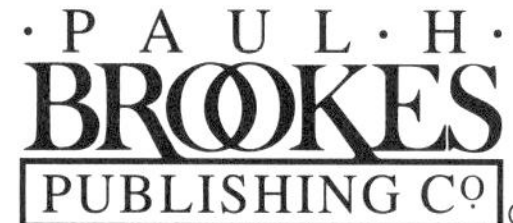

Paul H. Brookes Publishing Co.
Post Office Box 10624
Baltimore, Maryland 21285-0624
USA

www.brookespublishing.com

Typeset by Absolute Service Inc., Baltimore, Maryland.
Manufactured in the United States of America by Sheridan Books, Inc.

All vignettes in this book are composites. Any similarity to actual individuals or circumstances is coincidental, and no implications should be inferred.

Library of Congress Cataloging-in-Publication Data

Names: Sandall, Susan Rebecka, author. | Gauvreau, Ariane N., author. | Joseph, Gail E., author. | Schwartz, Ilene S., author.
Title: Building blocks for teaching young children in inclusive settings / by Susan R. Sandall, Ph.D., University of Washington, Seattle; Ariane N. Gauvreau, Ph.D., University of Washington, Seattle; Gail E. Joseph, Ph.D., University of Washington, Seattle and Ilene S. Schwartz, Ph.D., University of Washington, Seattle.
Description: Fourth edition. | Baltimore, Maryland : Paul H. Brookes Publishing Co., Inc., [2024] | Includes bibliographical references and index.
Identifiers: LCCN 2024000770 (print) | LCCN 2024000771 (ebook) | ISBN 9781681257990 (paperback) | ISBN 9781681258003 (epub) | ISBN 9781681258010 (pdf)
Subjects: LCSH: Children with disabilities—Education (Preschool)—United States. | Children with social disabilities—Education (Preschool)—United States. | Inclusive education—United States. | Individualized education programs—United States. | BISAC: EDUCATION / Inclusive Education | EDUCATION / Special Education / General
Classification: LCC LC4019.2 .S26 2024 (print) | LCC LC4019.2 (ebook) | DDC 371.9—dc23/eng/20240123
LC record available at https://lccn.loc.gov/2024000770
LC ebook record available at https://lccn.loc.gov/2024000771

British Library Cataloguing in Publication data are available from the British Library.

2028   2027   2026   2025   2024
10   9   8   7   6   5   4   3   2   1

Contents

Appendices **213**

About the Online Materials

Purchasers of this book may download, print, and/or photocopy the Appendices and Modules for professional or educational use.

To access the materials that come with this book:

1. Go to the Brookes Publishing Download Hub: http://downloads.brookespublishing.com.

2. Register to create an account (or log in with an existing account).

3. Filter or search for the book title *Building Blocks for Teaching Young Children in Inclusive Settings, Fourth Edition.*

Appendices

A   Quality Classroom Assessment Form
B   Classroom Action Worksheet
C   Child Assessment Worksheet
D   IEP/IFSP Planning Worksheet
E   Child Planning Worksheet
F   Child Activity Matrix
G   Classroom Activity Matrix
H   Staff Matrix
I   Evaluation Worksheet
J   ELO-at-a-Glance
K   Instruction-at-a-Glance
L   Inclusion Collaboration Checklist
M   Clarifying the Schedule Checklist
N   Clarifying the Child's Objective
O   Curriculum Modification Planning Form
P   Curriculum Modifications Checklist
Q   Teaching Episode Checklist
R   Embedded Learning Opportunities Checklist
S   Child-Focused Instruction Strategies Checklist
T   Online Resources

Modules

Module 1: Overview and Getting Started With the Building Blocks Framework
Module 2: Ongoing Child Assessment
Module 3: Planning for the Individual Child
Module 4: Visual Supports: Strategies to Facilitate Access, Participation, and Learning
Module 5: Using the Building Blocks Framework for Math and Science
Module 6: Applying the Building Blocks Framework to Address
    Challenging Behavior
Module 7: Using the Building Blocks Framework for Infants, Toddlers, and
    Their Families

About the Authors

Susan R. Sandall, Ph.D., Professor Emeritus, College of Education, University of Washington, Seattle

Dr. Sandall is professor emeritus at the University of Washington. She directed personnel preparation projects, developed curriculum materials for all age groups, and published materials on educational practices to facilitate optimal outcomes for infants, toddlers, and preschoolers with disabilities. Her scholarly interests are effective instructional practices for young children with disabilities in inclusive settings, the changing roles of teachers of young children, and effective approaches to professional development and knowledge utilization. She was principal investigator of the National Center on Quality Teaching and Learning for the Office of Head Start. Dr. Sandall served on the Division for Early Childhood (DEC) Commission on Recommended Practices and edited publications on the practices. She is on the editorial boards of *Journal of Early Intervention* and *Topics in Early Childhood Special Education.* She received an honorary doctoral degree from Stockholm University.

Ariane N. Gauvreau, Ph.D., BCBA-D, Senior Director of Professional Development, Haring Center for Inclusive Education, University of Washington, Seattle

Dr. Gauvreau is the senior director of professional development at the Haring Center for Inclusive Education at the University of Washington. Dr. Gauvreau has extensive experience as a training facilitator, teaching professor, special education teacher, home visitor, behavioral consultant, and coach. She has developed and facilitated training on early intervention and autism, inclusive education, multi-tiered systems of support, universal design for learning, social-emotional learning, and family-centered practices. She has published many articles on inclusionary practices in early learning and serves on the editorial board for *Young Exceptional Children.* Her professional interests include effective professional development and inclusionary practices for all children and families.

Gail E. Joseph, Ph.D., Bezos Family Professor of Early Learning, College of Education, University of Washington, Seattle

Dr. Joseph is the Bezos Family professor of early learning at the University of Washington. She teaches courses, advises students, provides service, and conducts community-engaged research on topics related to early care and education. Dr. Joseph has been involved in a number of research projects and training and technical assistance activities at the local, state, and national levels related to child care quality, teacher preparation, and promoting children's social-emotional development as well as preventing challenging behavior in early learning settings. She is the founding executive director of Cultivate Learning and was the principal investigator and director of the Head Start Center for Inclusion (Headstartinclusion.org) and co-principal investigator of the National Center for Quality Teaching and Learning funded by the Office of Head Start. At Cultivate Learning, she oversees the work of quality ratings in all licensed child care and state pre-K programs in Washington.

Ilene S. Schwartz, Ph.D., BCBA-D, Professor of Special Education and Director, Haring Center for Inclusive Education, University of Washington, Seattle

Dr. Schwartz is professor of special education and director of the Haring Center for Inclusive Education at the University of Washington. Dr. Schwartz is also the director of project DATA (Developmentally Appropriate Treatment for Autism), a school-based early intervention intensive behavioral intervention program for children with autism. She has an extensive background working with young children with special needs and their families, specifically with young children with autism and related disabilities. Dr. Schwartz is on the faculty of the Applied Behavior Analysis Program at the University of Washington. She is dedicated to creating inclusive schools so that all children, regardless of their background or ability, can attend the school of their choice and receive a high-quality education. Dr. Schwartz has published numerous chapters and articles about effective instructional strategies for children with autism, ethics in applied behavior analysis, and inclusive education.

Foreword

A high-quality early childhood program is, in part,
one that is inclusive, culturally and linguistically responsive,
and provides a sense of belonging for all children and their families.

—U.S. Department of Health and Human Services &
U.S. Department of Education (2023)

While preparing this foreword, I reflected on the complex issues involved in designing high-quality, inclusive early childhood learning environments to meet the needs of each and every child and family. These issues include, but are not limited to, 1) how we prepare personnel with the knowledge, skills, and dispositions to meet each child where they are and design learning experiences that are developmentally appropriate, culturally affirming, and appropriately challenging; 2) how we build systems to support the inclusion and belonging of each child and prohibit the use of exclusionary practices; and 3) how we work across systems to ensure every child has access to high-quality, inclusive settings. I also reflected on the evidence that we, as a field, are not doing a great job of making this vision a reality. This evidence includes the following:

1. We have made almost no progress in the percentage of preschool children who are served in inclusive settings (Barton & Smith, 2015).

2. We continue to suspend/expel preschoolers at high rates, and we disproportionately suspend/expel young children of color and young children with disabilities.

3. Teachers continue to report their most significant training needs are related to supporting children with disabilities and children who engage in persistent, challenging behavior.

Although it is beyond the scope of a book to systematically address these issues, *Building Blocks for Teaching Young Children in Inclusive Settings, Fourth Edition* exemplifies the type of tools that, when used collectively and within supportive systems, have the potential to change the way we provide education to our youngest learners. At the heart of *Building Blocks* is the recognition that young children learn in different ways, have different areas of strength and need, and have varied interests, experiences, and assets. Although the previous editions focused on instruction for children with disabilities, the authors recognized that in inclusive settings, all young children will need varying levels of support at different points in time. While having a "disability" is one reason children might need more support, other children might need different levels of support because they are learning English, they have experienced trauma, or they have never been in a group care setting (to name a few). This led the authors to change the title from *Building Blocks for Teaching Preschoolers with Special Needs* to *Building Blocks for Teaching Young Children in Inclusive Settings* and to describe *Building Blocks* as a multi-tiered system of support (MTSS). These changes help the user understand the need for high-quality universal practices for supporting all children as well as more targeted and intensive practices to meet the needs of small groups of children and, in some cases, individual children. These changes also dispel common misunderstandings, such as the belief that effective instruction and developmentally appropriate practice are somehow inconsistent with one another or that it is not possible to meet the intensive support needs of some children while also providing a high-quality environment for all children.

Although the change in title and alignment with MTSS represent "big picture" changes, the authors have been intentional in ensuring these changes are operationalized by providing concrete supports for programs. The *Building Blocks* framework provides a step-by-step planning process for designing high-quality learning experiences while also delivering increasingly more individualized supports to meet the needs of each and every child in an inclusive classroom. The book also includes practical strategies and ideas that are grounded in a planning process that recognizes the complexity of delivering instruction to all young children in a way that promotes participation, inclusion, and belonging. By including a framework for planning instruction, the book avoids being just a toolbox of good ideas with no understanding of how to use those ideas systematically to affect children's outcomes. The fourth edition expands on these key features by including a chapter on ongoing assessment and instructional decision making; developing new checklists and planning forms; and expanding vignettes, examples, and content. These changes provide more focused information on how to implement the framework AND how to determine if it is working. This edition acknowledges and addresses the complexity of providing instruction in inclusive classrooms and provides guidance on issues that often are barriers to effective instruction, such as strategies for preventing challenging behavior, strategies for minimizing the impact of bias on classroom decisions, and the need for implementation supports. I was excited to see the expansion of information on how to work with coaches to ensure teachers have the support they need to implement practices with fidelity. These changes reflect an acknowledgment that high-quality inclusion is about more than what the teacher is doing in the classroom and places responsibility on program leadership to ensure the necessary supports are in place.

I could not be more excited about the fourth edition. Since the first edition came out, I have consistently turned to *Building Blocks* for practical information to share with teachers and those supporting teachers. The author team has a deep commitment to inclusion that shows in their work. Their understanding of the challenges associated with promoting inclusion and belonging of all children is based on years of experience administering and teaching in early childhood programs, preparing teachers to work with young children with disabilities, conducting research, and building systems of support. The fourth edition reflects this experience as well as their commitment to information that is useful to those who work directly with young children and their families. One of the greatest challenges in our field is bridging the gap between research and practice. *Building Blocks* reflects this unique combination of experience with and commitment to translating research into information that changes the way teachers teach and thus changes outcomes for children.

Mary Louise Hemmeter, Ph.D.
Vanderbilt University

REFERENCE

U.S. Department of Health and Human Services & U.S. Department of Education. (2023). *Policy statement on inclusion of children with disabilities in early childhood programs.* https://www.acf.hhs.gov/sites/default/files/documents/ecd/policy-statement-on-inclusion.pdf

Acknowledgments

What does it mean to provide specially designed instruction in inclusive early childhood settings? What are evidence-based practices and how do they apply to young children with and without disabilities? These are questions that we were asking in 2002 when we wrote the first edition of *Building Blocks for Teaching Preschoolers With Special Needs,* and they are questions that we are still asking today. *Building Blocks* has turned out to be a user-friendly guidebook for students, teachers, child care providers, supervisors, coaches, and professionals in personnel preparation who are interested in helping young children in inclusive early childhood settings succeed. We are delighted with the response *Building Blocks* has received and with the ideas and innovations that people have drawn from our work. We know, however, that our work is not done. We have witnessed dramatic change in the early learning landscape since the work began, yet the teaching and learning challenges facing teachers every day in early childhood classrooms remain the same. Teachers are underpaid, programs are underresourced, and many children arrive at the school door with even greater needs. Many teachers, children, and families are struggling in the aftermath of the pandemic. But the overall hopefulness of early childhood educators is undiminished, and we are proud of how our students and colleagues play an important role in the lives of young children.

The title of the book has changed. *Building Blocks for Teaching Young Children in Inclusive Settings* represents a better understanding of early learning contexts and the practices to support learning for all children. We hope this new edition is valuable and sparks even more innovation and good teaching.

Every book has many authors. Some of these authors are acknowledged publicly, and others may be unaware of the influence they have had on the text. First, we would like to thank those people who have been actively involved in the process. We have been lucky to work with a talented group of co-authors, students, and colleagues throughout the development and field testing of *Building Blocks.* We extend our deep appreciation to previous authors who have moved to new stages of their lives.

The Building Blocks framework grew out of work that was conducted by the Early Childhood Research Institute on Inclusion (ECRII), funded by the U.S. Department of Education. As principal investigator, Sam Odom assembled a multitalented group of investigators who were committed to work together despite distance and methodological boundaries to understand the barriers and facilitators of inclusion for young children with disabilities. We worked together for more than 5 years to collect, analyze, and make sense of a wealth of data about inclusion that parents, teachers, and children shared with us so generously.

To ensure that this study addressed the ethnic and cultural diversity of America's young children, a group of researchers in different regions of the country collaborated on its development. The investigators included Paula Beckman, Marci Hanson, Eva M. Horn, Joan Lieber, Jules Marquart, and Ruth A. Wolery. We thank them for their spirit of inquiry and their collaboration.

We have also been very fortunate to have many colleagues, teachers, and mentors whose influence can easily be seen in the Building Blocks framework. In previous editions, we acknowledged some of these people by name. To those colleagues and to those who have strengthened our work in recent years, we extend our sincere thanks. We add a special thank you to the children, families, teachers, and colleagues at the Haring Center and Cultivate Learning at the University of Washington. You continue to inspire us.

We sincerely thank our friend and colleague Mary Louise Hemmeter, Vanderbilt University, for writing the forewords for all four editions. Her insights set the tone for this volume in just the right way.

We thank our families for their enduring support and patience.

Finally, a number of people helped us bring this edition to fruition. They include Matthew Zabel at Cultivate Learning and Melissa Solarz and Heather Shrestha at Paul H. Brookes Publishing Co.

Using the Building Blocks Framework

The Building Blocks framework is the basis for planning for and providing individualized support and instruction for children with identified disabilities, developmental delays, and diverse abilities in their early learning programs. The framework grew out of extensive experience with teachers attempting to address the wide variety of children's learning needs within active, busy classrooms, including child care centers and homes. The Building Blocks framework also grew from our experience as researchers with the Early Childhood Research Institute on Inclusion.

In this section, we describe the Building Blocks framework and provide an overview of the evidence that informs the essential components of the framework. The foundation for all children is participation in a quality early childhood program. Key ingredients for a quality early childhood program include promotion of children's active engagement, participation, and learning. Quality programs also recognize and support the importance of relationships. There are many important relationships to consider in early learning programs, including relationships among children, teachers' relationships with children, family partnerships, and collaboration among colleagues. Quality programs create a caring environment. Nonetheless, for some children or for some of their learning needs, this quality foundation, while necessary, is not sufficient. The Building Blocks framework offers levels of support that differ in intensity and specificity to help teachers and teams address children's learning needs. For many needs, curriculum modifications and adaptations will provide appropriate levels of support. If modifications alone are not effective in helping children accomplish their learning objectives, then teachers and teams can use specially designed instruction. Such instruction can be embedded in learning opportunities that occur in typical activities and routines in the classroom, home, and community. Specially designed instruction can also occur more intensely, which we call child-focused instruction. Two more components are necessary to make the framework effective. One of these components is ongoing data collection to monitor individual children's progress and to make instructional decisions. The other essential component is collaboration. Collaboration is at the heart of effective inclusive programs to ensure that engagement, participation, learning, and belonging occur for all children and their families. The first four chapters of the book will give you, the reader, an understanding of the Building Blocks framework and will outline the steps so that you can use the framework in your program.

Chapter 1

Introduction

Building Blocks for Teaching Young Children in Inclusive Settings, Fourth Edition, describes examples of educational practices that support and enhance the inclusion of young children with identified disabilities, developmental delays, and diverse abilities in community-based classrooms and early learning programs. It is designed for two primary audiences. First, teachers, caregivers, and other team members who work in community-based programs that include children with diverse abilities will find the book useful for their planning and teaching. Second, itinerant or consulting teachers and coaches will find the book useful in their work with teachers in the community.

This book contains the Building Blocks framework—a set of educational practices designed to help teachers do a more effective job of including and teaching young children with diverse abilities in early childhood classrooms and programs. It provides teachers with a variety of methods and strategies to ensure that children learn important skills in their early learning environments. Teachers can use these practices to complement their current curriculum. For example, these practices fit nicely with widely used curricula, such as the Creative Curriculum (Teaching Strategies, 2022), the HighScope Curriculum (HighScope, 2021), and the *Assessment, Evaluation, and Programming System (AEPS) for Infants and Children, Third Edition* (Bricker et al., 2022a), and support individualization within the curriculum.

The Building Blocks framework is based on research on early childhood inclusion and effective early educational practices (Barton & Smith, 2015a, 2015b; Guralnick & Bruder, 2016; Odom, 2001; Odom et al., 2011). For all children, but especially for children with identified disabilities, developmental delays, and diverse abilities, teachers and teams should use educational methods and strategies that match each child's needs. The methods and strategies vary in terms of intensity and specificity. The Building Blocks framework is designed to help teams select the appropriate level of assistance for children. The theoretical and empirical evidence supporting the Building Blocks framework is described in Chapter 2.

IMPORTANT TERMS

The Building Blocks framework uses a vocabulary that may already be familiar to many teachers; however, it is important to clarify what these terms mean in the context of the framework. This section defines several important terms that are used throughout the book.

Inclusion

Inclusion is often defined as the active participation of young children with and without disabilities in the same classroom (e.g., Head Start, child care, preschool) and in community settings. But it is more than that. Inclusion is about ensuring that all children, staff, and families who participate in a program feel supported in that program. In other words, children, teachers, and families feel that they belong to the program and its community. A less traditional way of defining inclusion is to say that inclusion is the celebration of diversity put into action. An inclusive program celebrates what every individual brings to that program and provides each with the support to be a successful member of that program. Inclusion is defined in a joint statement by the Division for Early Childhood (DEC) and the National Association for the Education of Young Children (NAEYC):

> Early childhood inclusion embodies the values, policies, and practices that support the right of every infant and young child and his or her family, regardless of ability, to participate in a broad range of activities and contexts as full members of families, communities, and society. The desired results of inclusive experiences for children with and without disabilities and their families include a sense of belonging and membership, positive social relationships and friendships, and development and learning to reach their full potential. The defining features of inclusion that can be used to identify high quality early childhood programs and services are access, participation, and supports. (2009, p. 1)

Children With Identified Disabilities, Developmental Delays, and Diverse Abilities

The term *children with identified disabilities and developmental delays* refers to children who are eligible for special education services and who have individualized education programs (IEPs) or individualized family service plans (IFSPs). The Building Blocks framework is also useful for children with *diverse abilities*, which are characteristics and needs related to varied factors such as language, culture, or approaches to learning. These children may need more individualized support or attention from their teachers. Throughout the book, we use people-first language. We believe it is important to emphasize that children with disabilities and/or diverse abilities are children first and should not be defined by a diagnosis.

Dual Language Learners

Children who are dual language learners (DLLs) are children who have a home language other than English and are learning two or more languages at the same time or learning a second language while continuing to develop their first language. Because children may be learning more than two languages simultaneously, the term multilanguage learner is also used. Research indicates that learning more than one language from an early age can have wide-ranging benefits and that early childhood programs should provide DLLs with the individualized supports that may be needed.

Individualized Education Program

An IEP is a document prepared for any student, ages 3 to 21, who is eligible for special education services. IEPs are required by the Individuals with Disabilities Education Improvement Act (IDEA) of 2004 (PL 108-446). Each IEP states 1) the child's present level of educational performance, 2) the child's annual goals and short-term objectives, 3) the special education and related services to be provided, 4) the extent to which the child will participate in the general education program, 5) the way in which the child's progress will be measured, and 6) the date of initiation and projected duration of services. The IEP also contains a plan for making the transition from high school to adulthood no later than age 16.

Individualized Family Service Plan

An IFSP is a document developed by the family and the team for a child age birth to 3 years who is eligible for early intervention (EI) under Part C of IDEA. Each plan includes the following: 1) the child's present level of development; 2) a statement of the family's resources, priorities, and concerns; 3) the planned child and family outcomes; 4) the specific EI services to meet the outcomes; 5) a statement regarding natural environments; 6) the length, duration, frequency, intensity, and delivery method for the services; 7) the name of the service coordinator; and 8) the steps toward transition at age 3.

Community-Based Classrooms

The term *community-based classrooms* refers to the types of early childhood classroom programs children typically attend. These include child care centers and homes, public school programs, Head Start programs, state and city prekindergarten (pre-K) programs, and private and cooperative preschools. Community-based classrooms do not include specialty clinics, laboratory classrooms, or other specialized schools. The term *natural environments* is found in Part C of IDEA. It refers to places and activities where children without disabilities spend time. There is an expectation that Part C EI services will take place in natural environments, such as the home and child care settings.

Head Start

Head Start is a federally funded, comprehensive early childhood program that serves children from families with low income. Early Head Start programs serve infants and toddlers under age 3, their families, and pregnant women. Head Start requires that at least 10% of their enrollment include children with disabilities.

Related Services

Related services include physical, occupational, and speech therapy; psychological services; and other services that a child who is eligible for IDEA services may require to receive the greatest benefit from their education. Such services are provided by or under the supervision of certified or licensed individuals (e.g., speech-language therapist, school psychologist).

Team

Special education, EI, and related services are provided by a team. The *team* consists of family members and professionals who work together to plan and implement the child's educational program. Collaboration is essential for effective team functioning.

Early Childhood Education

In this book, *early childhood education* (ECE) refers to educational programs and activities for young children prior to their formal school entry. The ECE teacher is an individual with training and preparation in child development and other content areas related to the education of young children. This individual may have certification in general ECE.

Early Childhood Special Education

In this book, *early childhood special education* (ECSE) refers to educational programs, activities, and services for children who are eligible for IDEA services who are age 3 to 6 years. ECSE is guided by the requirements of federal and state policies and by research on effective educational practices. The ECSE teacher has more specialized training and preparation for working with young children with identified disabilities, developmental delays, and diverse abilities. This person may work directly with children (e.g., an itinerant teacher) or in a consulting role. A special certification or endorsement is often required.

Early Intervention

Early intervention (EI) refers to services and supports for children with established conditions or developmental delays and, in some cases, children at risk who are under age 3 and their families. EI is guided by federal (Part C of IDEA) and state policies as well as research evidence. EI professionals include teachers and therapists. Services and supports occur in a variety of settings with a preference for natural environments.

Universal Design for Learning

The *universal design for learning (UDL)* approach guides teachers in designing learning environments from the very beginning for the widest diversity of learners. UDL encompasses the following three principles: 1) multiple means of representation to give learners a variety of ways to gain access to information and content, 2) multiple means of engagement to gain and maintain learners' interest, and 3) multiple means of expression to provide learners with a variety of ways to demonstrate what they know (Center for Applied Special Technology [CAST], 2018).

Specially Designed Instruction

Specially designed instruction is essentially what special education is all about. Specially designed instruction includes organized, planned, and individualized instructional activities needed by a child to accomplish IEP goals or IFSP outcomes and to help the child gain access to the general education curriculum. Specially designed instruction may include changes or adaptations to the content, methodology, or delivery of instruction to meet the child's unique needs.

Culturally Responsive Teaching

Culturally responsive teaching is an instructional approach that uses the cultural knowledge, prior experiences, frames of reference, and performance styles of ethnically diverse children to make learning experiences more relevant and effective (Gay, 2010; NAEYC, 2019). A related term is *culturally sustaining practices*, which are practices that center more specifically on nurturing and expanding historically devalued cultures to promote linguistic, literate, and cultural pluralism (Paris & Alim, 2017).

Tiered Supports

Education has adopted a promotion, prevention, and intervention approach from the field of public health. Such a tiered approach helps to organize teaching and learning for all children in ways that promote development and learning through a high-quality program and research-based curriculum (tier 1), deploy effective practices to prevent (pre-) academic and behavioral problems (tier 2), and provide intensive, individualized intervention practices if needed for children who struggle (tier 3). Universal screening and progress monitoring and collaborative problem solving are key components as well. Often referred to as the multi-tiered systems of support (MTSS) framework, this is a way to provide high-quality teaching and responsive caregiving through the delivery of differentiated support for all young children (DEC, 2021). Response to intervention (RTI) and positive behavioral interventions and supports (PBIS) are examples. Building Blocks is also an example of an MTSS in early childhood (Sandall & Schwartz, 2013).

Transition

Transition refers to the events, activities, and processes associated with key changes between environments and programs during the early childhood years and the practices that support the adjustment of the child and family to the new setting (DEC, 2014). Young children and families experience several transitions including from hospital to home, from home to EI, from EI to preschool, and from preschool into formal schooling. Some young children who are dually enrolled (e.g., in child care and in special services) may also experience numerous transitions from program to program.

THE CHILDREN

The stories of five children and their teachers enrich the descriptions of educational practices in this book:

Nhan is a 4-year-old boy who receives special education services because of delays in cognitive, language, and social skills. He attends a child care center 5 days a week from 7:30 a.m. to 6 p.m. His parents speak both English and Vietnamese. Both parents work outside their home. Nhan and his brother and sister were cared for at home by their Vietnamese-speaking grandmother until Nhan was 2 years old. He then began attending the child care center. His child care teachers became concerned about his slow progress and recommended to his parents that he be evaluated. He was identified as being eligible for special education and related services when he was 3 years old. Nhan and his family also received a comprehensive medical evaluation, and he was found to have a rare genetic disorder. Nhan continues to attend the child care center, and the school district provides an itinerant ECSE teacher and a speech-language therapist who visit Nhan in his child care classroom once a week. The district also provides a DLL consultant who provides services on request. There is one other child in the classroom who has an IEP, and another teacher comes to visit that child. Nhan's child care teachers use the Creative Curriculum (Teaching Strategies, 2022).

Tina is a 4-year-old girl with a medical diagnosis of Down syndrome and mild to moderate delays in most areas of development. Tina has been enrolled in special programs since she was 2 months old. When she was an infant, home visitors came to her home to provide services. As a toddler, she went to a program at a child development clinic. When she turned 3 years old, she went to a preschool class at a public school. This year, her mother transferred her to the Head Start classroom at the neighborhood center. This is the same program that her older brothers attended. There is one other child in Tina's classroom who has an IEP. An ECSE teacher and a speech-language therapist visit the classroom and work with the two children and the teachers once a week. A social worker provides family services for all families in the program. Tina's teacher, Dolores, has taught in Head Start for several years. All of the classrooms and teachers in this program use the HighScope Curriculum (HighScope, 2021).

Samisha is a 5-year-old girl with a medical diagnosis of cerebral palsy. She lives with her parents, grandmother, and three older siblings. She is learning to use a walker and, when motivated, can move quite quickly. In the classroom, she tends to move around by scooting on the floor. Samisha is very social, and she loves to be the center of attention. Her language skills are slightly delayed, and she does not demonstrate any cognitive delays. Although she is very interested in other children in her class, she is not very successful in peer interactions. She has a difficult time taking turns and sharing materials. She has good dramatic play skills when she suggests the story but has trouble changing her behavior to conform with a plan suggested by another child. Samisha attends a public school pre-K classroom that is team taught by ECE and ECSE teachers, Gia and David. She receives physical therapy once per week in the classroom. The classroom is composed of 15 children, six of whom qualify for special education services and have IEPs. The teachers use the Creative Curriculum supplemented with their vast collection of ECE activity books as resources.

Drew is a 3-year-old boy who lives with his parents and two brothers, one older and one younger. At 30 months, Drew was diagnosed with autism spectrum disorder at the multidisciplinary clinic at the regional children's hospital. His cognitive skills are near age-appropriate levels, but he has significant delays in social and communication skills. He has an extensive vocabulary and can use sentences to express wants and needs, but he rarely comments or engages in social conversation. Drew can play independently for long periods of time with a few preferred toys. His favorites are trains, Disney figurines, and markers. He has little interest in and few skills with other materials. Some people consider his play to be repetitive or stereotypical. Drew is also not very interested in his brothers or the other children in his classroom. He is very attached to his mother, however, and seeks her out for comfort and when he wants something.

In addition, Drew engages in behaviors that challenge his teachers and other adults, such as yelling, physical aggression, and running away. He has a very difficult time following even simple adult directions and will often start to yell and flail if anyone says "no" to him. Drew attends an integrated preschool classroom in a public school and an extended day program specifically designed for children with autism at the same school. The head teachers in both classrooms are dually certified in ECE and ECSE. There are 15 children in Drew's preschool class; nine children have identified disabilities and have IEPs. The classroom curriculum is the AEPS for Infants and Children. The extended day program has eight students with autism and four staff members and implements The Project DATA Model (Schwartz et al., 2017). Between the two programs, Drew is at school for 25 hours a week.

Mateo is an almost 2-year-old boy whose family has a complicated school and work schedule. He is enrolled in a family child care home with six other children who range in age from a few months to 5 years, with a few older children joining for after-school care. The lead teacher and owner, Dara, has operated her child care home for over 10 years. Mateo's parents, along with Dara, noticed that he was not meeting his early developmental milestones and alerted his pediatrician before his first birthday. He was then referred to the county's EI program and became eligible for services. Although Mateo's global developmental delay does not have a name, he has low muscle tone and does not yet walk. He is attentive to adults and peers but rarely initiates interactions. He uses a few gestures and vocalizations to communicate. Mateo's mother drops him off early in the morning, and his dad picks him up in the late afternoon. The visiting early interventionist, Kate, visits Mateo weekly, alternating between his family child care home one week and his home the next week. Mateo also sees a physical therapist at the EI center once a month. Mateo's older sister receives after-school care at Dara's home. Dara draws from a variety of curricula, state standards, and her own knowledge and experience to create learning activities for the children.

You will learn more about Nhan, Tina, Samisha, Drew, Mateo, their teachers, and their classmates as you use this book. Their stories and the practices described in the book are offered to provide you with support, guidance, and practical suggestions for including children with identified disabilities and other individualized support needs in your early learning program, which can enhance the development and learning of all young children.

In the following chapters, you will learn more about the tiers or levels of support that make up the Building Blocks framework. You will learn strategies for identifying specific educational practices to address the interests and needs of individual children. In addition, you will learn how to implement the Building Blocks framework in order to help each and every child participate, learn, and thrive in their early learning program. A set of seven professional development modules accompanies the book and provides even more information to extend and use the Building Blocks framework.

Chapter 2

Evidence-Based Practice and the Building Blocks Framework

Evidence, according to the *Oxford Dictionary of Current English, Fourth Edition* (Soanes, 2006), is information indicating whether something is true or valid. Those involved in education and early learning depend on evidence to help determine which interventions will best promote children's optimal development and learning. Although the use of evidence-based practices has been a cornerstone of special education for many years, use of evidence-based, or scientifically based, intervention programs in education is mandated by law for general education and special education. The Elementary and Secondary Education Act (PL 89-10) has consistently directed teachers to implement interventions grounded in research. The No Child Left Behind Act of 2001 (PL 107-110) required that educational practices must be "scientifically based." The reauthorization of the Individuals with Disabilities Education Act (IDEA) (PL 108-446) states that services should be based to the extent possible on peer-reviewed research. More recently, the Every Student Succeeds Act (ESSA) (PL 114-95) continues the commitment to evidence-based practice and encourages more local school responsibility for continuous improvement. Further, ESSA requires that *all* students be taught to high academic standards. The idea behind using evidence-based programs in education is really common sense. That is, educators want to know what works best to help children learn and then use only the most effective practices and interventions. Sometimes, however, determining which practices and interventions are evidence based is not so easy. Traditionally, research to identify evidence-based practices has involved large studies in which one group of randomly assigned participants receives the special or experimental intervention and a very similar group of randomly assigned participants receives the usual or comparison intervention. One of the problems with this approach to determining the scientific merit of an intervention is that it relies on looking at results for the "average" participant. This type of study offers information about how *groups* of participants on average respond to an intervention rather than information about the effects of the intervention on one specific child who comes from one specific family with one specific cultural and linguistic history and who is enrolled in one specific early learning center.

Although traditional group experimental research is helpful in identifying some effective intervention approaches, it is not the only strategy to determine the effectiveness of interventions for young children. Another strategy is to conduct smaller studies, using single-subject, mixed methods, or other research methodologies, to evaluate the components of the intervention. This is the approach we used with the Building Blocks framework. Building Blocks, as a package, has not been compared with other comprehensive approaches to early childhood inclusion or to comprehensive early childhood curricula. Rather, we have based each of the four building blocks that make up the framework (high-quality early childhood programs, curriculum modifications, embedded learning opportunities, and child-focused instructional strategies) on existing research as well as on our own studies (Odom, 2001) of individual components of the framework.

Understanding the evidence or research support for the specific instructional practices used is an important component of being an effective early childhood educator. It is even more important to know how to use this information to match instructional programs and practices to the needs of individual children. To truly be a data- or evidence-based teacher, you need to go beyond the research literature and collect information about the learning of your own students and use these data to make decisions about what to teach, how to teach, and where to teach.

In this chapter, we describe the Building Blocks framework. You will become familiar with the four blocks as well as with assessments for progress monitoring and data-based decision making and collaboration—essentials for using the Building Blocks framework. Along the way, we include evidence that supports our approach for helping early childhood teachers provide effective, appropriate intervention for young children. See Chapter 9 on implementation for even more guidance using the framework in your program or classroom.

THE BUILDING BLOCKS FRAMEWORK

The Building Blocks framework evolved from many research activities and experiences in a variety of early learning settings including classrooms, child care programs, play groups, and homes. The framework is guided by the goals of successful inclusion and improved outcomes for young children with identified disabilities, developmental delays, and diverse abilities in community-based programs. Using this framework, teachers can help all their students participate, learn, and thrive in their classrooms, homes, and communities.

What does "improved outcomes for young children" mean? An outcome is the result or consequence of the supports and services put in place for young children. A valued or meaningful outcome means that a child has received a benefit that improves their functioning in everyday life. Federal programs for young children with disabilities (Part C and Part B, Section 619 of IDEA 2004) are expected to document children's progress toward three outcomes, according to the Office of Special Education Programs (OSEP) of the U.S. Department of Education:

- Positive social-emotional skills (including social relationships)

- Acquisition and use of knowledge and skills (including early language, communication, and early literacy)

- Use of appropriate behavior to meet needs

Global outcomes, including improved quality of life (Schwartz & Kelly, 2021), are also important, in addition to the individual goals and objectives that appear on children's IEPs or IFSPs. Also, children enrolled in Head Start are expected to make progress toward indicators included in the Head Start Early Learning Outcomes Framework (U.S. Department of Health and Human Services, 2015). In addition, most states have early learning standards that define the desired outcomes and content of young children's education (https://qualitycompendium.org).

To accomplish valued or meaningful outcomes for individual children, teachers must match an individual child's goals and objectives with appropriate teaching methods and materials, decide what amount of help or assistance the child needs, assist, and determine whether the assistance helped. Fortunately, people (e.g., therapists and other specialists) are available to help the teacher and family. Collaboration and teamwork involving quality interactions, relationships, and collective responsibility are essential.

In addition, the successful inclusion of young children assumes that the early childhood settings in which the framework will be implemented are already of high quality—places where children are nurtured and their developmental and learning needs are met. The first step in using the Building Blocks framework is to assess what is currently happening in the early learning setting using the Quality Classroom Assessment Form (see Figure 4.1 in Chapter 4), that is, whether the basic features of a high-quality early childhood program are already in place. *Assessment* is the process of gathering information to make decisions. Assessment of the early learning setting recognizes the influence of the environment on children's behavior. By assessing the classroom or other setting, the education team can determine the extent to which that environment is likely to facilitate children's development and learning. If the assessment reveals that important factors are not present or are not optimal, the team can plan changes in the environment.

Second, the education team considers children's individual goals and objectives. Using an activity matrix is an easy way to consider the individual child's learning objectives when planning activities and routines (see Chapter 4 for more details and examples of activity matrices).

Third, the education team plans for those children who have IEPs/IFSPs or who have difficulty participating in the activities and routines. Each child should have an individualized plan that considers their particular strengths, interests, and needs. Planning for a child who has disabilities, delays, or diverse abilities requires thoughtful teamwork. It may also require adaptations to the usual curriculum or more planned opportunities for the child to learn and practice new skills and behaviors.

Figure 2.1 depicts the Building Blocks framework. There are four key components to the Building Blocks framework. The foundation—a high-quality early childhood program—is important for all children. The remaining blocks—curriculum modifications

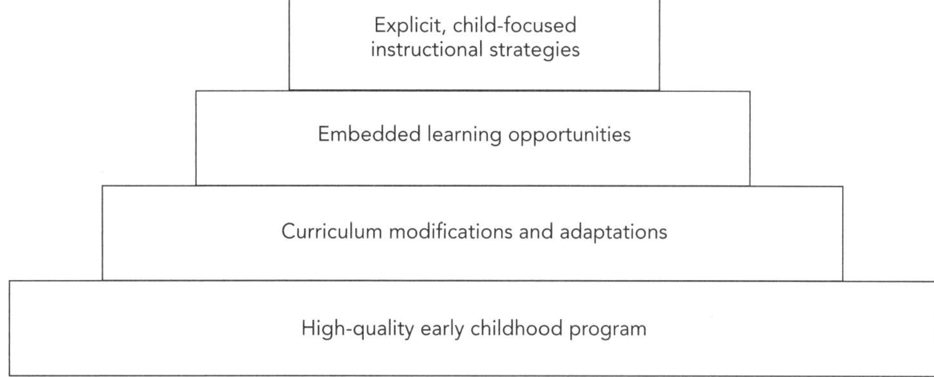

Figure 2.1. The Building Blocks framework.

and adaptations; embedded learning opportunities; and explicit, child-focused instructional strategies—represent educational practices that may be appropriate for some children for some of their learning objectives. The framework also indicates that as the blocks become smaller, the intensity and specificity of the practices increase.

The following sections describe each of the Building Block components in more detail. Each section is followed by the evidence base that underlies the component discussed.

HIGH-QUALITY EARLY CHILDHOOD PROGRAMS

A high-quality early childhood program meets principles of developmentally appropriate practices. Those practices are based on current knowledge about child development and learning; the strengths, interests, and needs of each child in the group; and the social and cultural contexts in which the children live (NAEYC, 2022). High-quality early childhood programs and developmentally appropriate practices are described in detail in a variety of resources (e.g., Bredekamp & Joseph, 2024; Brillante et al., 2023; Grisham-Brown & Hemmeter, 2017). Research and experience have uncovered some necessary components of a developmentally appropriate learning environment:

- Engaging interactions

- A responsive and predictable environment

- Many opportunities for learning

- Intentional teaching

- Developmentally and culturally appropriate materials, activities, and interactions

- Safe, hygienic practices

- Appropriate levels of child guidance

- Meaningful involvement for families

In other words, a developmentally appropriate environment means a caring community for all learners. These features are necessary, but they may not be sufficient to meet the unique needs of young children with identified disabilities, developmental delays, and diverse abilities. There are many ways teachers can adjust their curricula to include all children; these will be discussed later in this chapter. Note that we use the word *teacher* in its broadest sense and may refer to a classroom teacher or assistant, child care provider, home visitor, or other educator.

EVIDENCE BASE FOR A HIGH-QUALITY CLASSROOM

Several large national studies show that high-quality early learning programs result in better outcomes for children, both immediately and in the long term. Some of these studies were initiated many decades ago and have been following their participants for a long time. For example, the Abecedarian Project (Ramey et al., 2000) was conducted in North Carolina between 1972 and 1977 with children from low-income homes who were enrolled in a high-quality early learning program from infancy through age 5. Children who participated in this experimental early learning program tested higher on cognitive assessments on every test opportunity from preschool through age 21. In addition, the students who participated in the experimental preschool had positive lifelong effects. These students were less likely to be enrolled in special education, more likely to attend college, more likely to own their own home, and less likely to spend time in jail.

The Perry Preschool Project (HighScope Educational Research Foundation) was conducted in Ypsilanti, Michigan, in the 1960s and had the same overall goal as the

Abecedarian Project—to examine the short- and long-term effects of high-quality early learning environments on children living in poverty. The Perry Preschool Project yielded positive effects (Berrueta-Clement et al., 1984; Weikart et al., 1978). The children who participated in the intervention preschools scored better on subsequent cognitive testing than children in the same community who did not have access to the high-quality preschools. The results at the age 27 follow-up are also impressive (Schweinhart et al., 1993). Participants in the Perry Preschool study had better jobs, earned more money, were less likely to be receiving assistance from social service agencies, and were less likely to have been arrested.

Another study reinforced the finding that quality in early education matters. The Study of Cost, Quality, and Child Outcomes in Child Care Centers (Cost, Quality, and Child Outcomes Study Team, 1995) was conducted in the 1990s to examine the relationship between the quality of early learning programs and children's subsequent school performance. Researchers found that children who attended higher-quality child care programs performed better in school through kindergarten and that some of these differences were maintained until at least the second grade (Peisner-Feinberg et al., 1999). They also found that children who were at risk for school failure (e.g., students who lived in poverty) were more adversely affected by low-quality preschool programs and received greater benefit from higher-quality programs. Other studies in the early 2000s have also demonstrated that higher-quality early childhood programs can enhance early learning and development for all children (e.g., Barnett et al., 2007; Yazejian et al., 2020; Yoshikawa et al., 2013).

These findings offer convincing evidence that quality in early learning programs matters. Deeper analyses indicate that instructional content, teaching practices, and active engagement in learning opportunities are critical (e.g., Burchinal, 2018). In recent years, new, large-scale public early childhood programs have been launched by states and cities. Federal, state, and local funding contribute to efforts to build high-quality early learning systems and support ongoing evaluation of those efforts. A high-quality early learning program is the foundation of the Building Blocks framework. Extra supports for children with unique or complex learning needs are less effective if they are put into place in a setting that does not offer high-quality programming for all children.

CURRICULUM MODIFICATIONS

A *curriculum modification* is a change made to the existing activities, routines, or materials to achieve or maximize a child's participation. Teachers and others on the team can make intentional modifications, adaptations, and accommodations to activities, routines, and learning areas to include children with disabilities, delays, and diverse abilities, to ensure access, and to enhance participation. By increasing the child's participation and their playful interactions with toys and peers, the teacher can help the child take advantage of these opportunities to develop and learn. Of course, if the child is not able to learn through increased participation, the teacher must provide even more help. Chapter 5 provides more information on and many examples of curriculum modifications.

Think about the five children described in Chapter 1: Nhan, Tina, Samisha, Drew, and Mateo. All of their teachers modify the curriculum to address some of the children's individual learning objectives. For example, Nhan has a picture schedule to help him remember the daily schedule of events at his child care center. Tina takes a picture or toy with her to recall time so she has something to talk about. Samisha has a large block placed under her feet when sitting at the table to help her sit with better stability. Drew has his name written on his carpet square so he knows where to sit at circle time. And at Mateo's family child care, the staff put a container with his favorite small toys in the sensory table to encourage him to put them in and take them out.

EVIDENCE BASE FOR CURRICULUM MODIFICATIONS AND ADAPTATIONS

There is a good deal of research on what constitutes a well-designed early childhood environment (see Catalino & Meyer, 2016; Hamre & Pianta, 2005; Hemmeter et al., 2021; and Schwartz et al., 2002, for reviews). Use of this evidence base along with the principles of UDL guides teachers and their teams to create learning environments that welcome every child and family and plan for full and equitable access. Many of the modifications described in our framework help to ensure access for every child. Further, additional individual adjustments may be necessary to meet the needs of individual children.

Early childhood teachers view modifications and adjustments to classroom activities and materials as acceptable and feasible. In our own work at the Early Childhood Research Institute on Inclusion, we conducted group interviews with experienced teachers and therapists to identify specific types of modifications (Odom, 2001). These interviews, along with our review of the literature (see Sandall et al., 2016), resulted in the eight categories of modifications described in Chapter 5. Trivette and colleagues (2010) also completed a systematic literature review of various adaptations (e.g., changes to the environment, materials, and/or activities). Adaptations resulted in positive change to targeted behaviors including improved communication; improved cognitive, social, and motor behaviors; and increased child participation. Visual supports, such as photographs and pictures, are perhaps the most frequently researched modification. Use of visual supports is recommended practice for individuals with autism as well as young children with disabilities and delays (Gauvreau & Schwartz, 2013; Wong et al., 2015).

EMBEDDED LEARNING OPPORTUNITIES

Teachers can increase or enhance children's learning by embedding or integrating planned opportunities within the existing activities and routines. These planned opportunities are called *embedded learning opportunities* (ELOs). Teachers identify the opportunities most salient to the individualized learning objectives for a child and take advantage of the child's interests by embedding short, systematic instructional interactions or teaching episodes into the ongoing activities and routines. The teacher plans what to say and do and what materials to use within these interactions. These planned interactions or episodes occur often enough to enhance the child's learning. ELOs are both teaching and learning opportunities.

All the children in this book have some of their learning objectives met through ELOs. Nhan gets planned practice at asking simple questions during arrival and snack times. Tina works on sorting by size in the dramatic play area with dishes and at the manipulatives area with the building toys. Samisha works on following the rules in a game by playing games such as Lotto and Candy Land at the games table during free-choice time. Drew gets additional learning opportunities to increase his play skills (using building toys) during free-choice time and small-group time. Mateo gets planned opportunities to use words during diapering, eating, and arrival/departure routines.

The key characteristic of ELOs is that the instructional interaction is planned and embedded, as naturally as possible, within activities or routines that occur in classrooms, child care settings, or at home. Planning is also required so that the instructional interaction is repeated; the child must receive sufficient opportunities to learn. The effectiveness of the instructional interaction is evaluated and adjusted if necessary. That is, the teacher collects data to check on the child's progress to find out if the instruction has made a difference. One distinction between ELOs and curriculum modifications is that with ELOs, the individualized objective for the child may be different from, or more specific than, the general goal of the activity or routine. For more information on and examples of ELOs, see Chapter 6.

EVIDENCE BASE FOR EMBEDDED LEARNING OPPORTUNITIES

A strong evidence base supports the use of ELOs. Snyder and colleagues (2015) conducted a systematic review of the literature of this naturalistic instructional practice, a practice that goes by a variety of names including embedded learning opportunities, incidental teaching, activity-based instruction, routines-based teaching, embedded instruction, and natural developmental behavioral interventions. Hart and Risley's (1975) work on incidental teaching had an important influence on the development of this practice. Their work, much of which was conducted in Head Start classrooms, showed that children learned more complex language when their teachers systematically embedded teaching interactions into classroom routines. Effectiveness is maximized by embedding and distributing instruction throughout activities and routines (Schreibman et al., 2015).

The Snyder review, as well as other reviews by Gulbou and colleagues (2023), Hepting and Goldstein (1996), and Horn and Banerjee (2009), found that embedded instruction is an effective way to teach individualized skills across curricular domains. Embedded instruction is a recommended practice in early childhood (DEC, 2014). A variety of specific instructional practices are used, with most employing prompt and prompt fading procedures and reinforcement techniques (e.g., Daugherty et al., 2001; McBride & Schwartz, 2003). Some studies also found improved generalization (e.g., Wolery et al., 2002). This means that children can demonstrate the newly learned skill across a variety of settings. Teachers view embedded instruction favorably (e.g., Horn et al., 2000). In addition, professional development helps beginning and experienced teachers use embedded instruction (e.g., Phillips & Halle, 2004; Snyder et al., 2018). The important lesson running through all the evidence about the practice of ELO is that children's learning is related to the teachers' planning of ELOs, the use of multiple opportunities to learn and practice, and the quality instructional feedback the children receive.

EXPLICIT, CHILD-FOCUSED INSTRUCTIONAL STRATEGIES

Sometimes more explicit instruction is needed than is given through curriculum modifications or ELOs. Using *child-focused instructional strategies* (CFIS), ECE teachers or other specialists identify learning opportunities matched to a child's individual objectives and provide planned, consistent, systematic instruction to teach specific skills, behaviors, or concepts. These skills, behaviors, or concepts may be ones that the child is not able to learn from the usual curriculum, even with modifications or ELOs; or these may be skills, behaviors, or concepts that are unique to the child.

All of the children's teachers use CFIS to address some of the children's learning objectives. Nhan receives instruction to increase his concept knowledge every morning. He asks a classmate to join him so that he can use the concepts in conversation and play. Tina receives special instruction during her toileting time when she works on unfastening and fastening her clothing. Samisha has a specially planned instructional program to teach her to sustain interactions with peers. This program occurs every day at the beginning of free-choice time in the dramatic play area. Drew works on taking turns in conversation with peers at his small-group table. His teacher uses a systematic prompting strategy to increase the number and complexity of turns. Mateo's child care provider strategically places cube chairs on her covered patio. She uses verbal and physical prompts to elicit Mateo's "cruising" from chair to chair and reinforces his attempts to give him more systematic practice in upright mobility.

With CFIS, instructional interactions are even more systematic and more intensive than when using curriculum modifications or embedding more learning opportunities. Whereas the use of curriculum modifications and ELOs allows the teacher to continue to make use of ongoing activities and routines, CFIS are used when the child's individual objectives and learning needs are such that the objective drives the teacher's planning. The focus of instruction is on foundational skills that the child has not mastered, prerequisite skills, or barrier behaviors that interfere with learning. Many of the same instructional strategies that are used to deliver ELOs are used for CFIS; however, the specificity and intensity of instruction are greater, and the child's learning activity may look different from the learning activity for other children in the classroom. Chapter 7 provides more information about CFIS and when to use them in the early childhood classroom.

EVIDENCE BASE FOR CHILD-FOCUSED INSTRUCTIONAL STRATEGIES

Of all the blocks in the framework, CFIS has the most robust research support (see Collins, 2021; Schwartz et al., 2017; Snyder & Hemmeter, 2018; Wong et al., 2015). The majority of this support comes from single-subject research that demonstrates the effectiveness of such teaching strategies as positive reinforcement, response prompting, peer-mediated instruction, and corrective feedback. Much of this research involves people with disabilities; however, one striking exception to this is one of the first research studies documenting the effectiveness of the use of positive reinforcement to increase appropriate social behavior, published over 60 years ago. Eileen Allen and her colleagues (1964) systematically used positive teacher attention to increase the social interaction of a preschooler who was typically developing but who avoided his peers. The intervention was simple but effective. The teachers stopped interacting with the child when he was playing alone. When he was playing with or near other children, they would interact with him, encourage him, and provide lots of positive reinforcement. In a matter of weeks, the child was playing with his peers, and the teachers were able to decrease the amount of encouragement they provided. Playing with his friends became reinforcing to the child and was all the encouragement he needed.

Using peers in the classroom to help children learn is an area with strong research support. Peer-mediated interventions have documented effectiveness with young children with diverse learning needs and abilities (e.g., Milam et al., 2018; Strain & Bovey, 2011). For example, studies show that children with autism learn and maintain important social interaction skills and that children with and without disabilities have positive long-term effects from the intervention (Strain & Hoyson, 2000). A series of peer-monitoring studies in which children with and without behavior problems took turns acting as the peer monitor and receiving feedback found that both giving and receiving feedback were related to improved outcomes for all participants (Fowler et al., 1986).

Research demonstrates the strength of systematic response-prompting procedures (Ledford et al., 2012; Wong et al., 2015). Examples of response-prompting procedures include most-to-least, least-to-most, time delay, and chaining (Collins, 2021; Grisham-Brown & Hemmeter, 2017). Prompt hierarchies (i.e., most to least or least to most) are a way of organizing prompts so that the learner receives the amount of assistance needed.

Chapter 7 provides more information for using CFIS within the Building Blocks framework.

ASSESSMENT AND PROGRESS MONITORING

Ongoing assessment of child performance is a key feature of the Building Blocks framework and a recommended practice (DEC, 2014; McLean et al., 2020). Information about a child's performance relative to valued outcomes—both the child's individual outcomes and those deemed important for all young children—is gathered and used to decide what to teach and how to teach. To make good instructional decisions, the teacher and the team collect information about the child's performance within the context of the child's usual learning environments, such as the classroom, the playground, and the home. The teacher and the team regularly monitor the child's progress through systematic data collection to see how the child is responding to the supports provided (e.g., curriculum modifications, embedded teaching, more intensive instruction). They then use this information to make decisions about the child's continued need for instructional support. Chapter 4 introduces methods for collecting and using child progress information. Chapter 8 and the professional development module offer additional guidance.

COLLABORATION

The effective use of the Building Blocks framework requires that teachers and other team members work together through the process of *collaboration*. Collaboration is the cornerstone of effective inclusion (Lieber et al., 1997; Odom, 2001) and a recommended practice (DEC 2014; Winton et al., 2019). Collaborative teams hold shared beliefs, work toward common goals, have varying areas of expertise, use collaborative skills, and share the work involved in helping children move toward their goals. It is necessary to collaborate with family members as well as with other early childhood specialists to optimize child outcomes.

The five children, Nhan, Tina, Samisha, Drew, and Mateo, are enrolled in a variety of classrooms with a variety of teaching arrangements, yet all their teachers work collaboratively with other team members. These teams differ in membership depending on the goal of or reason for the collaboration. Nhan's child care teachers, an itinerant teacher, a speech-language therapist, and his parents meet regularly to plan for and discuss his progress in learning to communicate with adults and peers, as well as strategies for maintaining his home language. Tina's teacher, Dolores, and the assistant teacher, Maggie, meet at the end of every school day to talk about the day and to plan Tina's next school day. Samisha's teachers and the physical therapist meet every other week to talk about her progress. Drew's teacher, Jennie; Jennie's assistant, Marlene; a speech-language therapist; an occupational therapist; Drew's mother; and a behavior specialist meet to develop a plan to decrease Drew's tantrums. Mateo's early interventionist visits his home and his family child care home and organizes virtual meetings that also include his physical therapist. For each of these children, their teachers, parents, related services providers, and school or program administrator develop the child's IEP and/or IFSP as a team.

Collaborative skills can be difficult to acquire and require a good deal of practice, but these skills are essential for successful inclusion. Chapter 3 provides more information and strategies to enhance collaboration among the people who care about young children.

SUMMARY

This chapter introduces the structure of the Building Blocks framework and describes the evidence base that supports it. The aim of the framework is to help teachers identify, plan, and use educational practices that provide individual children with the assistance they need to develop and learn within their early childhood classrooms, child care programs, and homes. Like an RTI approach, the Building Blocks framework gives teachers strategies to determine if children are making progress and information on how to provide additional support if they are not. The Building Blocks framework is compatible with RTI and other tiered approaches to intervention (Buysse & Peisner-Feinberg, 2013; DEC, 2021). The Building Blocks framework gives teachers a practical, feasible, and evidence-based approach to meeting the needs of all their children and providing specialized instructional support for individual children who need it.

The Building Blocks framework is consistent with the DEC Recommended Practices that provide guidance on effective practice based on empirical evidence as well as the wisdom and experience of the field (DEC, 2014). Although it is important to ensure that the instructional strategies being used in early childhood programs are grounded in strong research evidence and that teachers are familiar with that evidence, it is also important not to assume that just because an intervention is supported by research evidence it will automatically be effective with every student. Teachers need to collect and analyze data on instruction that occurs in their programs and use those data to make decisions about a child's educational program.

The Building Blocks framework requires that teachers and teams work together to 1) provide a high-quality education for all children, 2) watch for children who are not making progress, 3) provide the amount and type of support(s) each child needs using teaching strategies that are likely to be effective, and 4) carefully monitor all children's progress. Subsequent chapters offer more information about each of the educational practices described in this chapter and the tools needed to put them into action.

Chapter 3

Keys to Teaming and Collaboration

Collaboration refers to working together in service of a common goal. There are many ways early childhood providers can collaborate in addition to formal and informal face-to-face meetings. We might use technology for virtual check-ins about a child, develop shared plans during nap time, communicate about child progress via an electronic document, share information about lesson ideas via text message, or use an informal sticky note system to document children's progress on IFSP or IEP goals. Regardless of the form of collaboration, the intention is to provide high-quality, seamless services to children and their families as we work together across disciplines, backgrounds, and perspectives. As noted in the DEC Recommended Practices Teaming and Collaboration Strand, programs serving young children with disabilities and their families will always involve more than one adult, and these adults must communicate and work well together to ensure the best outcomes for children (DEC, 2014). Additionally, reviews of the literature on early childhood inclusion have identified collaboration as the cornerstone of effective inclusive programs (Barton & Smith, 2015a; Bricker et al., 2022b; National Professional Development Center on Inclusion [NPDCI], 2009; Odom, 2001), yet collaboration among adults, who often represent different agencies, programs, and perspectives, can be one of the greatest challenges to successful implementation of inclusive practices.

Early childhood programs and services are situated within a larger context and complex ecological systems. Young children spend time across a range of settings before they enter K–12 systems, including community programs, child care settings, and Head Start or state-funded preschool programs. Children with identified disabilities or delays participate in all these settings. In this chapter, we focus on how adults, including educators, therapists, family members, program leaders, and other professionals who work directly with children and families, can collaborate in the most efficient and effective manner. Of course, this requires administrative coordination and support, especially related to time and resources for collaboration. Additionally, teachers and team members must recognize and appreciate the potential differences across programs, agencies, and people, in terms of procedures, funding, and philosophy, as they work together to meet the needs of each child every day.

Family and caregiver participation is a crucial part of high-quality early childhood programs, especially when serving children with identified disabilities and delays (DEC, 2014). Further, a strength of collaborative teams is their ability to represent a range of cultural, linguistic, and experiential identities and backgrounds. Collaborative teams may represent a family's background and home culture but also bring forth the perspectives of different disciplines and providers. However, for a team to be truly collaborative, the members must be in good and just relationships with one another. Collaborative teams value, respect, and support one another. Each member of a collaborative team should feel heard, safe, and appreciated. This all begins with relationships, and as our team often says, "Relationships are the heart of our work." Teams must have time to get to know one another, including protected time to communicate, plan, review child data, and have problem-solving discussions. Team members may have different ideas about how children learn, disability, inclusion, service delivery, expectations for children across activities, and so on, that can create tension. Good and just relationships among a team are a protective factor that enables teams to have difficult conversations when members have differing ideas about children's needs, behaviors, or other classroom issues.

WHAT DO EFFECTIVE COLLABORATIVE TEAMS DO?

1. Build Good and Just Relationships

Effective teams begin by developing meaningful and trusting relationships with one another. Although building relationships is an ongoing process, getting to know one another is always the first step. Teams might do quick ice breakers before meetings, use a structured getting-to-know-you form (see Hemmeter et al., 2020), or begin the day with a check-in to see how everyone is doing and feeling before working with children and families or starting a meeting. Some check-in questions might include the following: "What has your attention today?" "What is on your heart and mind right now?" "Share a one- or two-word intention you hold for today's meeting."

2. Have a Shared Vision

Teams must be aligned in their goals and overall vision for the whole classroom, program, or child and family. Starting off the year with a conversation about what the team wants for each family and each child (when the team involves several teachers) or the overall vision for one child (if the team includes one therapist and one teacher) is a great way to discuss the similarities in visions across all team members. Teams can even create an electronic or paper "vision board" for the child or children, with photos and written words that convey their hopes and dreams for the child and family.

3. Establish Clearly Defined Roles and Responsibilities

For teams to function collaboratively, all members must know what their expectations are across the day. Early childhood classrooms are lively, dynamic places that require setup and cleanup, different adults leading and supporting activities, and adults providing individual instruction to children as needed. Teams can create these plans together to ensure everyone has the opportunity to be in the areas or do the classroom jobs they enjoy the most and share the burden of the less preferred tasks (see Figures 3.1 and 3.2 for examples).

4. Communicate Effectively and Often

Effective teams must communicate regularly, clearly, and efficiently. Sometimes, this communication is related to one child needing extra support in the moment or an update on a new skill a child has learned. Effective, frequent communication also must involve classroom or program goals, changes in instruction, or necessary modifications to the daily schedule. As mentioned earlier, this communication may take all forms, depending on what works best for the team (e.g., text messages, electronic documents, virtual meetings). To determine which forms of communication work best for all, teams can reflect on their participation style (Razzetti, 2022). Do they like to process things aloud or prefer to think before talking? Do they consider themselves quiet or outspoken? Once each team member identifies their participation style, the team can reflect on how to become more aware of their colleague's style and can discuss how everyone can adjust their behaviors to create a team environment that feels supportive and welcoming to all.

5. Support One Another to Have Hard Conversations

Finally, the most effective teams support each other to have reflective and sometimes difficult conversations about how to interpret and respond to children's behavior, collaborate with families, deal with difficult societal issues that affect staff and families, and more. To equitably serve all children and families, teams must reflect on and discuss how they are supporting everyone in the classroom or program.

HOW TO FORM A COLLABORATIVE TEAM

All programs can be inclusive. An inclusive program is one in which a child with a disability or delay receives the instruction and support that they need to learn and participate with their peers. At minimum, a team supporting a child with an IFSP or IEP includes the general education teacher, a special education teacher or therapist, and the caregiver(s). Sometimes, children may have larger teams including multiple teachers, therapists, administrators, and caregivers. The ways in which specialized services are designed and delivered vary across programs, and as such, the collaborative team will look different depending on who is supporting the child in these settings. Table 3.1 describes the various early childhood programs, how children with disabilities may be supported within each model, and which professionals might make up the team.

To be a well-functioning team, members must come together to develop shared goals about children's learning priorities. Teams often expand or contract to meet particular purposes to address particular goals, and identifying these goals will also guide the team's membership. Team members may include the teacher(s) as well as classroom assistants or paraprofessionals; related service providers, such as physical therapists, occupational therapists, speech-language pathologists, social workers, and other specialists; the child's caregivers; and the program administrator. For IFSP or IEP planning, the team may be large, and membership is determined in part by legal requirements. For other goals such as ongoing curriculum and lesson planning, the team may be smaller.

Table 3.1. Inclusive early childhood education models

Early childhood setting	Program description	How are IEPs or IFSPs supported?
Center-based child care program	Program serving young children; fee based with possible vouchers. Programs usually have multiple classrooms.	ECSE itinerant teacher, therapist, or early intervention provider collaborates with the child care providers.
Family child care	Program serving young children; fee-based with possible vouchers. Usually smaller programs are held in the owner's or provider's home.	ECSE itinerant teacher, therapist, or early intervention provider collaborates with the child care providers.
Publicly funded prekindergarten	Publicly funded, full-day programs for 4-year-old children, sometimes called universal prekindergarten.	Co-teaching with ECE and ECSE teacher or by an ECSE itinerant teacher.
County, state, or federally funded programs	State-, county-, or city-funded programs for 3- to 5-year-old children. Head Start is a federally funded program for income-eligible children age 3 until entry into kindergarten and their families. Early Head Start serves infants, toddlers, and pregnant women.	Co-teaching with ECE and ECSE teacher or by an itinerant ECSE teacher.
Community-based preschool	Local preschool serving young children; may be fee based. Some may be privately owned, faith-based, family cooperative model, or other arrangements.	Itinerant ECSE teacher, therapist, or early intervention provider collaborates with teaching team.
Developmental preschool	Publicly funded preschool program designed for 3- to 5-year-olds served on an IEP, led by an ECSE teacher. May or may not have children without disabilities enrolled.	ECSE teacher and therapists provide instruction.
Natural environments	Most toddlers and families receiving IFSP services do so within their homes and communities.	EI providers and therapists provide instruction.

Key: ECE, early childhood education; ECSE, early childhood special education; EI, early intervention; IEP, individualized education program; IFSP, individualized family service plan.

TOOLS FOR CLASSROOM COLLABORATION

As discussed earlier, finding time for collaboration can be very challenging. We offer two tools to support collaboration in busy early childhood classrooms: 1) the Staff Matrix and 2) the Classroom Zoning Map. The Staff Matrix is a tool for establishing clear expectations and roles for each team member across the day. Figure 3.1 illustrates the Staff Matrix in Nahn's child care classroom. As you can see, each teacher's breaks, before- and after-school prep time, and free-play zoning details are included. This can be posted in the classroom so teachers can easily check in on their responsibilities during the day. Teams should create these together so everyone can provide input into their preferred areas and tasks and share the burden of the less preferred duties. (See Appendix H for a blank Staff Matrix; this is also available as a download.)

The Classroom Zoning Map is another resource for collaboration. This is used during free-play and recess/outdoor times and helps teachers organize where they will be in the classroom environment. Figure 3.2 illustrates an example of a Classroom Zoning Map in Nhan's classroom. The teachers, Nourhan and Vicki, created a map of their classroom and decided to split it into two main zones. The first zone includes dramatic play, library corner, writing and art center, and the bathroom. The second zone is the sensory table, science and meal tables, and block area. Each week, Nourhan and Vicki trade off on which zone they are in. During free choice, each teacher remains in their general area, playing with and providing instruction to the

Schedule	Nourhan	Vicki	Nhan's speech-language pathologist and itinerant special education teacher
Classroom:			
Team members: Nourhan and Vicki			
Morning prep	Nourhan	*Vicki arrives at 8 a.m.*	
Morning meeting	Lead	Support hand washing	
Free play	Blocks, dramatic play	Art, sensory table, science	Kelsey, the speech-language pathologist, visits Tuesdays to work on concepts and vocabulary
Snack	Yellow table	Green table	
Outside	BREAK (Rajni, program manager to support outside time)		
Bathroom/hand washing	Nourhan - toileting	Vicki - diapering	
Lunch	Green table	BREAK (Sami to support yellow table)	
Lunch cleanup/dishes		Dishes to kitchen	
Nap	BREAK		
Free play	Zone A	Zone B	Jill, the ECSE teacher, visits here to work with Nhan and Cam
Snack	Yellow table	Green table	
Outside	Play structure	Sand area	
Classroom cleanup	*Nourhan leaves at 3 p.m.*	Vicki	

Figure 3.1. The Staff Matrix in Nhan's child care classroom. (*Key:* ESCE, early childhood special education.)

children in those spaces. This helps them organize how they are managing the group of children and the materials in each area. Having a zoning map ensures that teachers have opportunities to interact with children in a variety of activities and materials but within a manageable amount of space. Team members can refer to the activity matrix to know the curriculum modifications, embedded learning opportunities, or more child-focused specialized instruction that is planned for their areas of the classroom. Similar zoning maps can be created for the playground, meal tables, or other spaces to guide team functioning.

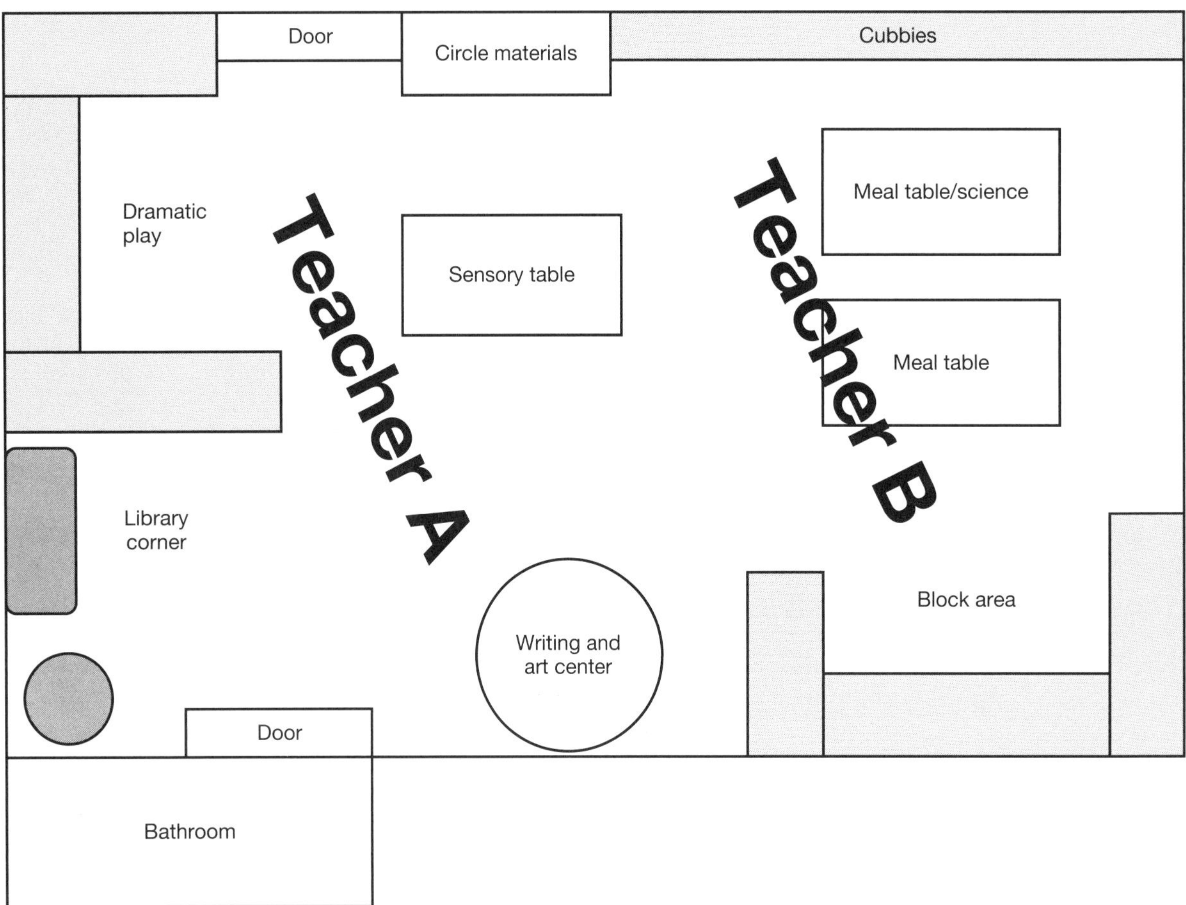

Figure 3.2. Example classroom zoning map.

STRATEGIES FOR MEETING AS A TEAM

Although regular meetings and communication are critical for teams, finding time to meet is one of the most difficult and complex problems. Teams might have time before or after school or during nap time, or programs may have a roving substitute who supports the classroom while a teacher attends a meeting. For school district–run programs, meetings may occur during children's music or physical education classes or during an early release day. Telephone, e-mail, video conferencing, shared electronic documents, and various telecommunication applications are useful communication tools to assist in the collaboration process especially for interagency and community collaboration. However, many teams prefer some face-to-face meeting times and feel that these enhance the development of trust and understanding of others' perspectives. Some teams use a hybrid model, with both virtual meetings and face-to-face check-ins.

Team meetings can vary in their degree of formality or structure. Daily debriefings with the teacher and classroom assistants may be relatively unstructured, whereas IEP or IFSP meetings are usually much more formal. Once a team is organized and has established meeting times, a general structure or framework for the meetings helps ensure they run smoothly and productively and provides all team members clarity on their roles. Although the following steps may seem somewhat rigid for team members who work together every day, the added structure is valuable for supporting active participation for members who are present less often or are members of many different teams. The first step is to establish a meeting facilitator. The facilitator drafts and shares the agenda, keeps the meeting moving and on topic, and solicits participation from each team member. Each meeting also needs a recorder to note what was discussed during the meeting, including all decisions that are made and who is responsible for specific follow-up activities. Finally, every meeting needs a timekeeper to make sure that the meeting starts and ends on time and to let team members know when time is up for discussing each agenda item.

The second step is to create an agenda. The facilitator takes the initiative in setting the agenda, sharing it with other team members, and inviting their input (electronic documents are especially useful for this). If an agenda item refers to changing or altering a child's learning objectives or instructional approach, it is essential that the child's performance data be shared at the meeting. Team members take responsibility for bringing needed information to each meeting.

The third step is the facilitation of the meeting and discussion of the agenda items. The facilitator begins the meeting by welcoming the team, introducing a team-building exercise or simply asking each team member to share how they are doing that day, and summarizing the last meeting as described in the meeting notes. As previously discussed, effective teams have members that are in good and just relationships with one another, and this can be supported by regularly checking in and acknowledging everything team members have going on outside of work. The facilitator is also responsible for keeping team members moving toward the stated purpose of the meeting, redirecting team members who digress from the topic, and in some cases, encouraging discussion of any disagreements. Toward the end of the discussion of agenda items, the facilitator should restate, reflect, and summarize the discussion, and whenever a decision is imminent, they should summarize the decision for the team. This allows team members to hear the decision articulated in someone else's words and can help clarify any miscommunication.

The final step is ending the meeting. During this step, the facilitator, with the help of the recorder, makes sure that all team members know what tasks need to be accomplished before the next meeting. Many effective teams end meetings with a brief checkout (Boyes-Watson & Pranis, 2015), where each person takes a turn answering a simple question such as, "How did you feel about the meeting today?" or "What are you going to take away from our meeting today?" The checkout is a brief opportunity for team members to share thoughts and acknowledge positive learnings from the meeting or areas that might need to be addressed to ensure the team continues to function well. (For more information on structuring a meeting, see Friend and Cook [2013].)

ACHIEVING THE TEAM'S GOALS

Before teams begin to work toward their goal, they should be sure that all team members share an understanding of what the goal means and how they will know when the goal has been met. For example, an ECE teacher and an ECSE teacher are working together in a Head Start classroom, and their goal for the meeting is to plan learning activities for the classroom. They first need to agree about what "plan learning activities for the classroom" means to them. Following are some of the questions the team members might ask themselves:

- Will we write lesson plans together?

- Will we be responsible for jointly delivering the instruction?

- Will the ECE teacher plan each activity and the ECSE teacher plan the modifications?

- Will the ECE teacher and the ECSE teacher take turns and plan independently for certain activities or days?

There are no right answers to these questions, and each team will approach them differently. The point of this exercise is for team members to agree about the meaning of the goal and ensure that everyone is clear on their role and responsibility pertaining to the goal. This team decides to meet each Friday during nap time and develop joint lesson plans for the following week. They will know the goal has been accomplished when they leave the meeting with completed plans.

THE COLLABORATIVE DECISION-MAKING PROCESS

Team members often encounter challenges, issues, and problems that require collaborative decisions. They must identify and solve problems related to children's learning and instruction and may have different ideas about the best path forward for a child. The following problem-solving steps are described in detail by Friend and Cook (2013):

1. Identify the issue or problem.

2. Generate solutions as a team.

3. Evaluate the solutions.

4. Implement the solution you choose.

5. Evaluate the outcome.

Tina's team is made up of Dolores, her ECE teacher; Maggie, the assistant teacher; Lou, the consulting ECSE teacher; Janet, the consulting speech-language pathologist; and Beth, Tina's mother. Dolores facilitates the meeting and has shared an agenda via e-mail earlier. The main topic for discussion is how to accomplish the goal of meaningfully including Tina in all classroom activities. They are meeting because Tina often refuses to walk from the playground to the classroom, which constitutes a barrier to the team's expressed goal.

The first step—problem or issue identification—is probably the most important step in the process. The team needs to define terms, as was done in the goal statement, so that all team members agree.

When this team came together, Maggie shared Tina's classroom data. She has counted how many transitions Tina completed on her own (1/10 over the past 5 days). Dolores posed other questions for discussion: How does Tina refuse? What does she do and say? How long does the situation last? How often does the behavior occur? Does it happen at any other time? Does Tina make other transitions independently? What is the same and what is different about this transition? What do the adults do?

Once the team members reach a consensus regarding the problem, the next step is generating solutions. There are several different ways to engage in brainstorming that promote the participation of and input from all team members (Friend & Cook, 2013).

Tina's team generated the following potential solutions: 1) pick her up and hold hands while walking back to class; 2) let Tina ride in a wagon; 3) use a peer buddy to walk with Tina; 4) let Tina carry a favorite toy back to class; 5) make sure that Tina's favorite activity is available when she gets to class; 6) let Tina walk with her favorite teacher; 7) wait with her without talking until she stands up and walks to class; and 8) give Tina some kind of tangible reinforcer when she gets to class. Following their discussion of the positives and negatives of each potential solution, the team decided to try a peer-buddy system. Janet, the speech-language pathologist, took notes on the shared electronic document. Dolores assigned tasks to be accomplished, and Lou e-mailed the team a link to the notes.

- Dolores will introduce the option of a "buddy line" at circle and invite all children to find a buddy when lining up.

- Dolores or Maggie will remind Tina at the end of playground time that it is time for her to pick a buddy.

- Lou will make a picture card that has photos of Tina's buddies for her to choose from.

- Dolores will make a simple data collection chart.

The final steps in problem solving are to implement the selected solution, collect data, and at the end of some specified period of time, evaluate to see if the solution worked. If the solution is successful, the team will continue. If not, the team will meet again and decide on another option. The team can use the Evaluation Worksheet (a blank form appears in Appendix I; it is also available for download) to keep track of and evaluate the plan.

This example illustrates the use of collaboration skills and team-meeting skills when the "problem" is a challenging behavior. The same approach works for other classroom challenges. For example:

Nhan's team has been embedding opportunities for Nhan to learn new concepts during free-choice time. However, the team is concerned that his concept knowledge is not increasing. His teacher and speech-language pathologist put their concern on the team agenda and will bring Nhan's progress data to the meeting for discussion.

Or, as another example:

During a home visit, Mateo's parents comment that he doesn't seem to be making much progress in walking. Mateo's home interventionist organizes a meeting with Mateo's parents; Dara, his child care provider; his physical therapist; and herself. In person and via video conference, the team examines Mateo's progress on walking to adjust their current plan.

SUMMARY

Successful adult collaboration creates inclusive opportunities and early learning environments that support all children. In this chapter, we presented ways and strategies that help adults effectively work together. Collaboration takes real effort and means working across agencies, programs, and boundaries and, much like inclusion, requires intentionality and ongoing work. You can use the Inclusion Collaboration Checklist in Appendix L to review and reflect on this aspect of your work. As publicly funded early learning programs expand, collaboration at the state and community level is equally important. With effective collaboration, *any* early learning program can be inclusive.

Chapter 4

Getting Started

The Building Blocks framework is designed to help teachers identify concerns for children who are not making adequate progress in any early learning setting and plan strategies to assist them on individual learning objectives. The format is useful for any child, not just children with identified disabilities, who may not be meeting learning objectives or who engages in behaviors that interfere with full participation in the early learning setting. The Building Blocks framework can also be used for children who are identified for special education services and who have IFSPs or IEPs.

This chapter describes the procedures for using the Building Blocks framework in early learning settings. These step-by-step procedures guide the team from the initial concern (e.g., how to teach the individual learning objectives, what to do about a challenging behavior) to a useful, practical plan. The goal is to help the team transform the IEP, other individual learning plan, or learning/behavioral concern into actual teaching and learning opportunities in the classroom. This chapter helps the team to do the following:

- Assess the classroom to ensure that it provides a high-quality learning environment for all children.
- Identify and clarify the classroom schedule.
- Gather information on children's individual goals and objectives.
- Assess the learning needs of an identified child.
- Clarify the concerns about the individual child.
- Create a plan.
- Construct a Child Activity Matrix that shows when the plan will be used.
- Implement the plan.
- Evaluate the plan and monitor child progress.

Many forms are included to help teams reach these goals. Although we provide forms in this text, teams should use only those that work best for them—it is not necessary to use each of these forms. This chapter contains filled-in example forms; blank forms that teams can photocopy and use are in the Appendix and electronic forms are available to download on the Brookes Download Hub. The following sections describe each of the steps. Although we use the word *classroom*, the Building Blocks approach and the various forms are adaptable to a variety of early learning settings, including center-based or family child care, home visiting programs, and play groups. Chapter 9 includes more examples of Building Blocks implementation and checklists to support each step in the blueprint.

STEP 1: ASSESSING THE QUALITY OF YOUR CLASSROOM

The Building Blocks framework and the specialized practices described in this book, such as curriculum modifications, embedded teaching, and child-focused instructional strategies, are built on the foundation of a high-quality early childhood program. Child outcomes are directly linked to classroom quality. Therefore, the first step in using the framework is for the teacher or classroom team (i.e., the people who work together to implement the program) to assess the early childhood classroom for 10 basic quality indicators using the Quality Classroom Assessment Form. It is especially helpful to list examples for each of the 10 indicators on the form. The results of the assessment will indicate whether the classroom is interesting and engaging to children, offers a balance of activities and learning arrangements, and provides children with both physical and emotional security. Figure 4.1 shows how Tina's (described in Chapter 1) teachers completed the form for their classroom. (See also Table 4.1.)

Some teachers or teams may already use another rating form to assess the classroom environment or as part of an accreditation process—for example, the Environment Rating Scales (Harms et al., 2007, 2015, 2017) or the Classroom Assessment Scoring System (CLASS; Hamre et al., 2014; La Paro et al., 2012; Pianta et al., 2008). Checklists or guidance materials designed for families to use in selecting a program for their child are also available from sources such as the NAEYC and Early Childhood Technical Assistance (ECTA) Center. In addition, the Inclusive Classroom Profile (Soukakou, 2016) is an observation tool that measures indicators of daily classroom practices that support the unique learning needs and characteristics of young children with disabilities. Any of these tools will yield information helpful for assessing the classroom environment.

What to Do

Strive to make your classroom a vibrant, engaging, supportive learning place for all children. If any foundational features are weak or missing, describe actions that the team can take to address the problem. Pay particular attention to the social-emotional climate of the classroom and the instructional support provided by the teacher(s). The Classroom Action Worksheet (see the filled-in version by Tina's teachers in Figure 4.2) may be used if you answered *no* or *not sure* to any items on the Quality Classroom Assessment Form. Next, the team implements these actions. This will help to ensure a high-quality environment for all the children in the classroom.

Quality Classroom Assessment Form

Date: _1/16_   Classroom: _Head Start_

Team members: _Dolores Sherman (teacher), Maggie Ong (assistant teacher)_

Goal: _Assess the classroom environment_

Indicator	Yes	No	Not sure	Examples
1. Do children spend most of their time playing and working with materials or with other children?	X			Children are busy and active most of the time.
2. Do children have access to various activities throughout the day?	X			We schedule different sorts of activities.
3. Do teachers work with individual children, small groups, and the whole group at different times during the day?	X			Scheduled small groups and snack; meeting times with whole group; individual time during plan-do-review
4. Is the classroom decorated with children's original artwork, their own writing, and stories they've dictated?		X		Lots of artwork; no writing
5. Do children learn within meaningful (i.e., relevant to their home cultures, interests, and experiences) contexts?	X			Classroom organized for HighScope, learning centers, projects based on children's ideas and family input
6. Do children work on projects and have periods of time to play and explore?	X			Small-group projects; plan-do-review at their pace
7. Do children have an opportunity to play and explore outside every day?	X			Always scheduled

(page 1 of 2)

Figure 4.1. Quality Classroom Assessment Form, as completed by Tina's teachers. *(A blank version is available in Appendix A and as a download.)*

Figure 4.1. *(continued)*

Indicator	Yes	No	Not sure	Examples
8. Do the literacy materials used in the classroom reflect the diversity of the children and families in the program?		X		For some learners, but not everyone. We are looking for more books that represent a range of family makeups (foster families and single-parent families)
9. Is the curriculum adapted for those who are ahead as well as those who need additional help?			X	We use HighScope. We're not sure we're meeting all of Tina's needs.
10. Do the children and their families from all cultures, languages, and backgrounds feel welcome, safe, and secure within their early childhood program?	X			Most children are happy when they arrive; lots of parents attend parent activities.

Notes: _We need to complete the Classroom Action Worksheet for Questions 4, 8, and 9._

Table 4.1. Quality Classroom Assessment Form indicators

Indicator	Examples
1. Do children spend most of their time playing and working with materials or with other children?	*Children spend the majority of their day actively engaged with one another, materials, toys, and the classroom environment. Children do not spend a lot of time listening to teacher explanations, waiting for activities, transitioning between activities, or waiting for teachers.*
2. Do children have access to various activities throughout the day?	*There are a range of things for children to do, including different play areas in the classroom (e.g., blocks, dramatic play, sensory table, books, games, science) and different activities across the day (e.g., large-group time inside and outside, mealtimes, shared reading times, planned art and science activities).*
3. Do teachers work with individual children, small groups, and the whole group at different times during the day?	*Teachers provide flexible grouping and work with children one on one (e.g., providing individual support or spending positive time with a certain child), support small groups of children (e.g., join a group of children in play in the block area, help extend a group of children playing outside, read to a group of children during free play), and provide whole-group instruction (e.g., circle times, shared reading, free play).*
4. Is the classroom decorated with children's original artwork, their own writing, and stories they have dictated?	*The classroom provides both windows and mirrors (Style, 1996) for all children, representing their home cultures, backgrounds, and identities. Children and their families are represented in photos, via their artwork, and in the stories they have shared. Teachers label children's art, including their descriptions (e.g., "This is a picture of my cat!" next to a child's drawing).*
5. Do children learn within meaningful (i.e., relevant to their interests and experiences) contexts?	*Teachers have learned about families' home cultures and identities and embedded them into the classroom curriculum in meaningful ways. Children's and families' identities are represented in classroom materials, such as books, classroom decor, visuals, dress up clothes, pretend play food, musical instruments, games, songs, meal formats, etc. Children's interests are incorporated in the curriculum (e.g., a class that is very interested in spiders found on the playground does an exploration on spiders as a unit).*
6. Do children work on projects and have periods of time to play and explore?	*Children have ample time to engage in uninterrupted play, without adults interfering. Free choice is at least 45 minutes, and there is an extended outside time as well. The classroom environment supports extended play, with interesting, relevant, developmentally appropriate materials that inspire children to remain engaged in play. The classroom works on projects that can extend over multiple days.*
7. Do children have an opportunity to play and explore outside every day?	*Every day, children spend time outdoors. The outdoor space includes materials that support play, such as playground equipment, sensory tables, bikes/trikes, balls, and materials for games. Children have opportunities to move their bodies and explore nature as much as possible.*
8. Do teachers read books to children individually or in small groups throughout the day?	*Literacy activities occur every day. Teachers read to children at large and small group, using universal design for learning (UDL) strategies to promote active child engagement (e.g., visuals, props, encouraging children to act out certain parts of a book). There is a classroom book area or library section full of a range of different books in children's home languages and texts that represent the families in the classroom.*
9. Is the curriculum adapted for those who are ahead as well as those who need additional help?	*Teachers use curriculum modifications to support children who are not engaged or interacting with the curriculum and classroom activities. Materials such as pictures, communication devices, and adaptive seating are readily available in the classroom. Teachers expand on the curriculum by offering choices, aligning to child interest, when creating plans to adapt the curriculum, and promoting active child engagement across all activities.*
10. Do the children and their families feel safe and secure within their early childhood program?	*Children and families feel welcome, safe, and that they belong in the classroom or program. Adults have positive, supportive, responsive interactions with children, providing social-emotional support. Teachers develop relationships with families and solicit their feedback on the classroom or program.*

STEP 2: PLANNING THE CLASSROOM SCHEDULE

One way to help ensure a safe and secure learning environment for children is to have a schedule. A schedule provides a predictable routine for children and should include the following characteristics. See Appendix M for the Clarifying the Schedule Checklist (also available as a download).

- Be divided into time segments that are appropriate to the children's needs and abilities

- Offer a balance of active and quiet times

- Offer a balance of child-initiated activities and teacher-directed activities

- Provide times for large- and small-group activities and time to play alone or with others

Classroom Action Worksheet

Date: __1/17__

Team members: __Dolores and Maggie__

Indicator*	What's the problem?	What can we do?	Who will do it?	By when?
4. Class decor	We have artwork but no writing.	Ask children to talk about their art. Write their stories, and post with their art.	Dolores Maggie	Start on Monday and continue
8. Book reading	We have storytime for whole group. Not everyone listens or participates.	Make the library corner more interesting. Have an adult in this center to read to small groups and one to one. Add props to storytime.	Maggie will make changes to the physical environment of the library corner, including props. We'll have our volunteer in library on Wednesdays.	Next week
9. Adaptability of curriculum	Tina doesn't seem to be making progress in her fine motor skills.	Ask consulting special education teacher to provide more information and to break down the objectives into smaller parts. Ask her to demonstrate for us.	Dolores will talk with the consulting teacher and schedule a time during visits so that she can show us.	In 2 weeks

* Abbreviated from Quality Classroom Assessment Form.

Figure 4.2. A Classroom Action Worksheet, as completed by Tina's teachers. *(A blank version is available in Appendix B and as a download.)*

- Include outdoor time
- Include adequate time for routines (e.g., toileting, snacks) and transitions
- Maximize teaching and learning time and minimize waiting time

What to Do

If the classroom does not have a consistent schedule or if the current schedule is not working, your team should work together to design a new classroom schedule.

Steps 1 and 2 are aimed at designing and enhancing the classroom learning environments for all the children. By taking a universal design for learning (UDL) perspective, the teacher and team provide all children with a variety of ways to access and participate in the classroom, curriculum, and learning activities. It is also assumed that the team uses a research-based curriculum and family input to guide the development of culturally relevant, engaging, and meaningful learning activities for all the children. See the section on the general early childhood curriculum at the end of this chapter for more on the importance of a curriculum that emphasizes key content.

STEP 3: PLANNING FOR AN INDIVIDUAL CHILD

With an inviting classroom environment and a consistent schedule, the next step is to plan for an individual child. The Building Blocks framework helps teams identify and provide individualized assistance to support a child's active participation and learning. Teams should begin by gathering each child's current individual learning objectives. A learning or behavioral objective contains the following components:

- The learner's name
- The behavior
- The criterion (e.g., how many, how often, how much of the time, or how long)
- The conditions

Learning objectives come from at least three sources. First, some children's objectives will come directly from their IFSPs, IEPs, or other individual plans. Second, the curriculum checklist (e.g., the *AEPS for Infants and Children* [third edition; Bricker et al., 2022a], the Child Observation Record [COR] Advantage [HighScope Educational Research Foundation, 2015], or Teaching Strategies GOLD [Heroman et al., 2010]) that is used for all children in the class may help identify an individual child's learning needs. Third, the team's observations of the child's current participation in classroom activities (using the Child Assessment Worksheet; see the blank form in Appendix C, which is also available as a download) may uncover additional learning needs.

Here are some individual learning objectives Tina's and Drew's teams devised:

- When given a mixed group of objects, Tina will sort all of the objects into smaller groups according to some physical attribute (e.g., color, size) six different times using six different sets of materials (e.g., colored dishes, big and little cars).

- During free-play times, Drew will demonstrate five new play skills (e.g., painting, doing puzzles, building with blocks) on three different occasions for at least 10 minutes each time.

Sometimes, a teacher's concerns about a child seem so overwhelming that it is difficult to clarify the actual problem areas, which makes it even more difficult to design an effective plan. For example, a child may have so many objectives on their IEP that the team members wonder how they can possibly find the time needed to work with the child on all of them. Another child may display so many behavioral challenges in the classroom (e.g., running away, grabbing toys, engaging in physical behaviors) that the adults feel that they are spending all their time trying to regain order. Or sometimes the child's IFSP outcomes or IEP goals are drawn from standardized measures and seem unrelated to the classroom or daily life.

The Child Assessment Worksheet can help pinpoint the concerns for a particular child and link those concerns to the daily routine and ongoing activities. This form guides the collection of information to determine how the child is doing within the context of the classroom and whether the child's learning needs are being met.

Drew's teacher and the rest of the classroom team met together and used the Child Assessment Worksheet to help them plan for Drew (see Figure 4.3). They wanted to incorporate his IEP goals within the classroom activities and routines and to better understand the function of his challenging behaviors.

What to Do

The team should work together to complete the Child Assessment Worksheet. First, fill out the first column with the classroom schedule. Then, in the next column, list classroom expectations for the child in question during each scheduled event. For example, at snack time, do you expect the child to find their seat, remain seated, ask for food and drink, and clean up? Do you expect the child to start this on their own or wait for directions from the teacher? Include some of the concepts and skills the child is expected to learn and practice during classroom activities. Each classroom will be different, and each teacher may have different ideas about children's participation. Doing this as a team helps ensure that all adults have similar expectations for children and activities during the day, providing needed continuity and structure.

In the third column, reflect on the child's current performance during each of the scheduled activities and routines. Is the child's current performance a strength, average (not a concern), or an area of concern? Again, it is best if the team does this together because it allows everyone to share their perspectives and come to a consensus. Note that the Child Assessment Worksheet will work in family child care home settings as well as classrooms. Use the daily schedule of activities and routines. Home visitors and families can identify home routines and use a similar planning process.

STEP 4: CLARIFY THE PROBLEM, ISSUE, OR CONCERN

After compiling a picture of the child's performance throughout the day, think about the following questions: What are the areas of concern? When does the child do well? When do the problems or concerns occur? Which concerns have the highest priority? The Planning Worksheet helps to plan a course of action for meshing classroom concerns with a child's IFSP/IEP objectives within the general early childhood curriculum. The Planning Worksheet is designed to guide the team's discussion of the individual child. The team aims for careful description of the concern (e.g., grabbing materials from peers, struggling to maintain engagement at circle time, not yet able to manipulate learning materials like crayons or books) and the team's current response. This leads to a problem-solving discussion and the team's best ideas for addressing the concern.

What to Do

There are two Planning Worksheets. The IEP/IFSP Planning Worksheet allows the team to use the child's IEP to list the goals and the related current learning objectives.

Child Assessment Worksheet

Date: 1/17

Teacher's name: Jennie   Child's name: Drew

Classroom activities	Classroom expectations	Child's level of performance
Arrival	Be able to wait with other children until everyone gets off bus. Walk to class with the group without holding teacher's hand.	Strength _______ Average _______ Area of concern ___X___
Circle time	Sit on his mat. Watch the teacher. Participate in songs and fingerplays. Practice counting and learning names. Answer general knowledge questions.	Strength _______ Average ___X___ Area of concern _______
Small-group time	Participate in planned activity. Attend to concepts and skills taught in planned lessons. Share materials. Sit at the table.	Strength _______ Average _______ Area of concern ___X___
Free-choice time	Try activities in the different areas. Play with minimal teacher support. Apply concepts and skills. Explore all centers.	Strength _______ Average _______ Area of concern ___X___

(page 1 of 2)

Figure 4.3. A Child Assessment Worksheet for Drew. *(A blank version is available in Appendix C and as a download.)*

Figure 4.3. *(continued)*

APPENDIX C *(continued)*

Classroom activities	Classroom expectations	Child's level of performance
Cleanup and transition	Put away toys when asked by teacher. Match toys to symbols on shelves. Stop playing when asked.	Strength _______ Average _______ Area of concern ___X___
Snack time	Sit at a table. Try food. Interact with peers as appropriate.	Strength _______ Average _______ Area of concern ___X___
Outdoor time	Run and play. Explore equipment. Play near or with others. Share toys.	Strength ___X___ Average _______ Area of concern _______
Departure	Follow teacher directions. Take care of clothes and belongings. Walk with the groups to bus.	Strength _______ Average _______ Area of concern ___X___

This section can be adjusted for children with IFSPs or behavior plans. It is intended to lay out the child's individual goals and objectives so that the team sees them in relation to the child's actual strengths and areas that need improvement in the context of daily routines and typical activities in the classroom. The Child Planning Worksheet guides the team to concentrate on the child's participation needs within the ongoing classroom or daily routine. This form is useful for children with or without an IEP or IFSP because it helps to define individual concerns and leads to a plan for teaching. In the first column, list the classroom activities that are areas of concern for the child in descending order of priority based on the Child Assessment Worksheet.

After completing the Child Assessment Worksheet for Drew, the team identified three scheduled activities that were areas of concern (see Figure 4.4). After discussing Drew's needs, his IEP, the needs of the other children in the classroom, and the available resources, the team decided to focus attention on small-group time, free-choice time, and transitions. They reasoned that if they and Drew could be successful during these times, Drew would have many more opportunities to learn and participate in the classroom.

In the second column, describe the problem or concern as carefully as you can. Make your description specific to the classroom activity identified in the first column. Write down exactly what the child does. Sometimes, it is important to capture what the child does *not* do, as well. For example, one child stands or sits by their cubby during free-choice time but never chooses an activity. Another child makes choices and plays creatively with toys but never speaks to the other children; the child only nods and points. The team should identify these issues collaboratively.

In the third column, describe what the team currently does about the concern. What kind of assistance is provided (e.g., physical help, repeated instructions)? Is it consistent? What sorts of environmental supports (e.g., pictures, special equipment) are currently in place? If the concern is a challenging behavior, how do the adults and children respond to the behavior?

In the fourth column, indicate your plan or your ideas for assistance or instruction. Use collaboration skills (e.g., idea sharing, listening, problem solving) to arrive at your plan (see also Chapter 3). Chapters 5, 6, and 7 contain more information about using curriculum modifications (CMs), embedded learning opportunities (ELOs), and child-focused instructional strategies (CFIS). Chapter 9 includes checklists for implementation.

These worksheets require teams to discuss and summarize the child's special or individual learning needs, including the child's IEP or IFSP objectives (or objectives from another individual plan) and concerns identified through an assessment of the child's current level of participation in the classroom. The Child Assessment Worksheet serves an additional function. By identifying the classroom activities or routines that are already areas of relative strength for a child, the team can use those times for embedding opportunities to learn new concepts and skills.

Drew's team—his classroom teacher, assistant teacher, the speech-language pathologist, the occupational therapist, and the behavior specialist—met together after school to discuss the results of their assessment and to figure out a plan. Drew's mother was not able to join them that day. She sent her notes and asked that Drew's teacher, Jennie, call her at the end of the meeting. Drew's team summarized current elements of his level of participation:

- Transitions are difficult for Drew.

- He grabs materials from peers and struggles to participate in small-group activities.

APPENDIX D

IEP/IFSP Planning Worksheet

IEP Today

Date: 1/17

Teacher's name: Jennie   Child's name: Drew

The "IEP Today" is based on the child's complete individualized education program (IEP) and tells the team the child's individual goals and the associated objectives that are the current focus of instruction.

Goal/domain	Current objective(s)
Interacts appropriately with materials during small group activities for 10+ minutes independently	Interacts appropriately with materials during small-group activities for 5 minutes with prompt
Follows routine directions from adult in group setting	Follows 1-step direction from adult in group setting with visual cues
Maintains conversation with peer or adult in topic for 2–3 turns	Responds with words to others' initiation of conversational topics with verbal prompt
Plays in small group with peers independently for 5+ minutes	Shares or exchanges objects with peers on peer request with prompt
Demonstrates five new play skills (different types of play)	Demonstrates one new play skill for 3+ minutes independently
Responds appropriately to variety of general knowledge questions	Responds appropriately to questions about name and age

(page 1 of 1)

Child Planning Worksheet

Date: __1/17__

Teacher's name: __Jennie__   Child's name: __Drew__

This planning guide will help you collect more specific information for areas of concern for specific children. Using the Child Assessment Worksheet, identify three activities on which you would like to focus your attention. Once you identify the problem, collecting information is the next step for instructional planning for children in inclusive settings.

Key: CM = curriculum modification; ELO = embedded learning opportunity; CFIS = child-focused instructional strategy.

Activities	Define concern	What are you currently doing?	Ideas for instruction
Free-choice time	Drew will play for a long time with preferred materials but refuses to even try the majority of the materials in the classroom.	Drew is asked to make a choice about where he wants to play. He almost always chooses the trains and cars. When teachers suggest that he make a new choice, he often has a tantrum. Teachers usually let him stay where he is.	CM __X__ ELO ______ CFIS ______ Describe: Drew will go to at least three areas during free-choice time. We will make sure that trains is the last area he goes to and that he can spend the longest time there. Use picture schedule.
Small-group time	Drew grabs materials from children who are seated next to him and needs a great deal of adult attention to stay engaged with the activity.	Drew has an assigned seat at small group, and a teacher sits next to him. When materials are put on the table, he often grabs the most preferred ones and won't share. Then a teacher must intervene.	CM __X__ ELO ______ CFIS ______ Describe: Drew will work independently for at least 5 minutes and respect boundaries telling him what materials are his. We will put his materials on a tray and praise him when he is engaged with his materials.
Transitions	Drew does not respond to the transition signal if he is at a preferred activity. If he is at a nonpreferred activity, he runs or wanders around the classroom.	A teacher goes to Drew, repeats the instruction, and physically helps with the transition. He often has a tantrum.	CM ______ ELO __X__ CFIS ______ Describe: Drew will use a picture schedule. We will go through the picture schedule at the beginning of the day. At each transition time, we will show him the schedule and repeat the instructions.

(page 1 of 1)

Figure 4.4. An IEP/IFSP Planning Worksheet and Child Planning Worksheet for Drew. *(Blank versions are available in Appendices D and E and as downloads.)*

- He has a limited number of preferred play activities; this hinders his participation with peers during free-choice time.

- When the activity focuses on one of Drew's interests, he remains engaged for a long period of time.

- He loves trains, Disney characters, and markers.

Drew's team also listed his current IEP objectives:

- Interact appropriately with materials during small-group activities

- Follow teacher-given instructions

- Respond to others' initiations of conversational topics

- Share or exchange objects during play

- Demonstrate five new play skills (e.g., painting, doing puzzles, building)

- Respond appropriately to general knowledge questions (e.g., "How old are you?")

Drew's team also discussed his performance on his most recent curriculum assessment. His classroom team uses the AEPS (Bricker et al., 2022a) at the beginning and end of each school year.

Because Drew's classroom has several children with identified disabilities, the team wanted to use teaching strategies that were fairly simple but also likely to be successful. They realized that the various adults had tried different approaches and that none of them had been very good at follow-through. Team members knew they needed to be more consistent.

Drew's team decided that a curriculum modification was likely to help Drew keep his materials organized and his hands to himself during small-group time. They also decided that another curriculum modification—a picture schedule—could be used to help Drew participate in free-choice time and to complete transitions. As an ELO, the pictures also would be used as a prompt to teach Drew to follow directions. As part of this discussion, the team decided how they would know if they and Drew had made progress. Although Drew's team is large, Jennie and the consulting teacher could use the same process of taking notes and regular debriefing sessions for all other children with special needs in the classroom.

STEP 5: CREATE PLANS

An individual intervention or lesson plan helps teachers and teams describe what they are going to say and do and what materials they will need to provide the planned instruction focused on the child's individual objective. This is in addition to the classwide lesson or activity plans that are already in place.

What to Do

Two intervention plans are provided. The ELO-at-a-Glance is discussed in Chapter 6, and a blank form is in Appendix J (also available as a download). The Instruction-at-a-Glance form is discussed in Chapter 7, and a blank form is in Appendix K (also available as a download). These forms provide space to detail the child's learning objective, the context for instruction, and a description to guide the instructional interactions. Space for data collection is also provided. Descriptions of CMs are usually inserted into the activity matrix (see the following section), but sometimes teams will create an individual plan for a modification as well.

STEP 6: CONSTRUCT AN ACTIVITY MATRIX

An *activity matrix* helps teachers and teams plan for instruction across the day and ensure that teaching occurs. It is difficult to individualize for one child in a busy early childhood classroom. A matrix reminds the team of 1) their planned schedule, 2) the number of children and the planned activities, 3) the number of adults who are available to assist, and 4) the activities that require adult monitoring. These reminders help ensure that teaching important child objectives is both planned and implemented. Activity matrices also help the teaching teams use their time and resources in the best ways possible. Gauvreau and Sandall (2018) describe how the activity matrix is used to organize learning activities across various settings, including at home and in the community.

An activity matrix can be constructed in a variety of ways. Some teams photocopy or print the form or forms provided in Appendix F (available as a download) and write in the information for their class. Other teams use a computer to build an activity matrix. Still other teams like to draw a large matrix on butcher paper and use sticky notes to fill in the cells. Teams should use what works best for them. Regardless of the form, it is crucial for all team members to actively participate in creating the activity matrix. This is an important way teams collaborate, and it ensures that everyone is aware of children's goals and the plan for instruction. Teams also must revise the activity matrix as a child makes progress and as objectives, teaching plans, staffing, or the schedule changes.

What to Do

To make a matrix for one child, write the classroom schedule down the left-hand column. Write the child's name at the top and the child's current objectives across the first row. To make a matrix for several children or the whole class, write the classroom schedule down the left-hand column, and then put the names of the children across the first row. (Activity matrices are used throughout the book as basic planning forms. Look at them carefully. You will see variations of the activity matrix for one child, for many children, and for collecting information about children's progress. Matrices can be created for home routines as well as the classroom.) The activity matrix highlights individual child objectives. The classwide curriculum is also being implemented, so even when a cell is blank, the expectation is that the child is participating in the usual learning activities. Use the following codes for the matrices:

CM = curriculum modification

ELO = embedded learning opportunity

CFIS = child-focused instructional strategy

Figure 4.5 shows the Child Activity Matrix for Tina. Figure 4.6 shows a Classroom Activity Matrix for Tina's classroom. This matrix includes two children with IEPs, Tina and Tyrone, and a third child with challenging behaviors, Ricky. Figure 4.7 shows a Child Activity Matrix for Drew.

APPENDIX F

Child Activity Matrix

Date: 1/17

Teacher's name: Dolores   Child's name: Tina

Write the classroom schedule in the left-hand column. Write the child's current learning objectives across the top row. Fill in the appropriate cells with brief versions of the selected teaching strategy.

Key: CM = curriculum modification; ELO = embedded learning opportunity; CFIS = child-focused instructional strategy.

	Use short phrases to request and comment.	Use words to recall action event.	Respond appropriately during transitions.	Share or exchange objects with peers.	Sort objects by variety of attributes.	Fit things together and take them apart.	Unfasten and fasten clothing (e.g., snaps, zipper on coat).
Arrival			CM—use picture cards				CFIS—backward chain
Planning	CM—picture schedule of choices		CM—use picture cards				
Work			CM—use picture cards	CM—paired activities	ELO—sort dishes, sort building toys	CM—preferred materials	
Recall		CM—use picture card	CM—use picture cards				
Snack	CM—preferred materials		CM—use picture cards				
Outside		CFIS—use time delay	CM—use picture cards				
Small- and large-group time	CM—preferred materials		CM—use picture cards	CM—paired activities	ELO—plan sorting activities for small group		
Lunch	CM—preferred materials		CM—use picture cards				
Nap	CM—preferred materials						
Outside			CM—use picture cards				
Play	(teacher breaks so no planned instruction)						
Departure			CM—use picture cards				ELO—practice fastening

(page 1 of 1)

Figure 4.5. A Child Activity Matrix for Tina. *(A blank version is available in Appendix F and as a download.)*

Classroom Activity Matrix

Date: __1/17__   Teacher's name: __Dolores__

Write the children's names across the top row. Write the classroom schedule in the left-hand column, starting with the second row. Fill in the appropriate cells with brief versions of the selected teaching strategy.

Key: CM = curriculum modification; ELO = embedded learning opportunity; CFIS = child-focused instructional strategy.

	Tina	Tyrone	Ricky				
Arrival	CM—Respond with words, picture cards	CFIS—identify name	CM—Follow routine, picture schedule (all day)				
Planning	CM—request and comment						
Work	CM—share; fit together ELO—sorting (use preferred materials)	CM—play near peers, use preferred materials	CM—Make choice, stay at activity; use picture schedule and timer				
Recall	CM—use words; use picture cards	ELO—use descriptive words					
Snack time	CM—requests, use preferred food						
Toileting	CFIS—fasteners, backward chain						
Outside		CM—play near peers, use preferred social materials	CM—Make choice, picture schedule and timer				
Small- and large-group time	CM—requests; share ELO—sorting (use preferred materials)	ELO—use descriptive words					
Departure	ELO—fastering						

(page 1 of 1)

Figure 4.6. A Classroom Activity Matrix for Tina, Tyrone, and Ricky. *(A blank version is available in Appendix G and as a download.)*

APPENDIX F

Child Activity Matrix

Date: 1/17

Teacher's name: Jennie   Child's name: Drew

Write the classroom schedule in the left-hand column. Write the child's current learning objectives across the top row. Fill in the appropriate cells with brief versions of the selected teaching strategy.

Key: CM = curriculum modification; ELO = embedded learning opportunity; CFIS = child-focused instructional strategy.

	Interact with materials.	Follow teacher-given instructions.	Respond to others' conversational topics.	Share or exchange objects.	Demonstrate five new play skills.	Respond to general knowledge questions.	
Arrival			ELO—most to least prompt				
Circle time						CM—invisible support (follow preferred peer)	
Small-group time	CM—environmental support			CFIS—model, differential reinforcement	CFIS—model, differential reinforcement		
Free-choice time	CM—preferred activity is final choice; picture schedule						
Snack	CM—environmental support					ELO—most to least prompt	
Outdoor time				ELO—differential reinforcement			
Transitions		ELO—picture as prompt					
Departure							

Building Blocks for Teaching Young Children in Inclusive Settings, Fourth Edition by Susan R. Sandall, Ariane N. Gauvreau, Gail E. Joseph, and Ilene S. Schwartz. Copyright © 2024 Paul H. Brookes Publishing Co., Inc. All rights reserved.

Figure 4.7. A Child Activity Matrix for Drew. *(A blank version is available in Appendix F and as a download.)*

STEP 7: IMPLEMENT AND EVALUATE THE PLAN

And now comes the fun part. Try out the plan you have developed for a child in the classroom for at least a week. Happily, plans often work—for example, providing a new toy captivates the child's interest and encourages the child to join the group; using a coloring sheet with a favorite character entices another child to the writing center; or pairing a child with a buddy solves the problem of lining up at recess. But other times, and for various reasons, our plans just do not work. Perhaps it is the other children who like the new toy rather than the intended child, the preferred character has no effect, or you now have *two* children who dawdle after recess. If the plan does not work well, sometimes we need to give it more time—try it for one more day. Use verbal reminders to help the child understand what is expected. Talk up the new toy, the new coloring page, or any other change you have implemented. Make it as fun and engaging as possible! Then observe carefully. Some children need to get comfortable with a change before they try it out. Try again. Remember that what the team was doing before did not work, either. Teaching is a constant process of observing, assessing, making teaching plans, trying them out, monitoring the child's progress, and adjusting. The excitement is both in figuring out what works and in the child's accomplishment.

What to Do

At the end of the trial period, answer the questions on a copy of the blank Evaluation Worksheet provided in Appendix I (also available as a download): Did the plan work? What will you do next week? This worksheet suggests three ways to collect information to monitor the child's progress: counts, notes, and products. For more detailed information about how to monitor the child's progress, see Chapter 8 and the professional development module on ongoing child assessment.

Collect information in the way that works best for you and your classroom. The point is to regularly collect and use the information to determine if children are making progress on their goals. Remember, evaluation can let you know that the child is learning and that your teaching makes the difference. Figure 4.8 shows a completed Evaluation Worksheet for Drew.

A NOTE ABOUT THE GENERAL EARLY CHILDHOOD CURRICULUM

A high-quality early childhood program uses a high-quality, research-based curriculum. This curriculum serves as a guide for what to teach (the important content) as well as a guide for planning the day-to-day learning experiences, activities, and interactions that children have with their teachers, their peers, and their environment. A high-quality curriculum is comprehensive, developmentally appropriate, culturally and linguistically responsive, and predictable and builds upon children's funds of knowledge (NAEYC, 2022). The important content of the curriculum should include social and emotional competence; communication and language development; cognition and general knowledge; physical well-being and motor skills; self-help skills; approaches to learning; and subject matter areas such as science, mathematics, literacy, social studies, and the arts.

We must keep in mind that simply placing children with and without disabilities in the same classroom does not lead to an inclusive environment. Teaching teams must help young children with identified disabilities gain access to and make progress in the general early childhood curriculum.

Evaluation Worksheet

Date: 1/17

Teacher's name: Jennie   Child's name: Drew

Concern	Plan	Evaluation information
Grabs materials from others and needs a great deal of adult attention	Objective is to work for 5 minutes. Give Drew his own tray and materials. Praise when he is participating.	Counts ___________ Notes _____X_____ Products ___________ M—took Molly's glue bottle; Th—no grabbing today Did the plan work? (Yes) No What will you do next week? Drew is participating more fully. Continue with the plan
Plays for a long time with preferred materials but refuses to try other materials	Use a picture schedule with four areas, and make the final area trains and cars. Use timer, and strive for 7 minutes in each of the first three areas.	Counts ___________ Notes _____X_____ Products ___________ W—at the sensory table for 3 min, books 4 min, art 6 min. Did the plan work? (Yes) No (Drew did great in the art center!) What will you do next week? Continue
Has a tantrum or wanders at transition times	Give instruction for making the transition. Show the picture. Prompt using slight physical assistance.	Counts ___________ Notes _____X_____ Products ___________ (record data on Drew's transition chart) Did the plan work? (Yes) No What will you do next week? Continue

Figure 4.8. An Evaluation Worksheet for Drew. *(A blank version is available in Appendix I and as a download.)*

SUMMARY

This chapter introduced you to the Building Blocks framework for including all children in your classroom. Successful inclusion means that all the children in the classroom participate, learn, thrive, and feel as if they belong. Before you can create, implement, and evaluate a plan for doing this, you need to become more familiar with the rest of the book. Deciding whether to use CMs, ELOs, or CFIS takes practice. There are no hard-and-fast rules; it depends on the child, the objective, and the classroom. It is a team decision, so use collaboration and problem-solving skills. Here are some helpful tips:

- If the child needs a little bit of help, try a CM.

- If the child needs a lot of assistance and support, try a CFIS.

- If the need lies somewhere in between, try an ELO.

- If your evaluation data tell you that your first attempt was not successful, adjust and try again.

Teaching Strategies

Curriculum modifications and adaptations are relatively simple yet planned strategies for altering activities, routines, materials, and interactions to support all children to participate in meaningful ways and create a sense of belonging for all. The more children are actively participating and engaged, the more they are learning. Eight categories of curriculum modifications are described: 1) environmental support, 2) materials adaptation, 3) activity simplification, 4) child preferences, 5) special equipment, 6) adult support, 7) peer support, and 8) invisible support. This section discusses modifications by category and by common early childhood activities such as ideas for the book corner, block play, sensory table, and so on.

Curriculum modifications and adaptations are one way to guide children in early learning settings. However, if the child is still not making progress on specific learning objectives with curriculum modifications in place, then we must provide more teaching and learning opportunities. We call this level of intensity and specificity *embedded learning opportunities* (ELOs). With ELOs, we plan for specially designed instructional strategies that are embedded into ongoing activities and routines in the child's environment. Providing more planned opportunities to practice specific skills related to a child's goals and objectives helps ensure they are learning these new skills or behaviors in a variety of settings and activities. For those children or for those learning objectives that require more explicit instruction, we provide more explicit, individualized instruction using clear instructions, assistance, and consequences. We call this level of intensity and specificity *child-focused instructional strategies* (CFIS).

Taken together, the practices described in this section build on the foundation of a quality early childhood program. We must always keep in mind that a solid foundation must be in place before we add curriculum modifications, ELOs, and CFIS. Teachers and teams use their careful observation and assessment of children's learning and, when necessary, match children's learning needs with more specialized, evidence-based, and individualized support to help children learn and thrive.

Chapter 5

Curriculum Modifications

A *curriculum modification* is a change to the ongoing classroom activity or materials to facilitate or maximize a child's participation in planned activities and routines. Curriculum modifications make up the second block in the Building Blocks framework and, like all aspects of Building Blocks, rely on the foundation of a high-quality early childhood environment (see Figure 5.1, Building Blocks framework). All children learn more when they are actively engaged and interacting with peers, toys, and classroom materials. But we know that some children will need additional support to actively participate within classroom routines. Further, simply placing children with and without disabilities in the same classroom or program does not create an inclusive environment. Rather, we must plan and implement intentional instruction to help all children play, learn, and develop friendships with one another. Curriculum modifications are simple, easy-to-implement interventions that require thought and planning but often do not take up many other resources. With careful planning, modifications and adaptations are important tools to support inclusion, help children make meaningful progress, and create a sense of belonging for all members of the classroom or program. And, it's likely there are many curriculum modifications already in place in your classroom or program.

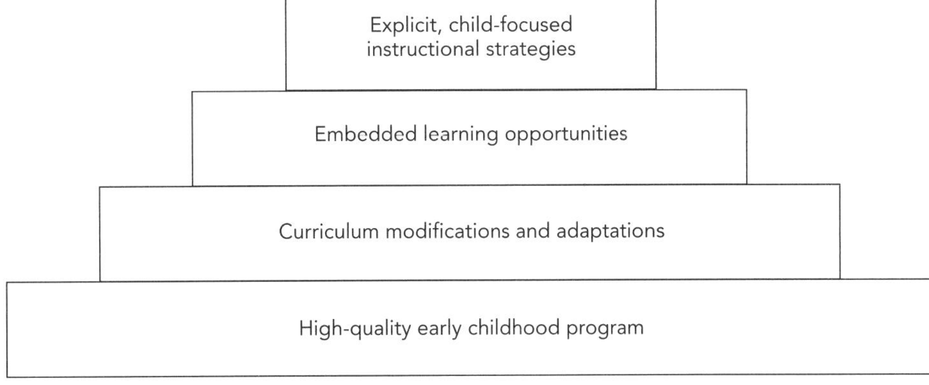

Figure 5.1. The Building Blocks framework.

Drew was having a hard time settling down in one spot at the beginning of large-group activities. The children in Drew's classroom all sit on carpet squares during large-group activities. Drew's teacher modified this for Drew by putting his name on his square so that he could be directed to sit at a particular spot in the group.

Samisha sometimes seems distracted by the effort of keeping her balance while sitting in a chair. Samisha has a large block placed under her feet, which helps her maintain her balance so that she can more easily participate in the ongoing activity.

WHEN SHOULD CURRICULUM MODIFICATIONS BE USED?

A modification to the curriculum is most effective when the child is interested in the ongoing activities but is not able to fully participate. One child may watch the other children and may try to participate without success. Another child may not stay with the activity long enough to take full advantage of the learning opportunities. Still another child may "tell" you they are having trouble with the activity by becoming frustrated, while another child may signal that they need help by becoming withdrawn. All these examples demonstrate children who need additional help, as they are not able to fully participate (for a range of different reasons).

TYPES OF CURRICULUM MODIFICATIONS

Table 5.1 lists eight types of curriculum modifications. The following pages provide numerous examples of each type of modification.

Teachers and therapists who work in inclusive early childhood classrooms have suggested the examples of modifications and adaptations in this chapter. These modifications are organized in two ways. First, they are organized by type. Second, additional modifications are matched to ongoing activities and routines that typically occur in early childhood classrooms (e.g., art center, meals, sensory table).

Some of these curriculum modifications may be considered assistive technology. *Assistive technology* is a broad term that refers to any item that supports a child's ability to participate actively in their school, home, or community setting (Sadao & Robinson, 2010). According to IDEA, all children who are eligible to receive special education or early intervention services are also eligible to receive assistive technology if it is included in the IFSP or IEP. There are additional assistive technology provisions under Section 504 of the Rehabilitation Act of 1973 (PL 93-112) and in the Americans with Disabilities Act (ADA) of 1990 (PL 101-336) that may be relevant for young children.

It is important to remember that a curriculum modification is used to help a child participate. If participating in a routine or activity is still not enabling the child to learn a specific skill or objective, try using an ELO or a CFIS (discussed in Chapters 6 and 7). Although curriculum modifications are a great option when a child needs a little bit of help to actively participate, teams must evaluate their effectiveness to determine if they are actually supporting participation. Many curriculum modifications will have a fairly immediate impact, but using ongoing child assessment (discussed in Chapter 8) will provide teams with the data they need to know for sure. For example, when Samisha's teachers put a block under her feet, they noticed that she sat up straighter and more securely and smiled as she played with the toys and materials on the table. Because the purpose of using a curriculum modification is to promote learning, the classroom team should also monitor the child's performance to determine if the child is becoming more independent in the activity or routine and if the child is learning the planned objectives for that activity. The Evaluation Worksheet (see Chapter 4, Figure 4.8) is one way to monitor children's progress.

Table 5.1. Types of curriculum modifications

Modification type	Definition	Strategies
Environmental support	Altering the physical, social, and temporal environment to promote participation, engagement, and learning	Change the physical environment. Change the social environment. Change the temporal environment (e.g., schedules and transitions).
Materials adaptation	Modifying materials so that the child can participate as independently as possible	Have materials or equipment in the optimal position (e.g., height). Stabilize materials. Modify the response. Make the materials larger or brighter.
Activity simplification	Simplifying a complicated task by breaking it into smaller parts or by reducing the number of steps	Break it down. Change or reduce the number of steps. Finish with success.
Child preferences	If the child is not taking advantage of the available opportunities, identify and integrate the child's preferences	Hold a favorite toy. Use a favorite activity. Use a favorite person.
Special equipment	Using special or adaptive devices that allow a child to participate or increase the child's level of participation	Use special equipment to increase access. Use special equipment to increase participation.
Adult support	Having an adult intervene to support the child's participation and learning	Model. Join the child's play. Use praise and encouragement.
Peer support	Utilizing peers to help children learn important objectives	Model. Pair the child with a buddy. Use praise and encouragement.
Invisible support	Purposely arranging naturally occurring events within one activity	Sequence turns. Sequence activities within a curriculum area.

COMMON CLASSROOM CHALLENGES: CURRICULUM MODIFICATIONS CAN SUPPORT BEHAVIOR

Sometimes, children might not actively participate (or participate successfully) in the ongoing classroom activities and routines because behaviors that are challenging interfere with participation. This section covers ways to consider the classroom environment and to modify it as needed to guide and support children to participate in group learning situations with their peers. We often describe the classroom environment as another teacher, and implementing meaningful curriculum modifications can provide children with additional structure and information that will ultimately support their relationships with peers, membership, and feelings of belonging.

One of the features of a high-quality early childhood environment is the use of developmentally appropriate practices that help children learn the expected classroom and social behaviors. These techniques are called *structural supports* because they involve careful planning or structuring of the environment, schedules, activities, and transitions, with the goal of successful and enjoyable participation and learning in the classroom. Here are several ways to structure the environment for success:

1. *Provide a balance between child-directed and adult-directed activities.* Provide opportunities for children to have autonomy and make authentic choices.

2. *Design a variety of areas in the classroom that are easily viewed and have boundaries.* The teacher should be able to view the entire classroom. The children should be able to recognize the boundaries of the learning areas.

3. *Make sure materials are organized and in good working order before children arrive.* Materials should be interesting and culturally relevant to the children, organized, and easily accessible.

4. *Offer activities that provide many ways for children to respond.* Use universal design for learning (UDL) to provide a variety of ways for children to participate, demonstrate their understanding, and engage with materials.

There are also several ways to structure your classroom schedule for success:

5. *Create a clear and consistent schedule.* Have a visual schedule that is easily understood by children and reference it during transitions and throughout the day.

6. *Use staff schedules.* Display and use a schedule for the adults that shows them where they should be and what they should be doing. (See Chapter 9 for staff matrices.)

You can also structure activities for greater success:

7. *Support participation.* Use a variety of ways to help children join activities and sustain participation. Provide a variety of interesting materials to entice children to the activity.

8. *Have high expectations for everyone.* With intentional planning, you can help all children participate and learn new skills and concepts. Use your curriculum to plan meaningful activities, implementing modifications for children who need them.

9. *Be consistent.* Children need consistency to feel safe and secure. All adults should provide consistent expectations and responses across all activities.

10. *Give positive, clear directions.* Positively state directions using clear, concise language (e.g., "use walking feet" versus "no running"). Break down more complex directions into shorter ones.

11. *When children are participating, provide feedback on their performance and efforts.* Feedback should be frequent, sincere, authentic, and behavior specific.

Transitions can be the most troublesome part of the day because they are often less structured and more difficult for a child to understand than other classroom routines. Here are several suggestions for structuring transitions for success:

12. *Teach children your expectations for their behavior during transitions.* Be specific in teaching children what to do during transition times, using modeling, visuals, or even puppets.

13. *Use pictures or other salient cues.* Some children have difficulty following verbal directions, so add pictures or other cues to illustrate what children should do during the transition or what is coming next.

14. *Begin the activity when a few children are ready.* If the activity is interesting and enticing, the other children will join, and those who made the transition quickly will not need to wait.

15. *When in doubt, teach the routine.* If children are still having difficulty with making a transition, teach them—specifically and systematically—what to do and what you expect during the transition. Use lots of feedback to celebrate success!

Even when all the elements of a structural support base are in place, some challenging behaviors will probably still occur. When this happens, curriculum modifications can be very helpful and require less time and resources than more intensive plans. In many cases, using a curriculum modification (or two!) can decrease a behavior that is challenging and help a child participate more independently. Figure 5.2 provides a lengthy list of common challenges experienced by teachers, with a corresponding list of possible modifications that have a high probability of supporting a positive behavior. You can use this resource to find a challenge a child may be experiencing and the corresponding possible modification(s). Then, you can turn to the section in this chapter on that type of modification for ways to develop a plan for the child. Of course, sometimes a curriculum modification is not sufficient, and you may need to try an ELO or a CFIS. Remember that sometimes children engage in a behavior that is challenging because they have not learned how to participate in a certain routine or engage in a specific skill. It is our responsibility to teach these behaviors so all children can be successful in our inclusive classrooms.

Classroom Conversations About Curriculum Modifications

Some teachers worry that using a curriculum modification may single out a child, may distract other children, or in some way may seem unfair to the others. The point of using a curriculum modification is to provide support so each child can participate in the activities and routines of the classroom, and everyone needs this help at some point! In inclusive and equitable classrooms, everyone gets the support they need to participate. This also gives teachers the opportunity to talk with all children about how everyone has different strengths and needs and that all of us need support from time to time. In many cases, it helps to explain a certain modification and encourage all children to determine if they need that type of support. We want all children to grow up being able to advocate for what they need to be engaged, active learners. It's okay for children to try out a piece of equipment, a visual support, or another way of engaging in an activity. There is usually no reason that a modification needs to be off limits to the other children. In some classrooms, everyone can access specific modifications, such as fidget toys, visual supports, or special seating at circle time.

Some children in Samisha's classroom are curious about her walker and the block she uses under her feet at table activities. Children are especially interested in her walker, and a few have even tried it out when they thought Gia and David (the teachers) weren't looking. At circle time, Gia decides to read the children's book *We All Move Together* (Fritsch & McGuire, 2021), a book that features children and adults from diverse backgrounds and abilities, some using special equipment to move, such as a walker. Samisha points to the picture of the child using a walker and says, "That looks like mine!" And another child exclaims, "That looks like Samisha's," and then Gia adds, "You're right. That is so cool!" Samisha shows the children how her walker works. Gia and Samisha explain that the walker helps Samisha move around independently and the block helps her be more stable and strong at the table. Gia asks the class if they have anything that helps them move around, and some children mention using training wheels on bikes, using a stool to reach something up high, and wearing a life jacket in a pool or lake. Gia emphasizes that in their classroom, everyone gets the help they need to play and learn.

Challenge	Environmental support	Materials adaptation	Activity simplification	Child preferences	Special equipment	Adult support	Peer support	Invisible support
Child does not actively participate at large-group time			✔	✔				
Child does not want to join large-group time	✔			✔		✔	✔	
Child is not interested in participating in a certain learning center or environmental area	✔		✔					
Child has difficulty making a transition from one area or activity to the next	✔			✔				
Child does not follow directions	✔					✔		
Child runs in the learning environment	✔		✔					
Child puts nonfood items in their mouth	✔	✔				✔	✔	
Child grabs items from others	✔							
Child engages in physical behaviors toward others	✔	✔						
Child does not attend to teachers	✔							✔
Child engages in self-stimulatory behavior				✔		✔		
Child engages in self-injurious behavior	✔					✔		
Child bites others	✔	✔						✔
Child is unstable when walking	✔		✔		✔			
Child has difficulty with stairs				✔	✔		✔	
Child has difficulty remaining with the group			✔	✔			✔	
Child dawdles	✔			✔			✔	
Child knows an answer or skill but does not demonstrate it				✔		✔		
Child does not participate in large-group activities			✔	✔				
Child has difficulty separating from their caregiver	✔							
Child will not remain seated on the bus or in car	✔			✔				✔
Child will not keep their seat belt fastened on the bus	✔			✔			✔	
Child screams in the classroom	✔							
Child bullies others						✔		

Figure 5.2. Ways to address common classroom challenges.

Challenge	Environmental support	Materials adaptation	Activity simplification	Child preferences	Special equipment	Adult support	Peer support	Invisible support
Child does not maintain proximity to peers	✔			✔				
Child falls out of chairs	✔				✔			
Child has difficulty sitting at circle time	✔				✔			
Child bothers others at circle time				✔				✔
Child has difficulty beginning and ending projects	✔		✔	✔				
Child has difficulty washing hands		✔	✔					
Child is not yet using verbal communication (speech)		✔						
Child runs out of the classroom	✔							
Child needs help to eat independently					✔			
Child does not respond to transition cues	✔							
Child does not follow classroom routine	✔					✔		
Child is easily frustrated and gives up easily			✔	✔		✔	✔	
Child demonstrates low rates of engagement			✔	✔				
Child has difficulty with lining up	✔							
Child needs support to clean up	✔		✔	✔				
Child is easily overstimulated	✔		✔					
Child will not come to group activities				✔				

Curriculum Modifications by Type

This part of Chapter 5 discusses numerous examples of each type of modification. You will find the definition of the modification, the general strategy (i.e., what to do), and examples of when the modification might work. There is also space for you to write your own ideas at the end of this section.

Environmental Support 63

Alter the physical, social, and temporal environment to promote participation, engagement, and learning.

Materials Adaptation 66

Modify materials so that the child can participate as independently as possible.

Activity Simplification 70

Simplify a complicated task by breaking it into smaller parts or by reducing the number of steps.

Child Preferences 73

If the child is not taking advantage of the available opportunities, identify and integrate the child's preferences.

Special Equipment 76

Use special or adaptive devices that allow the child to participate or increase a child's level of participation. This includes homemade equipment or devices as well as commercially available therapeutic equipment.

Adult Support 78

Have an adult intervene in an activity or a routine to support the child's participation and learning.

Peer Support 81

Utilize peers to help the child learn important objectives or participate in certain routines.

Invisible Support 84

Purposely arrange naturally occurring events within one activity.

Change the physical environment.

If a child pulls things off the toy shelves and then plays in front of the shelves, blocking other children's access . . .

> . . . put tape on an area in front of the shelf. Remind children that they can play with the toys outside the taped area. Sometimes, this is called a "Safe Building Zone."

If a child has difficulty keeping their hands to themselves when working on individual activities or projects . . .

> . . . provide individual workspaces by using trays, box lids, placemats, or masking tape on the table.

If a child has difficulty with putting toys and equipment away . . .

> . . . use pictures or symbols on shelves and containers. Make cleaning up a matching game.

Your ideas:

____

____

____

____

____

____

____

____

____

Change the social environment.

If a child has difficulty playing near other classmates . . .

> . . . plan cooperative small-group activities with engaging and highly motivating materials so that the child is close to peers while engaging in fun activities such as bubbles, cooperative block structures, and so on.

If a child has no play partners . . .

> . . . build friendships by seating a peer next to the child every day at a planned activity, such as snack or circle time.

If a child is unstable while walking . . .

> . . . arrange for the child to hold hands with buddies during transitions. With a buddy on one or both sides, the child will be more stable.

Your ideas:

____

____

____

____

____

____

____

____

____

____

____

Change the temporal environment.

If a child does not participate in learning centers during the free-choice time . . .

. . . create a picture schedule for the child. The picture schedule can have pictures or symbols representing the various learning centers organized in a certain order (e.g., art first, dramatic play second, blocks third). The child can be taught to check their schedule each time they finish an activity or have played in a certain learning center for a specified amount of time.

If a child has difficulty making transitions . . .

. . . just before a transition, provide the child with a picture or an object representing the area or activity that the child should go to next. The child could even take the picture or object to the next area.

If a child quickly finishes with the meal and then has difficulty waiting for the next activity . . .

. . . open one or two quiet centers (e.g., library, the art area) after mealtime so that the child can leave the table and engage in a new activity when they are finished.

Your ideas:

____

____

____

____

____

____

____

____

____

____

Put the materials at the optimal level for the child.

If a child has to reach up to the counter to put away the dishes and utensils after snack time . . .

. . . place plastic washtubs on child-size chairs or benches for cleanup.

If a child has difficulty standing in a way that makes using the art easel a problem . . .

. . . lower the easel and give the child a chair or buy or make a tabletop easel.

If a child's feet do not reach the pedals of the tricycle or Big Wheel . . .

. . . tape wooden blocks to the pedals to give them extra height.

Your ideas:

____

____

____

____

____

____

____

____

____

____

____

____

____

Teaching Strategies

Stabilize materials using tape, Velcro, nonskid backing, and so forth.

If a child's arm movements make the art paper slide off the table . . .

. . . tape the paper to the table.

If a child has trouble using one hand to hold a toy and toys (e.g., a jack-in-the-box, hammering toys) fall over when the child tries to use them . . .

. . . use clamps or Velcro to attach the toy to a hard surface.

If a child seems to slip and slide on the wooden chairs in the classroom . . .

. . . attach bathtub appliqués or a section of a rubber bathmat to the seat.

Your ideas:

____

____

____

____

____

____

____

____

____

____

____

____

____

If the skill or response required by a toy is too difficult for a child, modify the response.

If a child has difficulty turning the pages of a book . . .

> . . . glue a small piece of Styrofoam or tongue depressor to the pages; this will separate each page, making it easier to turn them.

If a child does not choose the art center because actions such as gluing and pasting are still too difficult . . .

> . . . use contact paper or other sticky paper as the backing for collages. The child only has to put things on the paper. (Work on gluing and pasting at other times.)

If it is difficult for a child to grasp markers and paintbrushes . . .

> . . . wrap pieces of foam around the markers and paintbrushes to make them easier to hold.

Your ideas:

____

____

____

____

____

____

____

____

____

____

____

Make the materials larger or brighter to attract the child's attention or interest.

If a child shows little interest in art activities such as making a collage or other activities using paper . . .

> . . . include pieces of shiny paper, feathers, or textured material in the collage box.

If a child shows little interest in the storybook during large-group time . . .

> . . . use a "big book" or use large illustrations painted or drawn by the children.

If a child with visual impairments has difficulty attending to objects or pictures . . .

> . . . use pictures and books that are bold and uncluttered.
> Use high-contrast colors in visual images.

Your ideas:

____

____

____

____

____

____

____

____

____

____

____

Break down the task or activity into smaller, more manageable parts.

If when playing with manipulative toys (e.g., puzzles, beads), a child is easily distracted by the pieces and often drops, bangs, or scatters the pieces rather than trying to put the pieces in or on something . . .

> . . . hand the pieces to the child one by one. Gradually increase the number of pieces the child has at one time.

If a child is overwhelmed by activities such as cooking projects, craft projects, and table games and is rarely successful at them . . .

> . . . break down the activity into several parts. Describe the steps in clear terms. Draw pictures of the steps to make it even clearer.

If a child has a long walk from the car or bus to the classroom and then dawdles, complains, and sometimes stops and drops to the floor . . .

> . . . put photos, posters, or other interesting displays at strategic points along the way. Encourage the child to go to the next spot and praise their efforts. Then, direct the child to the next spot, and so forth.

Your ideas:

____

____

____

____

____

____

____

____

Change or reduce the number of required steps.

If the soap dispenser is on the wall and requires that a child reach across the sink and make an upward motion with the hand and the child can barely reach it or needs to stand on tiptoes . . .

. . . use a plastic bottle with a pump top as a soap dispenser. Place it on the counter or attach it to the sink with a suction cup or strong Velcro.

If a child has difficulty with craft projects that have multiple steps . . .

. . . prepare the craft activity with individual children in mind. Some children may do the entire project. Others may receive projects that have been started, and they do some of the steps.

If a child plays repetitively in the house corner and rarely acts out multiple-step scenes . . .

. . . make photographs of three- or four-step play scenes (e.g., put the pot on the stove, stir, and take it to the table). Use the photos to help the child lengthen their play.

Your ideas:

____

____

____

____

____

____

____

____

____

____

Break down a complicated task into its parts and have the child finish with success.

If a child gets mixed up when trying to sort the placemat, dishes, wastepaper, and scraps after mealtime . . .

> . . . help the child do each step of the cleanup process until you get to the last step. Have the child do this step alone. Gradually increase the number of steps that the child does independently.

If a child has difficulty washing and drying hands . . .

> . . . help the child do each step until you get to the last step. The child does this step alone. Gradually increase the steps the child does independently.

If a child has difficulty pedaling the tricycle . . .

> . . . help the child place their feet on the pedals and start the rotation. Let the child finish the rotation (i.e., push down) by themselves.

Your ideas:

____

____

____

____

____

____

____

____

____

____

____

 Teaching Strategies

Let the child hold a favorite quiet toy.

If a child protests or fusses and tries to leave large-group times such as circle time . . .

. . . let the child hold a favorite quiet toy (e.g., stuffed animal, fidget toy). Give the toy to the child at the beginning of group time.

If a child has difficulty making a transition from one area or activity to the next . . .

. . . allow the child to carry a favorite toy from one activity to the next.

If a child has difficulty remaining on their nap mat during rest time . . .

. . . let the child hold a favorite quiet toy or a favorite book.

Your ideas:

____

____

____

____

____

____

____

____

____

____

____

____

____

Incorporate the child's favorite activity or toy into a specific area or activity.

If a child does not come readily to circle time or another large-group activity . . .

. . . begin large-group time with a favorite activity, such as blowing bubbles or singing the child's favorite song.

If a child has difficulty paying attention to books, pictures, or play materials . . .

. . . incorporate the child's favorite item into the activity as appropriate. For example, if the child likes a certain cartoon character, check out books with this character from the library, print off photos and tape them to blocks, and put figurines of this character in play areas.

If a child has difficulty engaging in new activities or learning centers or perseverates on one activity (i.e., does the same action over and over) . . .

. . . incorporate the child's favorite toy into the area or activity. For example, if a child loves trains and never goes to the dramatic play area, create a train station in the area, or create a fast-food restaurant and use toy trains as the prize that comes with the kid's meal.

If a child shows little interest in art activities such as making a collage or other activities using paper . . .

. . . include pictures of the child's favorite items to color, cut out, or use in their collage.

Your ideas:

____

____

____

____

____

Incorporate the child's favorite person into a specific area or activity.

If a child does not participate in certain learning areas of the classroom (e.g., the child rarely, if ever, goes to the library or writing center) . . .

. . . assign the child's favorite teacher to this area.

If a child has difficulty returning to the classroom after outdoor playtime . . .

. . . have the child's favorite person tell the child when outdoor playtime is over and then walk to the classroom. Have the person tell the child that they will see the child again in the classroom.

If a child has trouble staying interested in large-group or circle time . . .

. . . have the child's favorite person lead the final circle-time activity. Introduce this activity while the child is still paying attention.

Your ideas:

____

____

____

____

____

____

____

____

____

____

Use special equipment to increase access to activities and play areas.

If the outdoor play area is a long walk from the classroom, and a child who is not yet a skilled walker takes so long to get to the play area that the child does not have time to use the playground . . .

> . . . use a wagon that is big enough for two. Make it a treat to ride in the wagon with the child as well as to pull it. (Make sure the child gets ample practice at walking independently at other times during the day.)

If a child who uses a wheelchair or walker is not able to get close enough to the sensory table to participate . . .

> . . . there are a number of possibilities. If the sensory table is strong and sturdy, the child can sit on the table. If the legs on the table can be removed, placing the table on the floor may make it more accessible, or use a large plastic storage container (the kind designed to go under beds) as a sensory table. Consider giving children individual sensory tables made from plastic bins that can be placed on children's laps, a table, or the floor.

Your ideas:

____

____

____

____

____

____

____

____

____

____

____

Teaching Strategies

Use special equipment to increase participation.

If a child does not have the hand strength to cut with scissors . . .

> . . . use loop scissors or other adaptive scissors that require less hand strength.

If a child has poor sitting balance and seems to use all of their energy and concentration to sit in the chair, with little energy left to play with the toys or color or draw . . .

> . . . make sure the child has a chair with sides or armrests. If the child's feet do not touch the floor, make a footrest out of a sturdy cardboard box or a block.

If a child sits in an adaptive chair or a wheelchair and, during floor activities, is not at the other children's level . . .

> . . . use a beanbag chair or a cube chair in its lowest position so that the child is on the floor with the other children.

Your ideas:

____

____

____

____

____

____

____

____

____

____

____

Provide a model of another way to play or a way to expand on the child's play or other behavior.

If a child repeats the same play actions over and over without making any changes (e.g., if a child at the sand table dumps and fills and dumps and fills without seeming to pay attention to the effects of their actions) . . .

> **. . . show the child another way to do the action (e.g., dump and fill) but make small alterations from the way that the child currently plays. For example, hold the container up high while you dump it, or dump the contents through a funnel or short tube.**

If you provide props in the block area that are thematic but the child does not incorporate them into their play . . .

> **. . . take photographs of ways to use the props with the blocks. Place them in the block area, and occasionally draw the child's attention to them.**

If a child pounds and pokes at the playdough but does not use any of the tools . . .

> **. . . take one simple tool, such as a cylinder block. Demonstrate pounding and poking with it.**

Your ideas:

____

____

____

____

____

____

____

____

____

Join the child's play. By being there, you can show your interest and provide encouragement by your presence and through your comments.

If a child goes to the dramatic play area and watches the other children but does little more than observe . . .

> . . . go to the dramatic play area, see what captures the child's attention, and encourage them to explore the item. Play with the item or toy in an interesting and engaging way, and then offer it to the child.

If a child plays eagerly and enthusiastically but seems to become overwhelmed . . .

> . . . join the child in the same play area while their behavior is calm. Play in some of the same ways as the child. Try to slow the pace, redirect, or just give a gentle touch before the child's behavior escalates.

If a child is apt to run in the hallway on the way to the playground or bathroom . . .

> . . . position yourself near the child. Anticipate the child's behavior. Ask the child to hold your hand, or ask the child a silly question to keep them interacting with you as you walk together.

Your ideas:

____

____

____

____

____

____

____

____

Use praise and encouragement to help the child continue in an activity or a routine and to learn from their participation.

If a child repeatedly takes a book, flips the pages, and gets another book at the library corner and does the same thing . . .

> . . . make a positive comment about the child's play and ask if the child can show you another way to use the book, or demonstrate another way and ask the child to do the same action.

If a child usually tries to avoid cleaning up by immediately going to the next activity . . .

> . . . just as cleanup time is ready to begin, position yourself near the child and start your cleanup song with the child's name.

If a child is not an active participant during singing and other music activities . . .

> . . . keep a subtle eye on the child. Whenever the child does an action or sings, give the child full eye contact and a smile to provide positive feedback.

Your ideas:

____

____

____

____

____

____

____

____

____

____

     Teaching Strategies

Have a classmate model a way of participating.

If a child does not know how to play a new board game . . .

> **. . . pair the child with another child who is familiar with the game, and let the peer show the child how to play.**

If a child is learning how to request food by signing during snack time . . .

> **. . . make sure that the child is sitting at the table with children who know the signs for snack items.**

If a child is watching two children play with a new toy, and the child seems to be interested in the toy and wants to play with the two children . . .

> **. . . ask these two children to invite the child to join them and show the child how to play with the toy.**

Your ideas:

____

____

____

____

____

____

____

____

____

____

____

Pair the child with another child who can act as a helper.

If a child does not know when and where to line up during the transition to the playground . . .

. . . pair the child with another child who knows the routine and follows directions. Ask children to find their partner and hold their partner's hand when lining up.

If a child has difficulty lifting and putting the cover back on the sensory table during cleanup . . .

. . . ask other children to help. Make it a cooperative project.

If a child has trouble putting paint on sponges to make sponge prints . . .

. . . ask another child at the table to put paint on sponges for the peer, and then the child can make prints on the paper.

Your ideas:

Teaching Strategies

Have peers use praise and encouragement.

If a child is learning to use words or signs to request food items at snack time . . .

. . . have another child hold the requested food (e.g., a plate of orange slices). The child then needs to request the oranges from the friend instead of an adult. This can be a nice change of routine. One child is "in charge" of a plate of fruit, another is "in charge" of the basket of crackers, another has the pitcher of juice, and everyone has to ask a friend for what they would like to eat or drink.

If a child has difficulty with initiating and responding to peer interactions . . .

. . . create a "Classroom Greeter" job, where one child is in charge of warmly greeting the rest of the class each day. Help the identified child respond when the Greeter says hello and ensure they often have this job to provide more practice.

If a child always plays alone on the playground . . .

. . . identify a possible playmate who is fun and easygoing. Ask this child to play "follow the leader" with the other child. They can then take turns being the leader.

Your ideas:

____

____

____

____

____

____

____

____

____

Sequence turns to increase the likelihood of the child's participation.

If a child's hand strength is such that the child has difficulty during cooking activities that involve stirring or scooping . . .

> **. . . let the child take their turn after other children have stirred a bit or after another child has added liquid to the mixture so it's easier to mix. If the children are scooping out ice cream, let the child take a turn after the ice cream has melted a bit.**

If a child is a reluctant talker during group activities . . .

> **. . . give the child a turn after the turn of another child who is particularly liked or is particularly talkative. This can give the child ideas about what to say or do.**

If a child is learning to pour from a pitcher . . .

> **. . . let other children pour first so that the pitcher is not too full and heavy.**

Your ideas:

____

____

____

____

____

____

____

____

____

Teaching Strategies

Sequence activities within an activity or a learning center.

If a child needs more practice on a particular gross motor skill, such as walking on a balance beam . . .

. . . incorporate this skill into an obstacle course. Put a popular, interesting, or noisy item after the more difficult one. For example, let the children hit a loud drum after they walk along the balance beam.

If a child is working on matching . . .

. . . during the art activity of making collages, have the child's paper set up for matching (e.g., set up colors or shapes to be matched on the paper); after the child completes matching the items, they can make the collage.

If a child needs practice staying with the group during circle time . . .

. . . alternate active activities (e.g., songs with motions) with more passive activities (e.g., listening to stories).

Your ideas:

____

____

____

____

____

____

____

____

____

____

Curriculum Modifications by Learning Center and Routine

This section provides some additional examples of ways to modify the curriculum to help children participate, organized by the learning areas and the planned activities or routines often found in early childhood programs. These can be altered to fit the age group and setting, including the natural environments where toddlers spend time to prekindergarten classrooms serving older preschoolers. If a child in your classroom is having difficulty participating in a certain area or with a particular routine, find that section and explore the examples. Page numbers for each section are included in the next section. These ideas should help spark your own thoughts about what might work to promote the engagement, participation, and inclusion of children in your setting. This section is designed as a workbook where you can write your own ideas after each section.

LEARNING CENTERS

The specific learning centers may vary from setting to setting but generally refer to how the environment is arranged and how materials are placed in each area of the space. Learning centers encourage development across multiple domains, create more fluid, engaging spaces, and help children organize their play (NAEYC, 2021). These centers might include art, blocks, sociodramatic play, sensory play, book corner or library, science or STEM (science, technology, engineering, and math) area, and a game or manipulatives area. As with the routines and activities provided previously, if you have a child struggling in a specific area of your environment, go to that page number and explore the examples. Use the space provided at the end to jot down ideas you have for your own space.

Learning Centers

In addition to meaningful learning centers, high-quality early childhood programs also include meaningful, instructionally rich routines and activities. Large-group times (sometimes called circle or class meeting) are an important way to build community, friendship, and a culture of belonging. Small-group times enable us to focus on specific instruction related to our curriculum content or social-emotional learning. Many activities happen every day or several times a day in early childhood settings.

These routines help form the structure of the day and create valuable learning opportunities for children. We know that some of these activities can be particularly difficult for many children. Transitions inherently stop an activity that may be enjoyable for the child, and adaptive routines necessitate required learning opportunities for children as they gain independence with toileting, hand washing, eating, and so on.

Finally, we emphasize that each routine is intentionally included in the day because it provides a time for promoting the inclusion of all children and a chance to provide intentional instruction (discussed further in Chapter 6). If a child is having difficulty participating in a specific routine or activity, design an individualized modification. If several children are struggling, think about modifying the routine itself. This might include shortening the length of circle time or adding a "mini free playtime" as children begin the day, rather than having them start with an adult-directed activity. Although curricula and program standards or guidelines can help inform our daily schedule, it is just as important to create a plan that works for the children in your care.

Common Activities and Routines

Environmental Support

Alter the physical, social, and temporal environment to promote participation, engagement, and learning.

If a child messes up someone else's artwork or grabs things from a peer . . .

> . . . provide physical boundaries for the art project by allowing children to do their art in a box lid or on a plastic tray.

If a child mouths art materials . . .

> . . . use big art materials, such as big sponges to paint with instead of paintbrushes, and put all art materials in a bin with a "no eating" symbol on it.

Materials Adaptation

Modify materials so that the child can participate as independently as possible.

If a child has difficulty maintaining balance at the painting easel . . .

> . . . cut the legs off of an easel (or shorten them) and place the easel on the table; the child can sit while painting.

If a child has difficulty grasping a sponge or does not like to get messy . . .

> . . . glue a small block to the sponge so that the child can grasp the block instead of the sponge.

Activity Simplification

Simplify a complicated task by breaking it into smaller parts or by reducing the number of steps.

If a child is overwhelmed or frustrated with the multiple steps in watercolor painting . . .

> . . . break down the process into parts. Describe each step in clear single-word directions: "Water, paint, paper." Provide pictures of each step to make it even more clear.

If a child becomes frustrated with art or craft activities that require several skills (e.g., cutting, painting, writing name) . . .

> . . . partially complete the steps so the child only needs to demonstrate one skill and then is able to finish successfully. For example, for a project that requires children to cut out a shape, write their name on it, and paint it, provide the child with a precut shape with their name already printed on it so they only have to paint it to complete the activity.

 ## Child Preferences

If the child is not taking advantage of the available opportunities, identify and integrate the child's preferences.

If a child does not play or remain engaged long at the art center . . .

> . . . integrate a favorite item, activity, or person into the area. For example, if the child loves to play with cars and trucks, have some old cars and trucks at the art center. Let the child drive the cars through the paint and paint with the vehicles.

If a child does not choose the art center . . .

> . . . pair the child with a preferred peer and let them go to the art center together.

 ## Special Equipment

Use special or adaptive devices that allow a child to participate or increase a child's level of participation.

If a child doesn't yet have the strength or coordination to use a paint brush . . .

> . . . try out other painting utensils. Use old bath loofahs, kitchen tools, toothbrushes, or vehicles, or encourage the child to fingerpaint.

 ## Adult Support

Have an adult intervene in an activity or a routine to support the child's participation and learning.

If a child repeats the same action over and over again, such as pounding the markers on the table . . .

> . . . the adult can model how to do art another way while building on the child's action. For example, the adult could pound the marker in the shape of a circle or could pound two spots and draw a line between them.

 ## Peer Support

Utilize peers to help the child learn important objectives.

If a child is unsure what to do when going to the art area . . .

> . . . make sure the child goes to the area when other children are playing to provide models of different ways to use the materials.

If a child does not maintain proximity to peers . . .

> . . . plan cooperative art activities with motivating supplies (e.g., spray bottle with paint, bubbles tinted with food coloring) so the child needs to maintain proximity to peers while participating with engaging materials. This increases opportunities for the child to learn by watching peers model different ways to use the art materials.

 ## Invisible Support

Purposely arrange naturally occurring events within one activity.

If a child is unsure of how to complete or engage in an art activity . . .

> . . . sequence turns so that another child, who can demonstrate how to start the activity, takes the first turn.

If a child has difficulty with cleanup after art activities . . .

> . . . limit the number of transitions by having the child go to the art table for a messy painting project (that requires hand washing afterward) just before lunchtime so that they only needs to wash their hands once.

Your ideas:

____

____

____

____

____

____

Blocks

 **Environmental Support**

Alter the physical, social, and temporal environment to promote participation, engagement, and learning.

If a child becomes frustrated because children are getting too close to their block structure or are complaining to the teacher that the child is "in the way" of the blocks . . .

> . . . create a "no build" area with bright tape in front of the shelf.

If a child gets frustrated at cleanup time because they do not want to break down their construction . . .

> . . . provide the child with an "under construction" sign that can be gently placed in front of the structure and allow the child to return to their building later in the day or the next day. If it is not possible to save their structure, provide the child with a camera so they can take a picture of it and build it again tomorrow.

If a child spreads blocks across the room . . .

> . . . establish boundaries for the block area with a rug or brightly colored tape.

If a child is unsure of what to do in the block area or does not progress in block play skills . . .

> . . . display ideas around the block area, such as blueprints of buildings or photographs of simple block structures.

 **Materials Adaptation**

Modify materials so that the child can participate as independently as possible.

If a child with limited strength has difficulty using the wooden blocks . . .

> . . . provide large cardboard blocks. These can be made of milk cartons or other recycled material and covered with contact paper.

If a child with physical disabilities has trouble sitting on the floor and building . . .

> . . . put a table in the block area. Let the child stand at the table or sit in an adapted chair at the table.

 ## Child Preferences

If the child is not taking advantage of the available opportunities, identify and integrate the child's preferences.

If a child does not play or remain engaged long at the block area . . .

> . . . integrate a favorite item, activity, or person. For example, if a child loves animals, place animal props in the block area. If the child likes to pound on things, place workbenches and toy hammers in the block area.

 ## Adult Support

Have an adult intervene in an activity or a routine to support the child's participation and learning.

If all the child's building attempts fall down or get scattered and the child gets frustrated . . .

> . . . join the child's play. Hand the blocks to the child one at a time to slow the child's pace.

If a child is playing cars and blocks in the block area, repeatedly bangs the blocks together, and makes lots of sounds like car engines . . .

> . . . take a few blocks to build a road. Place a car on the "road" and imitate car engine noises while pushing the car along the road. Help the child use more blocks to make the road longer, and then push their car on the road and imitate the engine's sounds.

If a group of children are playing in the block area and some of these children get so excited that they may push and throw . . .

> . . . join their play, make comments, and provide affirmative, positive statements when children are playing safely. This can help prevent some problems.

Teaching Strategies

 **Peer Support**

Utilize peers to help the child learn important objectives.

If a child is trying to build a tower using interlocking or magnet blocks and cannot quite figure out how to fasten these blocks in a locked position, gets frustrated, and starts to throw the blocks . . .

> . . . ask another child in the same area to show the child how to put the blocks in the correct position so that they lock or connect together.

If a child moves the blocks around the area but has difficulty building things . . .

> . . . pair the child with a peer buddy who likes to build. Encourage the children to take turns as they work on the same building.

Your ideas:

____

____

____

____

____

____

____

____

____

____

____

____

____

Dramatic Play

 ## Environmental Support

Alter the physical, social, and temporal environment to promote participation, engagement, and learning.

If a child becomes overstimulated and does not engage in play . . .

> . . . limit the number of items in the dramatic play area to only a few things you know the child can be successful with. You can always add more later.

If a child does not engage in sociodramatic play . . .

> . . . provide the child with a playscript. A playscript can be developed using either photos or drawings. The idea is to script a two- or three-part play sequence that the child can follow during play. For example, 1) get a pot, 2) put food in pot, and 3) stir pot.

If a child perseverates on one play sequence or is disruptive in the dramatic play area . . .

> . . . use items from the dramatic play area during circle time and small-group time to teach new ways to play. This can provide direction and structure for children and can expand a child's play skill repertoire.

 ## Materials Adaptation

Modify materials so that the child can participate as independently as possible.

If a child uses a walker or wheelchair . . .

> . . . make sure there is enough space in the classroom for the child to maneuver. Try it out yourself. You may also need two tables in the area so that they are at varied heights.

If a child has difficulty gripping or handling tools . . .

> . . . stock the house area with easy-to-grip spoons, forks, and handles. Build up handles with foam or tape. Full-size, heavier utensils may be easier to hold than child-size utensils.

If a child has difficulty fastening clothes . . .

> . . . make sure the dress-up clothes are easy to put on and take off. Adapt with Velcro. Include items that are simpler to use, such as hats, sunglasses, or purses.

 ## Child Preferences

If the child is not taking advantage of the available opportunities, identify and integrate the child's preferences.

If a child does not play or remain engaged long at the dramatic play area . . .

. . . develop a prop box that reflects the child's interests. For example, if a child loves stuffed animals, create a pet station in dramatic play that includes animals, pretend food, vet supplies, and so on.

. . . integrate favorite toys, activities, or people. For example, if the child likes yellow, place yellow dress-up clothes, yellow dishes, and so forth in the dramatic play area.

 ## Adult Support

Have an adult intervene in an activity or routine to support the child's participation and learning.

If a child who is learning language skills plays with a tea set in the dramatic play area and they pretend to pour tea into a cup and drink it . . .

. . . bring a doll to the table. Pretend the doll is your guest, serve tea to the doll, and then begin a conversation with the doll.

If a child wanders in and out of the dramatic play area but never gets beyond trying one thing . . .

. . . join the child. Watch to see what the child looks at or does. Do the same thing, no matter how simple. Then, gradually take turns and expand on the child's play. For example, if the child looks in the mirror, you look in the mirror and say something.

If a child has a difficult time engaging with peers in the dramatic play area . . .

. . . before the child moves to dramatic play, ask them to point to or tell you three things they can play with a peer in the dramatic play area, and ask which they will try first.

 ## Peer Support

Utilize peers to help the child learn important objectives.

If children are washing baby dolls in the dramatic play area and a child wants to wash the doll but has trouble removing the small clothes from the doll . . .

> . . . ask another child to help them take off the baby doll's clothes, so the child can enjoy washing the baby doll.

If a child likes to go to the dramatic play area but often seems to get stuck after dressing a doll with clothes and shoes . . .

> . . . invite children with more advanced play skills into the area. They can show the child what else the doll can wear (e.g., a hat, a purse) and what else the child can do with the doll (e.g., talk to the doll, brush their teeth, walk the doll in a stroller, feed the doll food).

If a child does not often choose the dramatic play area . . .

> . . . pair the child with a peer who likes this area. Ask the peer to take the child to the dramatic play area so they can play together.

Invisible Support

Purposely arrange naturally occurring events within one activity.

If a child loses interest or always does the same thing in the housekeeping area . . .

> . . . add props gradually and naturally. For example, add a suitcase to the housekeeping area. Put a few new articles of clothing in it.

> . . . add props gradually and naturally to integrate themes. For example, add a large refrigerator box to the housekeeping area that can become a car to go to and from the house.

Your ideas:

____

____

____

____

Sensory Table

 ## Environmental Support

Alter the physical, social, and temporal environment to promote participation, engagement, and learning.

If a child does not like to get dirty or get their hands messy . . .

. . . provide child-size gloves that the child can wear while playing in the area.

If a child loses interest or does not engage at the sensory table . . .

. . . place novel items in the table each week or hide small toys children can look for.

If a child always gets wet or dirty during play in the sensory table . . .

. . . have smocks near the sensory table so that children can put them on as they enter the area and do not need to leave the area to get a smock and then come back. This can also serve to limit the number of children in the area (e.g., if there are only four smocks, the area is full when the smocks are all being worn).

 ## Materials Adaptation

Modify materials so that the child can participate as independently as possible.

If a child has difficulty grasping objects . . .

. . . provide easy-to-grasp tools, such as shovels, scoops, or large serving spoons. If necessary, build up the handles with foam and tape.

If a child uses a walker or wheelchair or is too short and has difficulty reaching into a table . . .

. . . let the child sit on the table, but only if the table is sturdy and strong. You could also put the table on the floor or give the children plastic tubs for individual sensory tables.

If a child has difficulty seeing the sensory materials . . .

. . . make sure the materials (e.g., sand, water) contrast in color with the table and the toys. Dye the water with food coloring to see if that helps the child.

 ## Child Preferences

If the child is not taking advantage of the available opportunities, identify and integrate the child's preferences.

If a child does not play or remain long at the sensory table . . .

. . . integrate a favorite item. For example, if a child loves fish, place water in the table with plastic fish. If a child likes spinning things, provide sand toys that have spinning parts.

. . . integrate a favorite motor action. For example, if a child loves to pound, place plastic hammers on the sensory table with golf tees and let the child pound "nails" into the sand; or freeze plastic animals in water and then let children pound the ice block with hammers to loosen the animals.

. . . station a favorite adult or encourage a preferred peer to play at the sensory table.

 ## Peer Support

Utilize peers to help the child learn important objectives.

If a child is pouring sand into a bottle but the child keeps tipping the bottle, gets frustrated, and starts to pour sand onto the floor . . .

. . . have another child stabilize the bottle on the sensory table so they can successfully pour sand into the bottle without tipping it over.

If a child is reluctant to play at the sensory table . . .

. . . pair the child with a peer. Give the pair a toy to share. For example, give them one bucket and give each of them a scoop, and encourage them to fill the bucket together.

If a child does the same actions over and over again at the sensory table . . .

. . . encourage the child to join children who are playful, interactive, and have lots of ideas.

 ## Invisible Support

Purposely arrange naturally occurring events within one activity.

If a child does the same thing over and over at the sensory table . . .

> . . . add items gradually and naturally. For example, if the child fills and dumps with the containers, add spoons, scoops, tongs, or shovels so they can try out new things.

If a child loses interest in the sensory table . . .

> . . . place a box or tub of new (or different) toys near the sensory table, such as plastic gems, small counting manipulatives, pom poms, and so on. Let the children "discover" the new toys.

Your ideas:

____

____

____

____

____

____

____

____

____

____

____

____

____

Book Corner or Library

 **Environmental Support**

Alter the physical, social, and temporal environment to promote participation, engagement, and learning.

If a child is distracted . . .

. . . carefully consider the arrangement of your book corner. It should be in a low-traffic area and near other quiet centers.

If a child is active and noisy in this area . . .

. . . carefully consider the materials that are available. Provide headphones for those who use audio players, tablets, or other devices. Limit the number of children who can use the area at one time.

If a child never uses the area during free-choice time . . .

. . . use the book corner at other times of the day, as appropriate, to introduce the child to the area. For example, have the child's small group meet in the book corner.

 **Materials Adaptation**

Modify materials so that the child can participate as independently as possible.

If a child has difficulty sitting on the floor . . .

. . . provide a child-size table and chair in the area for the child.

If a child has difficulty turning the pages . . .

. . . place bits of Styrofoam or popsicle sticks in the upper right-hand corner or on the side of the pages, making them easier to lift. You can also make or use cardboard books.

If a child is not yet interested in storybooks . . .

. . . include photograph albums with pictures of the children. Make photograph albums of children in the classroom and class activities. Ask families to share photos from home and make a book of the child's family members.

 Teaching Strategies

 ## Activity Simplification

Simplify a complicated task by breaking it into smaller parts or by reducing the number of steps.

If a child does not have the fine motor skills to write but has something to say . . .

> . . . use a text-to-speech app on a tablet or computer or use a tablet and app that enables children to write by using their finger on a touch screen.

 ## Child Preferences

If the child is not taking advantage of the available opportunities, identify and integrate the child's preferences.

If a child does not frequent or remain long at the book corner . . .

> . . . integrate a favorite topic into the book selections. For example, if a child loves horses, place several horse books in the book corner. If a child has favorite books at home, place copies of these books in the book corner.

> . . . integrate a favorite movement or motor action. For example, if a child loves to make noise, place some sound-producing books in the book corner.

> . . . place toys that go along with certain books in the book corner. For example, offer *The Very Hungry Caterpillar* (Carle, 1969) and add some plastic fruits and vegetables and a caterpillar puppet. (Socks with eyes on them work great, too.)

> . . . create family books for each child by inviting families to share photos and creating these books as a class (or send home materials for families to make their own).

 ## Adult Support

Have an adult intervene in an activity or a routine to support the child's participation and learning.

If a child rarely chooses the book/library corner . . .

> . . . station the child's favorite adult in the book corner.

If a child gets very loud or excited when listening to audio books . . .

> . . . have an adult join the child. The adult can use a gentle pat or touch to help the child control their excitement.

 **Peer Support**

Utilize peers to help the child learn important objectives.

If a child flips through the books and quickly leaves the book corner . . .

. . . pair the child with a classmate. Have the classmate "read" a story. Then have them switch.

If a child has difficulty using and listening to audio books . . .

. . . hook up two pairs of earphones to the CD/MP3 player, tablet, or other device. Have children listen to the book in pairs.

If a child is learning to talk and they choose to read books during free-choice time . . .

. . . encourage children to read stories to each other. The child will have more chances to observe how to tell a story and to practice talking.

Your ideas:

Science or STEM Area

 **Environmental Support**

Alter the physical, social, and temporal environment to promote participation, engagement, and learning.

If a child has difficulty waiting for a turn . . .

. . . have the children sign up on a dry-erase board or chalkboard for a turn. After a child finishes, they cross off their name. Prewritten names on pieces of paper backed with Velcro can also be used to indicate a child's turn.

If a child has difficulty using the science center independently and is not sure how to measure, compare, or explore materials . . .

. . . post visual directions at the center and create visuals to provide more information on how to engage with these materials.

 **Special Equipment**

Use special or adaptive devices that allow a child to participate or increase a child's level of participation.

If a child is disinterested in the curricular content . . .

. . . use a tablet to show images and video footage to illustrate concepts, such as showing children videos of different types of weather or different types of food.

If a child struggles to use a child-sized magnifying glass . . .

. . . add in a larger magnifying glass designed for adults.

If a child is unable to stack Unifix Cubes to measure materials . . .

. . . provide a variety of materials that can be used to measure things but do not require specific fine motor skills, such as pipe cleaners, straws, toilet paper or paper towel tubes, or magnet blocks.

 **Child Preference**

If a child is disinterested in the science area . . .

. . . include measuring and comparison materials that align with their interests, such as their favorite characters or figurines.

Science or Stem Area

 **Peer Support**

Utilize peers to help the child learn important objectives.

If a child has difficulty measuring or comparing objects . . .

. . . pair the child with a classmate who uses slower and more systematic strategies to explore these concepts.

Your ideas:

Manipulatives and Games

 ## Environmental Support

Alter the physical, social, and temporal environment to promote participation, engagement, and learning.

If a child is easily distracted by the more active centers in the classroom . . .

> . . . arrange the center to reduce distractions. Use L-shaped shelves. Place the manipulative center in a quiet part of the room.

If a child interferes with another child's materials at this center . . .

> . . . use trays or box lids as individual workspaces.

 ## Materials Adaptation

Modify materials so that the child can participate as independently as possible.

If a child has difficulty handling the string for bead stringing . . .

> . . . glue dowels to a board. Use spools or blocks with holes drilled in them as beads. Have the child place the beads on the dowels.

If a child has difficulty handling puzzle pieces . . .

> . . . provide a range of puzzle types. Glue spools or small blocks to the tops of puzzle pieces for handles.

If a child has difficulty handling game pieces or game pieces keep scattering during the game . . .

> . . . attach Velcro to both the play pieces and the game board. Or laminate the game board and pieces and use masking tape to keep things in place.

If a child has difficulty playing games and taking turns with peers . . .

> . . . create double-sided visuals that have a "my turn" sign on one side and a "wait" sign on the other. Put these visuals in board game boxes so they are available every time children play.

 ## Activity Simplification

Simplify a complicated task by breaking it into smaller parts or by reducing the number of steps.

If a child is interested in but overwhelmed by puzzles . . .

> . . . help the child learn the steps: Spill out the pieces, turn the pieces right side up, start with pieces that form the edge, and so forth.

If a child is interested in but overwhelmed by sequencing or patterning activities . . .

> . . . start the pattern and then let the child finish it.

 ## Adult Support

Have an adult intervene in an activity or a routine to support the child's participation and learning.

If a child has difficulty taking a turn or following the rules for table games . . .

> . . . join the children's play. Take turns with the children and use gentle coaching to help the children learn the rules.

If a child insists on selecting the most complex toy, gets frustrated, and throws it . . .

> . . . join the child's play. Hand the pieces to the child one at a time, talk through strategies for doing the activity, or model asking for help.

Your ideas:

____

____

____

____

____

____

____

Circle Time

Environmental Support

Alter the physical, social, and temporal environment to promote participation, engagement, and learning.

If a child has difficulty keeping their hands to themselves during circle time . . .

. . . provide children with individual boundaries by having them sit on individual carpet squares.

If a child has difficulty attending to stories . . .

. . . be sure that everyone can see the book. Sometimes, children cannot see the book because they are seated too close or too far away. Move the book close to children as you are reading, so they can see the pictures up close.

If a child has difficulty attending to songs or books . . .

. . . use objects, props, or puppets to act out songs to make them more meaningful. Pass out objects or props that align to concepts, such as small spider rings for children to explore while singing "The Itsy Bitsy Spider" or laminated pieces of a bus children can add to a felt board while singing "The Wheels on the Bus."

Materials Adaptation

Modify materials so that the child can participate as independently as possible.

If a child is disinterested in circle-time activities and does not yet use verbal language . . .

. . . allow the child to choose a song, book, or fingerplay by pointing to a picture of the selection or by selecting a certain activity card.

If a child is disruptive or passive during songs and rhymes . . .

. . . provide the child objects or flannel pieces associated with the song or rhyme and encourage them to hold them up during that part of the song (e.g., holding up a pigeon while reading *Don't Let the Pigeon Drive the Bus* [Willems, 2003]).

 ## Activity Simplification

Simplify a complicated task by breaking it into smaller parts or by reducing the number of steps.

If a child leaves circle time or is disruptive when stories are read . . .

> . . . read a story that is repetitive and has simple language (e.g., *Brown Bear, Brown Bear, What Do You See?* [Carle, 1967]; *The Napping House* [Wood, 2000]; *Go Away, Big Green Monster!* [Emberley, 1992]) every day for the week. As the child learns the story and begins to understand it, they will become more engaged. Other children will benefit because stories that are read repeatedly help children learn to read.

If a child has difficulty understanding stories . . .

> . . . use objects or flannel board pieces or even photocopied pages of the story that represent characters or objects in the story. The child can make connections between the physical objects and the story.

If a child struggles to pay attention to stories . . .

> . . . give the child a small board book of the same story you are reading to the class. Many common preschool books also come in a smaller, board book size, and holding their own version of the story will help the child participate.

 ## Child Preferences

If the child is not taking advantage of the available opportunities, identify and integrate the child's preferences.

If a child tries to leave large-group times such as circle time . . .

> . . . let the child hold a favorite quiet toy (e.g., stuffed animal, fidget toy). Give them the toy at the beginning of group time. Some teachers provide stuffies or fidget toys for all children in the group.

If a child is not willing to go to or participate during circle time . . .

> . . . begin circle time with a favorite activity or toy. For example, when only a few children are at circle time, begin blowing bubbles for them while saying, "Yehaya is at circle. He's playing with bubbles." Other activities include giving children a squirt of scented lotion, spraying water, blowing up a balloon, or giving children a turn with a novel toy, such as a whirligig. As soon as the identified child arrives at circle time, immediately give them a turn.

If a child is hesitant to go to circle time . . .

> . . . tape a picture of their favorite character to their carpet square and invite them to come sit with the character.

Special Equipment

Use special or adaptive devices that allow a child to participate or increase a child's level of participation.

If a child has difficulty remaining seated or struggles with their trunk stability at circle time . . .

> . . . provide multiple seating options. Cube chairs help children to sit in a more stable position. Wobble seats provide more input to children who need to move their bodies, while allowing them to remain at the circle area. Wedges help some children sit up more independently.

Adult Support

Have an adult intervene in an activity or a routine to support the child's participation and learning.

If a child does not transition to the circle area . . .

> . . . have an adult provide individualized directions and gentle support for the child to join the group.

If a child is unsure of what to do during circle-time activities . . .

> . . . have an adult sit next to the child and model exaggerated movements while praising and encouraging the child as they approximate the movements.

Peer Support

Utilize peers to help the child learn important objectives.

If a child is asked to choose the picture that shows today's weather and put it on the weather board but they do not know which one to pick . . .

> . . . create a "weather team" where one child picks a picture and gives it to another child who puts the picture on the board.

If a child is working on initiating and responding to peers . . .

> . . . have a "Class Greeter" each day who is in charge of warmly greeting each child. The "Class Greeter" can greet peers in verbal or nonverbal ways, using a stuffed animal, offering a high five or elbow bump, waving, and so on.

 **Invisible Support**

Purposely arrange naturally occurring events within one activity.

If a child often gives nonsensical or inappropriate responses to circle-time questions . . .

. . . call on a child who will model an appropriate response just before calling on that particular child.

If a child is unsure of what to do at circle time . . .

. . . seat the child between and across from or next to peers who will consistently model appropriate actions.

Your ideas:

____

____

____

____

____

____

____

____

____

____

____

____

____

Teaching Strategies

Small Group

 ## Environmental Support

Alter the physical, social, and temporal environment to promote participation, engagement, and learning.

If a child grabs objects from others . . .

. . . add physical structure to the activity by putting the child's project on a plastic tray or in a cardboard box lid. This way, the child has a reminder of which items are theirs and are relevant to the project.

If a child has difficulty making the transition to small-group time . . .

. . . assign seats at the small-group table. Post the child's name and photograph on the table or on their chair. This ensures that children know exactly where they need to sit at small-group time and eliminates transition chaos. Or give the child a name card to take to small-group time.

If a child has difficulty following directions . . .

. . . present only one step with the corresponding item at a time. Present another step only after the child has completed the first.

 ## Materials Adaptation

Modify materials so that the child can participate as independently as possible.

If a child is matching word cards to pictures of objects but the child's arm movements move the cards out of their correct places . . .

. . . put Velcro on the back of the cards and the pictures. Let the child attach the cards and the pictures to a board.

If the table is too high for the child . . .

. . . attach a foam board or cushion to the child's seat by using Velcro or tape or encourage the child to stand and take away the chairs.

If a child has difficulty holding a writing implement . . .

. . . wrap the tool with foam tape so that it becomes bigger and easier for the child to hold.

 ## Activity Simplification

Simplify a complicated task by breaking it into smaller parts or by reducing the number of steps.

If a child has difficulty with puzzles or games that have lots of pieces . . .

> . . . hand the pieces to the child one by one or start with a completed puzzle and gradually increase the number of the pieces taken out.

If a child is overwhelmed by the project the group is working on . . .

> . . . make picture cards to illustrate the steps or parts of the activity.

 ## Child Preferences

If the child is not taking advantage of the available opportunities, identify and integrate the child's preferences.

If a child protests the activity and tries to leave the small group . . .

> . . . let the child hold a favorite quiet toy or a material that will be used during the activity. Give the child the toy before the activity begins.

If a child is not willing to go to or participate at small group . . .

> . . . integrate a favorite item into the activity. For example, if a child loves trains, have the child run a toy train through paint to create their artwork instead of using a paintbrush.

If a child finishes the activity quickly and then wants to leave . . .

> . . . create "all done boxes" with motivating items inside that the child can use after they finish the activity, so they have something interesting to do while they remain at the small-group table with their peers.

 ## Adult Support

Have an adult intervene in an activity or a routine to support the child's participation and learning.

If a child seems to be confused by the steps involved in a cutting and pasting activity and does not know where to start . . .

> . . . have an adult sit beside the child and show them how to cut out a shape and glue it to the paper without telling them directly.

If a child appears to be getting frustrated with the activity . . .

> . . . provide encouragement by taking turns with the child.

Teaching Strategies

 ## Peer Support

Utilize peers to help the child learn important objectives.

If a child has difficulty putting the last few pieces of a puzzle in the correct places . . .

> . . . let another child who has put the puzzle together successfully tell or give clues to the child about where the pieces go.

If a child has difficulty opening a jar to get playdough or other materials out . . .

> . . . pair the child with another child so that the partner can hold the bottom of the container firmly on the table while the child takes off the cover.

If a child with fine motor difficulties becomes frustrated while stringing beads because the beads keep falling out of their hands when they try to hold the string in one hand and the bead in the other hand . . .

> . . . pair the child with another child and ask the partner to hold the beads for them so that the target child can focus on putting the string through the beads. Or ask the pair to figure out who will do which part of the task.

 ## Invisible Support

Purposely arrange naturally occurring events within one activity.

If a child spends most of small-group time standing or squirming in the chair . . .

> . . . move the small group to an area of the room where sitting at the table is not required.

If a child has difficulty understanding the teacher's verbal directions . . .

> . . . give the child a turn immediately after a child who is successful with the activity, so the peer provides a model.

Your ideas:

____

____

____

____

Adaptive Routines: Toileting, Diapering, and Hand Washing

 ## Environmental Support

Alter the physical, social, and temporal environment to promote participation, engagement, and learning.

If a child has difficulty following the hand-washing or toileting steps . . .

. . . illustrate the steps in each routine by using visuals. Place these above the sink and near the toilets so children can easily see them.

If a child struggles to transition to use the toilet while playing . . .

. . . use a visual timer or picture to provide a clear warning that it will be time to use the bathroom in 3 more minutes.

If a child squirms or protests diaper changing . . .

. . . post pictures of children in the class on the changing table, hang an interesting mobile, or attach images of the child's favorite things where they can see them during diaper changes.

Materials Adaptation

Modify materials so that the child can participate as independently as possible.

If a child has difficulty pumping the soap when washing their hands . . .

. . . create a study base on the soap dispenser by attaching it to the sink area with a suction cup or strong Velcro so it does not move when they push down.

Adaptive Routines: Toileting, Diapering, and Hand Washing

 ## Activity Simplification

Simplify a complicated task by breaking it into smaller parts or by reducing the number of steps.

If a child has difficulty setting up their cot and bedding . . .

> . . . set up the cot for the child (the most difficult part) and have them gather their bedding materials.

If a child has difficulty waiting to wash their hands . . .

> . . . attach pictures or interesting images made from contact paper to the counter area where children are waiting and encourage children to play "I Spy" or have them point out their favorite items or identify colors, animals, or shapes while they wait for their turn.

 ## Adult Support

Have an adult intervene in an activity or a routine to support the child's participation and learning.

If the child is unable to wash their hands or complete parts of the toileting routine independently . . .

> . . . provide gentle prompting for each step in the routines, and help the child with the beginning steps, decreasing your support as they become more independent.

 ## Peer Support

Utilize peers to help the child learn important objectives.

If a child does not lie down on their mat during the transition to rest time and instead wanders around the classroom . . .

> . . . make sure the other children lie down first before asking the target child to lie down.

If a child is resistant to using the bathroom or washing their hands . . .

> . . . encourage them to choose a friend to complete this routine with, or assign "potty buddies" or "hand-washing buddies" and have children do these routines together.

 ## Child Preferences

If the child is not taking advantage of the available opportunities, identify and integrate the child's preferences.

If a child is not interested in toilet training (but is showing signs of being ready) . . .

. . . ask the family about having the child pick out underwear with their favorite characters or colors on them.

If a child has difficulty transitioning to the bathroom . . .

. . . embed a choice in this routine by asking the child if they would like to go in "1 more minute or 3 more minutes" or if they would like to "fly to the bathroom like a butterfly or hop like a bunny."

 ## Special Equipment

If a child is unstable when using the toilet . . .

. . . provide a stool, handrails, or an inset toilet seat so they feel more stable and secure during this routine.

Your ideas:

____

____

____

____

____

____

 ## Materials Adaptation

Modify materials so that the child can participate as independently as possible.

If a child cannot reach the pedals on a tricycle or Big Wheel . . .

> . . . build up the pedals with blocks of wood taped to the pedals.

 ## Child Preferences

If the child is not taking advantage of the available opportunities, identify and integrate the child's preferences.

If a child does not participate . . .

> . . . do not limit the outdoor space to large-muscle activities. Add easels and paint, musical instruments, outdoor blocks, or a picnic table and board games.

If a child does not participate in certain areas of the playground . . .

> . . . assign a favorite adult to that area.

If a child does not engage with their peers outdoors,

> . . . invite specific children to begin playing with the identified child's favorite materials or activities, such as bubbles or chalk. Then, encourage the identified child to join their peers with this activity.

 ## Adult Support

Have an adult intervene in an activity or a routine to support the child's participation and learning.

If a child does the same thing day after day . . .

> . . . join the child's play but bring something new with you, such as a ball, chalk, or bubbles.

If a child runs excitedly and often gets in the way of the swings and slides . . .

> . . . make a running track with tape or chalk. Organize a "track meet" or other running event.

 **Peer Support**

Utilize peers to help the child learn important objectives.

If a child is trying to pull a wagon but it is too heavy for them . . .

. . . ask another child to help the target child so that together they are able to move the wagon.

If a child has vision problems and has difficulty going through the obstacle course . . .

. . . pair the child with another child who has strong vision and gross motor skills. Let the children figure out the best way to do the obstacle course together.

If a child is reluctant to try the slide or another piece of equipment . . .

. . . ask a classmate to invite the child to join them on the equipment.

Your ideas:

 ## Child Preferences

If the child is not taking advantage of the available opportunities, identify and integrate the child's preferences.

If a child does not participate . . .

. . . incorporate a favorite toy into the activity. For example, if a child likes trucks, have the children roll trucks back and forth in time to the music.

. . . have the children participate in groups of two or three. Assign this child to a group that includes a favorite peer or adult.

If a child does not do the hand motions in fingerplays . . .

. . . have the children look at themselves in mirrors while doing the activity.

 ## Adult Support

Have an adult intervene in an activity or a routine to support the child's participation and learning.

If a child does not try new movements or actions . . .

. . . imitate the child. Take turns. Eventually introduce a new movement and see if the child imitates you.

 **Invisible Support**

Purposely arrange naturally occurring events within one activity.

If a child does not participate during large-group music and movement activities . . .

. . . incorporate music and movement into other activities. For example, have the child hop or take "giant steps" to the next activity. Include several of these activities during the day.

If a child is not interested in music activities . . .

. . . have the children make their own musical instruments (e.g., drums, maracas, tambourines) during art or small-group time. The child may be more interested in music if they get to play their own instrument.

Your ideas:

 **Environmental Support**

Alter the physical, social, and temporal environment to promote participation, engagement, and learning.

If a child seems hesitant entering the classroom . . .

    . . . have the children's name cards or pictures available outside the classroom. Let the child take their name or picture card into the classroom and place it on a large picture of the school. At the end of the day, reverse the process.

If a child has difficulty getting settled into the daily routine . . .

    . . . place a picture card in the child's cubby of their favorite activity. The picture card indicates the child's first task of the day (e.g., going to the block area), so they can begin doing something they love.

If a child wanders or dawdles on the way to the bus at the end of the day . . .

    . . . give the child a picture symbol or a "bus pass" to take to the bus driver.

If a child is taking too long to complete the departure routine and get their things ready to go . . .

    . . . make this a fun game by encouraging the child to "beat the clock!" Set a timer for a few minutes (making sure to select a time that is close to the amount of the time the child currently takes to complete the task) and provide lots of verbal praise for the child to be quick.

Activity Simplification

Simplify a complicated task by breaking it into smaller parts or by reducing the number of steps.

If a child acts out while waiting for the other children to get ready to leave . . .

> . . . reduce waiting time. Arrange for an adult to supervise departure as soon as a few children are ready to leave.

> . . . embed engaging activities when children are waiting, such as singing songs or playing guessing games. Invite the child to select which activity they would like to do from a visual list of activities by the door.

If a child takes an excessive amount of time to complete the various departure tasks . . .

> . . . decide which tasks are most important. Have the child do these independently. Help with the others. Gradually increase the child's responsibility for all departure tasks.

If a child has difficulty greeting adults or peers . . .

> . . . provide a visual choice chart with pictures of different ways to greet, such as hug, high five, handshake, wave, say "Hi," and so on.

Child Preferences

If the child is not taking advantage of the available opportunities, identify and integrate the child's preferences.

If a child wanders or dawdles at departure time . . .

> . . . have the child take a picture of their favorite thing they did at school that day, using the classroom tablet or a smartphone. Then text or post to the classroom communication app so the child can talk about this with their family at home.

If a child is hesitant to enter the classroom . . .

> . . . begin the day with their favorite activity, such as welcoming them in with bubbles, a fun puppet, or a specific toy. Let them engage with their favorite activity for several minutes before getting started with the daily schedule.

If a child's transition from the bus or car to the classroom is slow . . .

> . . . have outdoor time as the first and last activity if possible.

　　　　Teaching Strategies

 ## Materials Adaptation

If a child is learning to zip a jacket . . .

>. . . enlarge the tab of the zipper by adding a ring or other zipper pull.

Your ideas:

Transitions

 ## Environmental Support

Alter the physical, social, and temporal environment to promote participation, engagement, and learning.

If a child tends to stay in one area and does not seem to explore other areas . . .

> . . . set a timer for the child. When the timer beeps, the child goes to another area so that they can explore all the areas.

If a child does not seem to know where they are going to sit before circle time begins . . .

> . . . put their name and photo on a mat and arrange it before the activity starts. Encourage the child to find their name and picture.

If a child has a hard time following classroom routines and does not seem to know what is going to happen in the classroom . . .

> . . . use a picture schedule. Let the child turn over the card after each activity is finished. Or move a clothes pin or arrow up and down the schedule to identify which activity is next. Have the child be the "schedule helper" and be in charge of notifying the group of upcoming transitions.

If a child continues to have difficulty following directions during transitions . . .

> . . . give a silly transition cue, such as using a novel musical instrument or asking children to stop and do a specific action (e.g., pretend to eat an ice cream cone, act like a dinosaur, roar like a lion).

 ## Child Preferences

If the child is not taking advantage of the available opportunities, identify and integrate the child's preferences.

If a child is wandering around in the classroom while the other children are lining up at the door to go outside . . .

> . . . let the child's favorite person (a teacher or a peer) tell them to come to the line and hold hands while the child is waiting or walking to the playground.

If a child has difficulty making transitions from activity to activity . . .

> . . . think of a favorite toy or activity the child likes to do, and then find or draw a picture of it. Cut the picture into as many pieces as there are transitions. Each time the child successfully makes a transition, give the child a piece of the puzzle. When the child puts all the pieces together, they get to do that activity or play with that toy.

  Teaching Strategies

 ## Adult Support

Have an adult intervene in an activity or a routine to support the child's participation and learning.

If a child does not seem to know what to do during the transition from small-group activity to free-choice time . . .

> . . . near the end of the small-group activity, tell the child what they can do after they finish. For example, you might say, "When you finish that, you can pick an area where you want to play. What areas do you want to play in? We have blocks, books . . . ."

If a child seems surprised at or hurried during transitions . . .

> . . . give the child an individualized warning about 5 minutes before the transition.

If a child does not seem to know what to do during a transition . . .

> . . . reflect on your own instructions. Be sure that they are clear, specific, and consistent.

 ## Peer Support

Utilize peers to help the child learn important objectives.

If a child does not seem to know what to do and where to go during transitions . . .

> . . . pair the child with another child who knows the routine well.

If a child is having difficulty getting a toy off a shelf . . .

> . . . teach the child how to ask one of their peers for help.

Your ideas:

____

____

____

____

Cleanup

 ## Environmental Support

Alter the physical, social, and temporal environment to promote participation, engagement, and learning.

If a child becomes confused and distracted during cleanup time . . .

> . . . place photos on shelves and toy bins so children know where the toys go. Label all materials in the child's home language.

If a child becomes frustrated during cleanup time . . .

> . . . use big buckets or bins that are labeled for blocks, toys, and so forth so that the child has a clear idea of where toys belong.

If a child refuses to clean up . . .

> . . . make cleanup tickets. Draw pictures or use photographs of various areas in the classroom and allow a child to pick a card or ticket. The card the child picks is where they clean up. When the child is done, they give the card back as a ticket to go to the next activity.

 ## Adult Support

Have an adult intervene in an activity or a routine to support the child's participation and learning.

If a child does not know where the big blocks go when cleaning up the block area . . .

> . . . pick up a few blocks and put them where they belong on the shelves to show the child where to put them.

If a child wants to help clean up the table after meals but does not know exactly what to do . . .

> . . . put a couple of lunch plates in the basket to give the child an idea of where to start.

If a child is trying to wash paint off their hands without using soap . . .

> . . . model this action by putting paint on your hands, too. Then, put some soap on your hands and rub them together to show the child how to get the paint off.

 ## Peer Support

Utilize peers to help the child learn important objectives.

If a child is cleaning tables after snack and struggles to spray and wipe down tables . . .

> . . . create a "Clean Team" and pair the child with another child so that one child can squirt the soap on the table and the other child can wipe the table clean.

If a child often does not wash their hands thoroughly after painting . . .

> . . . pair the child with another child who usually cleans their hands well. Ask children to check their partner's hands after washing them.

If a child does not help at cleanup time . . .

> . . . assign two children to a task. For example, one child holds the bin, and another gathers the cups and puts them in.

Your ideas:

 **Child Preferences**

If the child is not taking advantage of the available opportunities, identify and integrate the child's preferences.

If a child eats very little or will not try new things . . .

. . . have a favorite adult eat with the children at the child's table.

. . . incorporate child participation into snack or meal preparation. This can be something simple, such as watching cheese melt on toast, making the juice, or stirring the yogurt into the fruit salad.

. . . serve food in a novel, interesting way. Put cut up fruit on skewers or toothpicks, serve food in ice cube trays rather than on plates, or offer the child food picks instead of utensils.

If a child struggles to remain at the table during mealtimes . . .

. . . encourage them to bring a quiet toy to the table, such a figurine or book, and allow them to play with the item during mealtimes. Work to increase the amount of time the child remains at the table.

. . . make placemats for all the children with their favorite characters, colors, activities, and so on (or have children make their own), and encourage children to point to or talk about their favorite things during meals. This can provide something for children to do when they have finished eating or if the identified child does not eat very much and is finished before their peers.

If a child is learning to use a napkin . . .

. . . use napkins that are the child's favorite color or that have pictures of the child's favorite things on them.

 **Peer Support**

Utilize peers to help the child learn important objectives.

If a child is learning how to use utensils properly . . .

. . . make sure that the child is sitting at the table with other children who can use utensils so the target child can see how others use utensils during snack time.

If a child is learning to use signs to request something . . .

. . . ask another child, who also signs, what they want before giving them more food so that the target child can have a chance to observe a peer using signs to make a request.

If a child has difficulty pouring juice from a pitcher . . .

. . . ask another child at the same table to pour juice for all the children. Give the target child another job, such as passing out napkins or plates.

Your ideas:

____

____

____

____

____

____

____

____

____

____

____

____

Rest Time

 ## Child Preferences

If the child is not taking advantage of the available opportunities, identify and integrate the child's preferences.

If a child is restless and loud . . .

. . . let the child hold a favorite quiet toy or stuffed animal.

. . . have quiet books that children really enjoy in a basket that is available only at rest time. Even if the child does not nap, they can look at "special books" quietly.

. . . allow the child to listen to quiet music or an audiobook as long as they remain on their cot or mat.

If a child is distracted by peers during nap time and keeps other children awake . . .

. . . move their cot to a part of the classroom where they cannot see other children, such as in an area where shelves block their view.

If a child is not willing to lie down for nap time . . .

. . . let the child choose where they want to lie down. Offer a choice, such as, "Do you want to sleep on the red mat or the blue mat?" or "Do you want to set up your cot in the block area or circle area?"

 ## Adult Support

Have an adult intervene in an activity or a routine to support the child's participation and learning.

If a child wanders around the classroom . . .

. . . go to the rest area. Help children settle down by rubbing their back, talking quietly, or providing books or stuffed animals.

 **Peer Support**

Utilize peers to help the child learn important objectives.

If a child does not lie down on their mat . . .

> . . . make sure that some of the other children lie down first in the rest area. When the child sees other children lying down quietly in the rest area, they may want to do what their peers are doing.

If a child is learning how to put their things away after rest time . . .

> . . . pair the child with a peer who knows this routine. Have them help each other as they put away bedding, cots, and comfort objects.

Your ideas:

____

____

____

____

____

____

____

____

____

____

____

____

____

SUMMARY

This chapter provides many relatively simple examples of how to modify or adapt learning activities, materials, or routines using curriculum modifications so the individual child can actively participate. A high-quality early childhood foundation includes planned activities, routines, and learning centers that are interesting and engaging for all the children in the group. But even with this foundation in place, it is likely that some children may need additional support. Curriculum modifications enable teachers to help each child participate in a meaningful way, promoting more learning opportunities and creating environments that are truly inclusive. Although curriculum modifications can be powerful teaching strategies, they must be planned and used intentionally. That is, teachers must assess children's performance and create meaningful plans to support them. Use the Curriculum Modification Checklist in Appendix P (also available as a download) to review these components. In our own work with early childhood teams, we find that teachers can quickly and easily implement these into their classroom and report that, many times, such simple adjustments result in increased participation and engagement (Horn et al., 2000; Lee et al., 2010; Lieber et al., 2008). It is important to review the effectiveness of curriculum modifications about once a month to determine if a change is necessary. Some children will require additional instruction, with ELOs or CFIS. But for many children, curriculum modifications are a small change that can have a very large impact.

Embedded Learning Opportunities

Early childhood teachers use embedded learning opportunities (ELOs) to create short, intentional teaching episodes within ongoing activities and routines. The teaching episodes focus on a child's individual learning objectives and are embedded within existing activities and routines; the instructional component is planned ahead of time.

ELOs can be used when the child shows interest in ongoing daily activities and when there is a good match between the activity or routine and the child's learning objective. For example, if a child's learning objective is counting using one-to-one correspondence, then a daily activity that requires counting, such as counting the bowls for snack time, would be a good match.

Using ELOs has many benefits. First, because existing activities and routines are used, this strategy should not require big changes to the classroom. Second, a teacher can take advantage of a child's interests and preferences, which should enhance the child's motivation to participate and learn. Third, because the teaching takes place in natural settings, the child's ability to use the newly learned skill by themselves is increased. And fourth, if the teacher plans to provide ELOs several times during the day and during different activities, the child's ability to use the skill in a variety of situations is also encouraged.

ELO refers to the particular feature of embedding instruction. The use of ELOs is based on the assumption that the teacher and team are already using a high-quality curriculum and their knowledge of appropriate standards or benchmarks to guide their planning of engaging activities. Furthermore, these activities are intended to help *all* children learn valued concepts and skills. The reason for using ELOs is that some children need instruction and feedback to take advantage of the learning opportunities within these activities; therefore, the teacher and team plan teaching episodes so these children can more fully engage in activities and routines. The teacher and team make sure that the child has many opportunities to learn, practice, and accomplish their individualized objectives.

When planning and implementing ELOs, teachers and teams use instructional strategies that are likely to be effective, such as prompting and reinforcement. They use these strategies frequently so that the child learns the identified objective. Chapter 7 provides a discussion of these instructional strategies.

One of Samisha's learning objectives focused on increasing her cooperative play skills with peers. One of the ways Gia and David, Samisha's teachers, decided to work on this was to embed planned teaching and learning opportunities in the classroom's free-choice time. The classroom features a learning center where the children can play with board games, such as Lotto. During free-choice time, Gia and David planned to invite Samisha to this learning center when other children who were more skilled players would be there. David then used prompts and encouragement to help Samisha learn the game and play cooperatively with her peers.

Instead of setting up a special or separate time for Samisha to learn and practice cooperative play skills, her teachers did some extra planning so that they could embed the necessary instruction (in this case, using systematic prompting and encouragement) within the ongoing free-choice activities.

Just as teachers use ELOs to create short teaching episodes in their classrooms, families and other caregivers can use ELOs to increase teaching and learning opportunities within activities and daily routines at home or in the child care setting. The many activities and settings that make up the daily life of the family or the child care home or center are the sources and contexts in which learning opportunities are embedded.

One of Mateo's learning objectives is to use approximations of three to five single words. His visiting early interventionist, Kate, and Mateo's parents identified diapering, snacks and meals, and book reading as times in their daily routines to embed teaching. They chose a few words to focus on, such as *up*, *more*, and *book*. During the routines, Mateo's parents modeled the words and used wait time, or an extra pause, to give him time to try to use his words. When he made an attempt, they repeated his vocalizations, smiled, and said the word again. Then, Kate partnered with Dara at the family child care home to identify daily routines to use in the same way. They selected diapering, snacks and meals, going outside, and greeting Dad at the end of the day, and Dara began using modeling and wait time to help Mateo use words.

Instead of trying to find special teaching times during their busy days, Mateo's parents and his child care provider reviewed their daily activities and found times when they could insert short, intentional teaching episodes throughout the day. Figure 6.1 illustrates the teaching episode.

THE BASIC STEPS

Using ELOs sounds like a natural thing to do. However, teachers must plan very carefully to ensure that during ELOs, children with identified disabilities, delays, or diverse abilities are able to adequately practice the skills on which they need more instruction and feedback. Seven basic steps are necessary for planning and implementing ELOs:

1. Clarify the learning objective and determine the criterion.

2. Gather baseline information to determine the child's current level of performance.

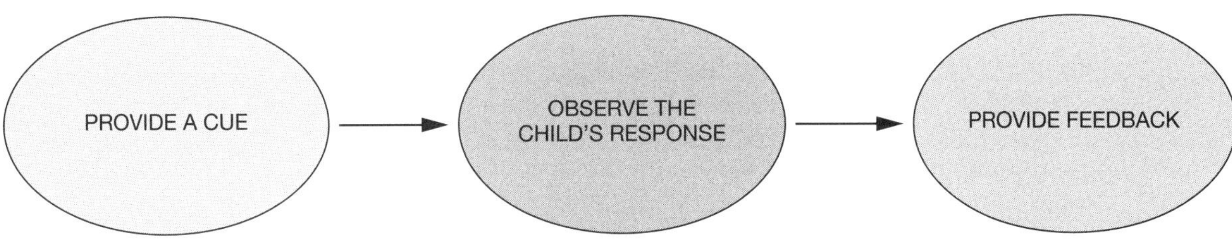

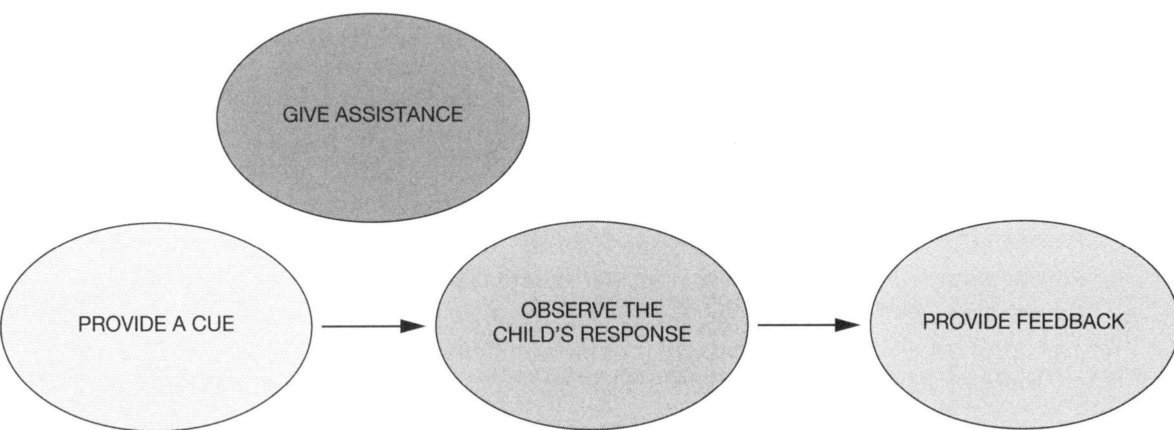

Figure 6.1. Teaching episode steps.

3. Use an activity matrix to select activities, learning centers, or routines in which instruction can reasonably be embedded. (See Chapter 4 for an example.)

4. Design the instructional interaction and write it on a planning form. You can use an ELO-at-a-Glance form (provided in Appendix J and also available as a download), which tells exactly what will happen during a teaching episode (adapted from McCormick & Feeney's "IEP-at-a-Glance" [1995]).

5. Implement the instruction as planned, remembering these tips:

    • Give clear instructions.

    • Let the child respond.

    • Provide feedback.

6. Keep track of the opportunities provided. Provide multiple opportunities every day.

7. Periodically (every week) check to find out if the child has achieved the objective.

Drew was learning to follow teacher-given instructions. His learning objective stated that during the typical classroom day, Drew would respond to the first request to begin or complete activities. He would respond to at least 80% of first requests and would do so for 2 days in a row. After completing the Child Assessment Worksheet and examining the daily schedule, Drew's teacher and team decided that they would work on part of this objective during transitions from activity to activity. Drew's teacher, Jennie, and her assistant, Marlene, took a couple of days to observe his current performance at following instructions. They made a simple chart listing each transition and the instructions they would give Drew for the transition (e.g., "Time for circle," "Go to small group with Jennie"). They left a place to write "yes" or "no" after each instruction to record whether Drew follows the instruction on the first request. They collected information for 2 days and found out that Drew always needs more than one instruction except when it is time to go outside.

Jennie and Marlene talked about the best way to teach Drew to follow instructions. They decided to use a visual or picture prompt with him to help him better understand the direction. Look at Drew's Child Assessment Worksheet and Child Activity Matrix in Chapter 4 to review the planning done by his team.

Identifying the opportunities for learning is not enough. Next, Jennie, with help from the team, discussed and wrote a plan for Drew (see Figure 6.2).

This plan, called an ELO-at-a-Glance, tells what will happen during a teaching episode. Good teaching includes 1) a careful description of the expected child behavior (i.e., the objective), 2) what the teacher or other adult will do before this behavior, and 3) what the teacher or other adult will do after the child's behavior. Drew's ELO-at-a-Glance shows all these parts. In addition, the form tells the teacher about any materials they may need or any changes they may need to make to the typical activity to embed instruction. For Drew, Jennie needed pictures that will tell him what to do next. For example, she or Marlene will show Drew a picture of children at circle time and say, "Drew, go to circle." Before snack, she or Marlene will show Drew a picture of the soap dispenser and say, "Drew, it's time to wash hands," and so forth. See Figure 4.7 to see how ELOs appear on the activity matrix.

Pairing the ELO-at-a-Glance with the Evaluation Worksheet to collect information is helpful in determining if the ELO strategy is effective. Information can be collected in many ways. (These are described in Chapter 8.) When using the ELO strategy, we suggest that child data are collected on a weekly basis.

Information about a child's progress is meaningful only if the teachers have actually embedded the instruction. Sometimes, it is necessary to keep track of the adults' behavior to make sure that planned instruction occurs. The space at the bottom of the ELO-at-a-Glance can be used for this purpose. Part of the team's planning should be to decide how many opportunities to provide each day. Having the opportunity to practice the skill with feedback one time a day is not enough; the team should try for 10 times or more. Plan for many learning opportunities and distribute the learning opportunities within and across the daily activities and routines. This will facilitate learning and ensure that the child uses the new skill in different settings and with different people.

Drew's example illustrates how to use ELOs to help a child learn a skill that is best acquired within the context of classroom routines. The example for Samisha (see p. 138) shows how to embed learning opportunities within free-choice time. In many early childhood classrooms and child care settings, free-choice time, or learning center time, accounts for a significant portion of the day. Thus, it is prime time for teaching and learning. It is not unusual for a young child with identified disabilities or a child with behavioral challenges to have difficulty during free-choice time. Sometimes, a child does not have adequate social, language, or play skills to participate during this time. Another child might have difficulty maintaining attention to the activities and does not grasp the concept or skill as the teacher might expect.

APPENDIX J

ELO-at-a-Glance

Date: _1/07_

Team members: _Jennie (teacher), Marlene (assistant)_

Child's name: _Drew_

Routines: _Transitions_

Objective: _When shown a picture and given an instruction to start an activity, Drew will follow the instruction the first time it is given. He will do this 80% of the time, 2 days in a row._

What are you going to do?
Show Drew the picture.

What are you going to say?
"Drew, go to circle."

How will you respond?
If Drew follows the instruction, praise and remind him of what he just did. If not, show picture, repeat instruction, and physically assist him.

What materials do you need?
Circle time   Drew's small group   Each play area   Bus   Soap dispenser
Juice and cookies   Slide and tricycle

How many opportunities will you provide each day?
(Use Drew's transition chart to track progress.)

Monday	Tuesday	Wednesday	Thursday	Friday
10	10	10	10	10

(page 1 of 1)

Figure 6.2. An ELO-at-a-Glance for Drew. *(Blank version available in Appendix J and as a download.)*

Samisha's learning objective states that during play times, Samisha will join her peers in play and maintain play with them for 10 minutes or more in cooperative play activities. She will demonstrate this in four different play areas. Samisha's teachers, Gia and David, completed the Child Assessment Worksheet, examined their daily schedule, and observed and took notes on Samisha's play during free-choice time (see Figure 6.3).

They noted that Samisha can take part in cooperative play in the dramatic play area but only if she initiates the storyline. Even then, her cooperative play lasts only a couple of minutes. Gia and David also noted that Samisha has started to watch other children play games in the table game center.

One of the important considerations for Samisha's teachers is that there are six children with IEPs in this classroom, and many of the children have objectives that could be embedded during free-choice time. Gia and David need to be creative and realistic about how to use their time and resources. They decided to embed instruction on cooperative play at the table game center. Once Samisha is successful, they will intentionally embed instruction on this objective in other play areas. The current plan means that one adult will work with three or four children. The structure of the game and systematic use of prompting will help Samisha learn to play with the other children. The teachers developed an ELO-at-a-Glance for Samisha (see Figure 6.4).

To maximize their time and resources, Gia and David could decide to use this same activity during free-choice time to embed instruction for another child in the class. Joey is one of Samisha's classmates. He also likes to play at the game table. This could be a prime time for the teacher (who is already there) to embed instruction on one of Joey's fine motor objectives: Joey will release a handheld object onto or into a larger target with either hand. The teachers select the game's playing pieces with Joey in mind and then use the slight physical assistance (the prompt) he needs to help him place the playing piece on the appropriate section of the game board.

TIPS FOR CONSTRUCTING EMBEDDED LEARNING OPPORTUNITIES

Consulting ECSE teachers find the ELO approach and the planning forms useful in their work with community-based teachers. Once a teacher learns the approach and how to use the forms, the approach can be easily transferred to other children and their objectives. However, sometimes the community-based teacher believes that the child needs highly specialized one-to-one time with the consulting teacher. Other times, the IFSP or IEP is written in a way that makes it difficult to translate the child's goals and objectives to functional classroom behaviors. The following are some guidelines that may be helpful in these situations.

Tailoring the Learning Objective

It is important to remember that learning objectives are not the same thing as activities. Likewise, planning an activity is different than providing instruction (see Giangreco et al., 1994). Community-based teachers are skilled at planning interesting, fun activities for groups of young children; however, in an inclusive classroom, they may not be as experienced at ensuring that an individual child's objective is embedded and that sufficient instruction is provided. For example, a child may have several learning objectives aimed at skills such as reaching, grasping, making a request, or comprehending people's names. These objectives are not activities. They are skills that children are expected to use during genuine activities to participate more effectively in those activities. The teacher's job is to teach the child to do those skills and to use them during genuine activities. Just presenting the activities is not enough; teaching must also occur.

Child Assessment Worksheet

Date: 1/17

Teacher's name: Gia

Child's name: Samisha

Classroom activities	Classroom expectations	Child's level of performance
Arrival	Stay with class when walking to classroom. Walk independently	Strength _______ Average _______ Area of concern ___X___
Circle time	Sit on own mat. Participate in music and movement games. Participate in literacy and numeracy activities.	Strength _______ Average ___X___ Area of concern _______
Small-group time	Stay at table. Participate in art and other small-group activities. Contribute questions and answers related to planned lesson.	Strength _______ Average ___X___ Area of concern _______
Free-choice time	Play independently. Play cooperatively with other children. Share and take turns. Explore all learning centers during the week.	Strength _______ Average _______ Area of concern ___X___

(page 1 of 2)

Figure 6.3. A Child Assessment Worksheet for Samisha. *(Blank version available in Appendix C and as a download.)*

Figure 6.3. *(continued)*

APPENDIX C *(continued)*

Classroom activities	Classroom expectations	Child's level of performance
Cleanup time	Clean area promptly when asked. Replace materials to shelves.	Strength _______ Average ___X___ Area of concern _______
Snack time	Stay at table. Eat snack. Talk with other children and pass items when asked.	Strength _______ Average ___X___ Area of concern _______
Outdoor time	Play on equipment in the playground. Play independently and with other children.	Strength _______ Average _______ Area of concern ___X___
Transitions	Follow instructions. Stay with group.	Strength _______ Average ___X___ Area of concern _______

(page 2 of 2)

ELO-at-a-Glance

Date: _1/17_

Team members: _Gia (teacher), David (assistant)_

Child's name: _Samisha_

Routines: _Free choice: Table game center_

Objective: _During play times, Samisha will join her peers in play and maintain play with them for 10 minutes or more in cooperative play activities. She will do this in four different play areas._

What are you going to do?
Point to or hand Samisha the game prop (e.g., car, ball).

What are you going to say?
"Samisha, take a turn," or other appropriate prompt

How will you respond?
If Samisha follows the instruction, praise and emphasize playing together. If not, hand Samisha the game prop and repeat instruction.

What materials do you need?
Table games that can be used by two or more children at the same time (e.g., Don't Break the Ice, Lotto, Hungry Hungry Hippos)

How many opportunities will you provide each day?

Monday	Tuesday	Wednesday	Thursday	Friday
Free-choice: table games 10+ minutes	Free-choice: table games 10+ minutes	Free-choice: table games 10+ minutes	Free-choice: table games 10+ minutes	Free-choice: table games 10+ minutes

(page 1 of 1)

Figure 6.4. An ELO-at-a-Glance for Samisha. *(Blank version available in Appendix J and as a download.)*

Sometimes, IFSP or IEP objectives are written in ways that may actually limit the potential for embedding the objective within genuine classroom activities. For example, a child's IEP objective may state, "Given the cue, 'Put the puzzle together' when presented with a three- to five-piece interlocking puzzle, Annie will disassemble the pieces and then put the puzzle back together on at least 80% of the response opportunities." This may lead a teacher to implement instruction on the objective by seating the child at a table and providing the child with repeated opportunities with a selected set of puzzles. This is unlikely to occur in an active, play-based classroom, and it may not be very motivating for the child. It is more likely that children will have opportunities to play with a variety of puzzles, various building or manipulative toys, and materials that involve identifying or reproducing designs.

As a member of the child's IEP team, the consulting ECSE teacher can help write objectives that are functional and generative. An example would be the following: "Annie will assemble toys or objects by putting pieces together. She will do this with at least five different toys available in the classroom, such as puzzles, LEGOs, or stringing beads." This new objective and the teaching procedures are stated on the ELO-at-a-Glance.

In preparing to use an ELO, the consulting ECSE teacher should work with the team to develop a learning objective or to modify the established learning objective so that it can be easily and naturally embedded in many activities (e.g., water play, cooking, art center) and routines (e.g., arrival, snack time, cleanup time). If a child needs instruction on a highly specific but necessary objective, however, using ELOs may not be the right approach. Here are some helpful hints for writing or tailoring learning objectives:

1. Do not limit a child's initiation of a skill or behavior to just one instruction or cue. Instead of using a single cue, such as "When a toy is rattled or shaken, the child will crawl 4 feet to obtain the toy," try "Child will crawl a minimum of 4 feet in response to any of the following: adult presence, peer presence, to obtain objects, to participate in an activity, and so forth."

2. Broadly define the child's response, if appropriate. Instead of saying "Child will request help in obtaining a favorite toy that is out of reach," try "Child will solve common problems by using more than one strategy, such as using a tool, requesting help, reaching around the barrier, and so forth."

3. Avoid limiting the objective to one type of material. Instead of saying "Child will stack three 1-inch cubes," try saying, "Child will stack a variety of small, stackable items, including blocks, small books, notepads, plastic cups, LEGOs, and so forth."

The purpose is to translate an objective from a child's IFSP or IEP to a learning objective that can be addressed more easily and effectively in the classroom, home, or child care setting. The important features of tailoring the objective are that 1) teaching can be implemented within routine and planned activities, 2) teaching can be implemented across multiple activities so the child receives sufficient learning opportunities, and 3) teaching is aimed at the acquisition of new concepts and skills, not just practice of already acquired skills.

Breaking Down Goals

Sometimes planning what to teach requires simplifying or breaking a large or annual goal into smaller, easier parts to help both the child and the teacher. Then, the steps can be sequenced for teaching. By breaking down the larger goal and teaching the steps or parts, the child makes progress toward the larger goal.

To break down a goal, first identify the child's current level of performance in relation to the large goal. There are at least four ways to break down a goal:

1. Break into smaller amounts. Specify a smaller quantity of items, toys, people, or locations for the goal. The skill stays the same, but the frequency or quantity of the skill is adjusted.

2. Provide help. Provide different levels of help until the child can perform the large goal independently. Be planful about the types and amount of help you provide and how you will gradually decrease your help.

3. Break down the goal into steps. Some goals are actually complex tasks with multiple steps. Break down a large goal or task into individual steps and teach each step.

4. Use logical order. Identify related skills that lead up to the goal. Teachers use their knowledge of child development and experience to figure out the subskills needed for the child to accomplish the large goal.

See Figure 6.5 for examples of breaking down larger goals into smaller parts.

After breaking down the large goal into smaller parts, the teacher and team sequence the parts or steps for teaching. The sequence may be easiest to hardest, first to last, or in logical order. The value of breaking large goals into smaller, teachable parts and then sequencing the steps is that both children and teachers will feel successful and teaching will be more efficient.

Method	Example
Smaller amounts	**Goal:** Samisha will join her peers and maintain play with them for 10 or more minutes in cooperative play activities. **Current level:** Plays for 1–2 minutes and then leaves the area. **Steps:** • Play for 3 minutes. • Play for 6 minutes. • Play for 10 or more minutes.
Providing help	**Goal:** Drew will respond to the first request to begin or complete activities for 8 out of 10 opportunities for 2 days in a row. **Current level:** Needs repeated individual instruction and physical assistance to begin or complete all activities except going outside. **Steps:** • Provide visual representation of every direction (e.g., photograph or drawing) plus individual instruction. • Provide visual representation plus instruction given to group; stand near Drew. • Provide visual representation plus instruction given to group. • Provide instruction given to group.
Step by step	**Goal:** Nhan will ask a peer to play a game or activity with him; he will be successful at asking and interacting with a peer at least once during free choice or outside play every day. **Current level:** Joins other children's play but does not initiate play with others. **Steps:** • Identifies a game, toy, or activity to play. • Identifies a peer to play with. • Approaches the peer. • Gets peer's attention. • Asks peer to play.
Logical order	**Goal:** When asked "What do you want?" or other natural cue, Mateo will use five different words to request (consistent word approximations). **Current level:** Vocalizes, smiles, and uses some gestures to communicate. **Steps:** • Imitates consistent vocalization and gesture. • Uses consistent word approximation and gesture. • Uses five consistent word or word approximations to request.

Figure 6.5. Method for breaking down goals.

Organizing the Learning Objectives

Planning is key to effective use of ELOs. In essence, the teacher and team are using specially designed instruction and doing so within the ongoing activities and routines of the day. The team prepares for learning by selecting learning opportunities that are likely to occur and that are distributed throughout the day and by preparing for learning by thinking carefully about the resources (including the people) that are available during class time. The team also prepares for learning by thinking about how they will monitor children's progress on their learning objectives.

Identifying or Creating Embedded Learning Opportunities   A child's process of learning the objectives is supported by planned teacher behavior. Teachers create opportunities for a child to perform the behavior, and they act in such a way as to accelerate the child's acquisition of the behavior. One way to do this is to take advantage of a child's interests or preferences (one of the curriculum modifications) when planning for ELOs.

One of Nhan's objectives is to increase vocabulary. Nhan has learned to smile, select a toy or activity, and look busy to avoid talking. However, his teachers also know that Nhan has some definite preferences in terms of toys. He likes to paint, build with blocks, and play ball on the playground. The teachers use the ELO strategy to teach Nhan to say the words for these toys. The teachers place the toys on shelves just out of his reach to encourage Nhan to ask for them by name. When he names the toy, a teacher gives it to him while repeating the word. Nhan's teacher also places pictures of all the children's favorite toys and people, as well as small toys, in her pockets. During transition times, she pulls these out to play naming games with Nhan and his classmates.

Creating Multiple Embedded Learning Opportunities   Multiple opportunities to practice targeted skills should be developed within and across activities. Children with identified disabilities, delays, and diverse abilities often require many opportunities to learn a new skill or concept. An important aspect of making ELOs work is to create many new opportunities to make certain that teaching and learning occur. Our examples so far show how to take advantage of the natural fit between certain objectives and activities or routines, as well as building on the child's interests and preferences. However, sometimes the child is reluctant to participate, or we need to create even more opportunities. A few other methods can be used to encourage participation in the activity and provide access to the learning opportunities. The environment can be arranged to set up opportunities. Think about seating arrangement, selection and placement of materials, and scheduling of activities. Wait time can be used to encourage initiation and participation. For example, Nhan's teachers place interesting objects in sight but out of reach to encourage his use of verbal language. Teachers can also start an activity and then pause and wait for the child to request more or another turn. Finally, choice making can encourage participation. There are lots of occasions when two or more choices can be offered. The child makes a selection and the learning opportunity can begin.

Any or all of these methods can be used to create and plan multiple learning opportunities. Use an activity matrix (see Chapter 4) to organize the learning opportunities.

Designing and Implementing Instruction

Selecting the appropriate teaching strategy can be difficult, but it is *so* important. The effective use of ELOs depends on designing and using instructional strategies that have a good chance of being effective. Fortunately, research and experience provide information to help make it easier to select good strategies (e.g., DEC, 2014; Sandall et al., 2005). Some of the things to think about in making selections include the following:

- Is the teaching strategy likely to be effective?

- Is it developmentally appropriate? (Is it similar to the approaches used with all children, or will it stigmatize the child?)

- Is it useful across environments?

- Is it respectful of the child?

There are three parts to a teaching episode—what the teacher says or does, what the child does (the behavior part of the learning objective), and how the teacher responds. What the teacher says or does involves the natural cue; it also includes a prompt. A prompt is what the teacher does, before the child responds, to help the child respond as expected. Examples of prompts include pictures, physical assistance or gestures, or a model.

The teacher or other adult must remember to complete the teaching episode by responding to the child and providing feedback. This is also called a *consequence*. It is planned ahead of time and might come in the form of praise, a comment, or a natural consequence, such as giving the child the toy they asked for. The consequence also includes a planned correction procedure or what the teacher does if the child does not respond as expected. Take a look at the ELO-at-a-Glance for Drew and Samisha (Figures 6.2 and 6.4, respectively) to see examples of simple but planned correction procedures. See Chapter 7 for more about instructional strategies.

Monitoring the Child's Progress   Collecting data about the use of ELOs has two components. First, it is important to keep track of the opportunities that are actually provided. It can be difficult to do this in a busy and action-packed classroom. On the ELO-at-a-Glance, the teacher can make a hash mark each time an opportunity is provided. Some teachers attach a blank piece of paper to the wall and make tally marks there. In one classroom, the teacher decided to provide at least 10 opportunities for a particular child each day. He put 10 paper clips in his pocket. Each time he provided a learning opportunity for the child, he moved a paper clip to his other pocket.

Second, teachers, of course, want to know if a child is making progress. Is the child learning the skill or concept? Every week, the teacher (or the consulting ECSE teacher) should collect child performance data. If the child is making progress, the instruction should continue. If the child has achieved the objective, practice opportunities may continue, but the team should think about what objective to teach next. If the child is not making progress, the team should make a change. Thus, the team will have information that is directly related to the child's IFSP or IEP. Chapter 4 introduced several ways to gather information about a child's progress: counts, notes, and permanent products. (See Chapter 8 for a more thorough discussion of these methods.) The data collection method chosen should match the objective, and it should be easy to implement in the classroom. The information is helpful only if it is collected and used regularly and systematically.

SUMMARY

ELOs have great natural appeal to teachers. This teaching strategy uses the existing activities, materials, and routines of the preschool classroom, home, or child care setting. Thus, it should be easy to incorporate a child's preferences and interests. ELOs naturally lead to the practice of behaviors that are distributed across the various times and events of classrooms and other learning environments.

It is important to remember, however, that ELOs are a way of providing specially designed instruction. It is not just about planning activities. ELOs must be carefully planned and carried out frequently enough to result in learning. They must also be matched to a child's individual learning objectives. The essential features of ELOs are contained on the ELO-at-a-Glance: the target behavior, what the teacher will do and say, how the child is expected to respond, and how the teacher will respond. It is vital that the teacher complete the teaching episode or learning opportunity by implementing all these parts. Children with identified disabilities, delays, and diverse abilities may have difficulty taking advantage of naturally occurring learning opportunities. Thus, an ELO is a specialized strategy that delivers the individualized, deliberate instruction that some children need. For more examples of planning and using ELOs, see the professional development modules on applying the Building Blocks framework to math and science and for infants and toddlers and planning for the individual child. The aim in using ELOs is for a child to learn their individual objectives and to use them in meaningful ways. Success is measured by the child's progress. If the child is not making progress, even more instructional support is warranted. The next chapter describes what the team can do if the child needs even more specialized assistance.

Chapter 7

Child-Focused Instructional Strategies

Sometimes, children with identified disabilities, developmental delays, and diverse abilities require directed, explicit instruction to achieve their individualized objectives and make progress in the typical early childhood curriculum and learning activities. In such situations, teachers must use instruction that is more systematic, more frequent, and even more carefully planned than that described in previous chapters. Child-focused instructional strategies (CFIS) are, for the most part, the same strategies that are used in embedded learning opportunities (ELOs). The difference is the level of intensity with which instruction is provided. To acquire necessary skills and concepts, some children may need more opportunities every day to practice the skill, more assistance from their teachers, explicit instruction in a setting with fewer distractions, positive reinforcement in a more consistent manner, and consistent guidance when they make errors.

These instructional strategies are techniques and methods for delivering instruction that have been demonstrated to result in improved child outcomes for children with different abilities and backgrounds. They help teachers transform opportunities for learning into successful learning interactions (for more information on CFIS, see Grisham-Brown & Hemmeter, 2017; Schwartz et al., 2017). This chapter describes when and how to use these instructional strategies for young children who need specially designed instruction and defines and describes the strategies.

WHEN TO USE CHILD-FOCUSED INSTRUCTIONAL STRATEGIES

CFIS can be used whenever you want to teach specific skills or concepts. Often, these specific skills or concepts come from the high-priority goals and objectives found on the child's IEP, IFSP, or behavior support plan. The strategies can be used in a number of different classroom and child care situations and during interactions that are child or teacher initiated. CFIS are used when a teaching team has identified a learning

Table 7.1. Instructional interactions using child-focused instructional strategies

Adult (antecedent)	Child (target behavior)	Adult (consequence)
"Samisha, walk to the snack table."	Samisha walks with her walker to the snack table.	"All right, Samisha. Have a seat right here." The adult gives Samisha a smile and a pat on the arm.
At the snack table, the teacher says, "Anyone wearing an orange shirt can clean up."	Drew looks at his shirt and says, "I'm orange" and gathers his snack dishes.	"Great job listening for directions, Drew."
As the teacher is reading a book during circle time, she stops, points to a picture of a baseball bat, and says, "What is a word that rhymes with *bat*?"	Three children call out in unison, "Cat."	The teacher responds, "You are correct. Cat rhymes with *bat*. Does anyone have another idea?"
Dara joins Mateo as he plays with a bin of sand and cars on the floor at child care. She holds up a car and models, "You can say *car*."	Mateo reaches for the car and says, "Ca, Ca."	Dara gives Mateo the car and says, "Car! Here's the car."

objective and has determined that for a particular child to learn the objective, the child needs specially designed instruction (e.g., "Samisha will use her walker or furniture to walk or step from place to place in the classroom"; "Nhan will use the Picture Exchange Communication System to request preferred art materials"; "Mateo will approximate words for his favorite items at home"). That is, CFIS are used when a child may need more intensive attention than can be embedded in ongoing routines and activities.

When using these teaching strategies, teams should remember that all instruction takes place in the context of an interaction or teaching episode. Most often, CFIS occur in the context of an adult–child interaction, but explicit instruction can also be used within peer-to-peer interaction. Either the child or the adult can begin the interaction, but the adult makes the decision to use this interaction as an instructional opportunity and uses the planned teaching strategy. When thinking about instruction occurring in the context of interactions, it is important to consider the sequence of turns that the people involved take; ideally, an instructional interaction includes an antecedent (what happens before or the teacher's cue), the behavior (the child's response or behavior), and consequence (what happens after the child's response). See Table 7.1 for examples as well as Figure 6.1 in the previous chapter.

These examples are explicit because they are planned by the teacher to help the child achieve the individualized objective. During CFIS, the same instructional strategies are used regularly, and the teacher evaluates the child's behavior and uses it as the basis for changing the teacher's behaviors. The purpose is to facilitate the child's success in learning the objective by providing many opportunities or trials to learn and practice the individualized objective and receive feedback.

THE BASIC STEPS

The first step is to decide whether to use specially designed instructional strategies in addition to ELOs or whether embedding instruction into the ongoing activities and routines will be sufficient for a child to learn the objective. Itinerant or consulting teachers or specialists contribute to designing and using CFIS by sharing their knowledge of effective strategies. Following are some of the criteria that the teacher and the team need to consider:

- *The child is making very slow progress despite the teacher's or the team's use of ELOs or curriculum modifications.* In other words, the child's response to the current intervention is not meeting the team's or the family's expectations. In this case, the team will make certain the objective is appropriate, break it into smaller parts if necessary, and add CFIS to provide the child with more opportunities to learn and practice the target skill with guidance.

- *The child must learn a skill or concept to succeed in the general early childhood curriculum.* In other words, the skill is a keystone skill that will help the child access the ongoing activities, routines, and curricular content. Examples of such skills or concepts that might need to be taught explicitly to a young child are establishing joint attention, imitating children or adults, playing with toys, and following simple directions.

- *The child must learn a foundational school skill.* That is, the teacher or the team teaches skills that help the child be as independent as possible in early childhood environments. Examples are playing or working independently for short times, managing materials, and following classroom routines, as well as age-appropriate adaptive skills that would be best taught in a private setting, such as toileting or dressing.

- *The child's objective is unique.* Other children in the classroom are not learning this skill or concept. Samisha's objective to learn to use her walker is one example; learning to use an augmentative and alternative communication system is another.

- *The child demonstrates a persistent behavior that interferes with participation and has an individual behavior support plan.* The child may need instruction to learn functionally equivalent replacement skills for such behaviors as whining, grabbing, and so forth. When a child engages in behaviors that are challenging to teachers, we examine what the child is trying to tell us and then use CFIS to teach a different way of communicating the unmet need.

Once the decision is made to use CFIS, the basic steps are similar to those outlined for ELOs:

1. Clarify the learning objective and determine the criteria.

2. Gather baseline information to determine the child's current level of performance.

3. Use an activity matrix to select activities or times of the day when the special instruction can be delivered.

4. Design the instructional interaction—the teaching episode—and write it on a planning form.

5. Implement the instruction as planned. Ensure that instruction is implemented correctly and frequently enough to provide multiple opportunities across the day for the child to respond, acquire, and practice the skill with teacher guidance.

6. Collect and review child performance data daily.

Notice that the final step has changed in intensity. That is, the teacher or the team needs to collect data on child performance every day so that informed teaching decisions can be made as soon as necessary. Because teacher and child time are valuable resources, the teacher needs to use classroom time wisely. Data are collected using one of the methods described in Chapters 4 and 8: counts, notes, or permanent products. Counting is often the preferred method when using CFIS.

Another way the use of CFIS differs from that of ELOs or curriculum modifications is the time that is identified for the specially designed instructional situation. The teacher may use a few minutes before or during an ongoing classroom activity for CFIS. For example, the teacher may join a child's play during free choice or outdoor time to work on a specific skill or behavior using CFIS. The aim is to increase the number of opportunities or trials that the child has to respond to explicit instruction on the learning objective. Many children with complex learning needs will require many opportunities to learn a new skill. The data collected by the teacher will answer the question about how many trials are necessary for the child to learn the new skill.

DEVELOPING CHILD-FOCUSED INSTRUCTIONAL STRATEGIES

Whether a teacher plans to provide instruction embedded within an ongoing activity or routine or as a specially designed part of the day, the basic instructional strategies are the same. The strategies can be divided into three categories: instructions, prompting strategies, and consequence (e.g., positive reinforcement, corrective feedback) strategies.

Instructions

The purpose of *instructions* or cues is to tell a child what they are expected to do. In a classroom, teachers may give instructions to a single child or to groups of children. An important step in giving good instructions is to know what it is that you want the child to do. Instructions guide the child to a specific component of a task or an activity or to the materials that you want the child to pay attention to. In general, good instructions are:

- Short

- Clear

- Focused on the observable behavior

- Positive (i.e., they tell the child to do something rather than to stop doing something)

Table 7.2 provides examples of instructions. Use the Child Assessment Worksheet in Appendix C (also available as a download) as a resource for team members to clarify shared expectations.

Prompting Strategies

A *prompt* is something a teacher does before the child responds in order to increase the probability that the child will respond correctly. Prompts are used in addition to the instruction or cue, and a prompt is considered effective only if it helps the child demonstrate the correct response or engage in the desired behavior. Many kinds of prompting strategies are useful in early childhood classrooms, but all should 1) help teach skills, 2) be removed as soon as possible (so the child can do the skill independently), and

Table 7.2. Examples of effective and not effective instructions

Effective instructions	Less effective instructions
"Point to the train."	"I see lots of pretty pictures. Do you see a picture of a train?" (*Note:* The probable outcome of this instruction is for the child to say "Yes," not point to the picture.)
"Nhan, come play baseball with us."	"Nhan, look, lots of kids are playing baseball. You like baseball, don't you? What would you like to do now? Would you like to join your friends?"
"Write your name on the sign-in sheet."	"Remember what we do every day when we come into the classroom? It is the first thing we do; we do it before we join morning meeting. Remember, you get to sign in with everyone else from the class. You need to write your name right here."
(To a child who is running around the room during free-choice time)	
"Drew, listen. Do you want to play at the sensory table or with the blocks?"	"Drew, stop running around and think about what you want to do. You need to make a choice."

3) be combined with reinforcement. Prompts may be verbal, gestural, a model, physical, or pictorial. Notice the different levels of support provided by the different kinds of prompts. Prompt hierarchies (most to least or least to most) can be used systematically to teach new skills.

Graduated Guidance   Using *graduated guidance,* a teacher provides the least amount of assistance (prompt) necessary to the child. The help should be removed as soon as the child can do the skill on their own.

Samisha is learning to put on her backpack by herself. This involves positioning the pack, putting one arm through the strap, pulling it to her shoulder, and then putting the other arm through the strap and extending her arm so that the strap is on her shoulder. The teacher uses a physical, hand-over-hand prompt for the steps of putting on the backpack that Samisha cannot do on her own and verbal prompts for the steps that Samisha can do but sometimes forgets. As soon as Samisha learns to do a new step on her own, the teacher no longer prompts that step.

Time Delay   Teachers can reduce and eventually eliminate the prompts they give a child by allowing the child a few seconds to do part of the behavior before giving a prompt. This prompting strategy, called *time delay,* can be very effective in teaching children to be more spontaneous in requesting and labeling toys, materials, or activities.

Mateo's child care provider uses time delay as a way to teach words to request favorite toys or activities. While pushing Mateo on the swing outside, she gently stops the swing, moves to Mateo's level in front of him, and gives him an encouraging and expectant look. She waits 3 seconds or until Mateo approximates the word "go" or "swing." If Mateo does not use a word approximation, Dara prompts him, "Go. Tell me go."

Time delay is also an effective prompting strategy for nonverbal responses.

If Samisha always waits for the teacher to start putting the backpack on her, the teacher could use time delay. The teacher stands near the children's cubbies and says, "Time to get your backpacks on." Then the teacher waits about 3 seconds while looking expectantly at Samisha. If Samisha begins the task, the teacher smiles and helps as needed. If Samisha waits, the teacher could give a more direct instruction, such as, "Samisha, put your backpack on," and wait another 3 seconds.

Backward Chaining   For some objectives, it may make more sense for the teacher to provide prompts or assistance for the entire sequence of steps at first.

Tina's teachers, Dolores and Maggie, use backward chaining to help Tina learn to fasten her clothing. At first, Dolores or Maggie uses hand-over-hand assistance to get the fasteners lined up and to apply some pressure. Next, they start to remove their assistance during the last step (e.g., snapping the snaps, finishing the zip). Then, they start to remove their assistance at the step of applying pressure. Finally, they will remove their help at lining up the fasteners, and Tina will be able to do the whole series of steps by herself. While she is learning this series of steps, Tina experiences success at the completion of the task of fastening.

Consequence Strategies

A *consequence* is a teacher behavior or an environmental event that occurs after a child behavior. For example, if a child asks for a glass of water and someone brings the water, the consequence for the behavior of asking is receiving water. A consequence also provides information; it is sometimes referred to as instructional feedback. The most commonly used and most effective consequence in early learning settings is positive reinforcement. Another consequence frequently used is corrective feedback. Both of these are discussed further in this section.

Research and experience provide evidence to support the use of reinforcement procedures to help children learn. *Reinforcers* are things (e.g., praise, activities) that follow a behavior. Whereas prompts occur before the child's behavior, reinforcers are what teachers do immediately after the child's behavior or response. The focus here is on the use of positive reinforcement.

Positive Reinforcement

Positive reinforcement is an action or event that follows a specific response and increases the likelihood that the response will happen again. Reinforcement is used extensively in educational environments and can be very simple and natural. For example, after a child asks for a ball, the teacher gives the child the toy and says something like, "Thanks for asking. Here's the ball." It may also be more systematic and formal. For example:

After Tina gets her clothes fastened, the teacher says, "Wow, Tina, you snapped your snaps!" and puts a star on her chart. When Mateo says, "Go," Dara says, "Let's go" and gives the swing a push.

Positive reinforcement is usually a pleasant consequence; it has a high probability of increasing whatever behavior it follows.

An important feature of positive reinforcement is that what functions as a reinforcer is very specific to each child and varies over time. Although teacher praise, encouragement, and smiles may be powerful reinforcers for most young children, we cannot assume that these will be effective for all children, especially with children with more complex learning needs. The only way to determine whether something is a reinforcer is to examine the effect it has on a child's behavior. For instance, if a child is not learning a skill in instructional sessions with teacher praise being used as the intended reinforcer, one interpretation may be that a more powerful reinforcer (e.g., access to a preferred toy, such as a music toy) may be needed. Families can also identify possible reinforcers through their knowledge of their child's favorite activities, events, and toys.

Differential Reinforcement of Other Behavior

The idea behind differential reinforcement of other behavior (DRO) is to catch and celebrate the child demonstrating behaviors that are valued at home and school and let the child know it! This technique is used when you want to decrease a challenging behavior in the classroom by providing the child with positive reinforcement for behaviors that are incompatible with the challenging behavior. For example, if a child is very active and moves rapidly from one activity to another without really playing at any activity, we could use a DRO procedure to provide feedback to the child when they stay at an activity and become engaged in play. Call attention to the child's appropriate behavior ("Drew, look at you and Rohan making a spaceship with the blocks. It's really getting big!"), rather than to the inappropriate behavior ("Drew, stop running around the classroom and find something to do!").

Table 7.3. Examples of corrective feedback

Context/setting	Child behavior	Corrective feedback
During free play, Tina is playing with dolls in the dramatic play area with two other children.	Tina grabs a doll from another child.	"Tina, Amanda was playing with that doll. If you want a turn, you need to ask."
During specialized instructional time, Drew is working on identifying colors. The teacher holds up a blue container of bubbles and asks, "What color?"	Drew says, "Green."	"It is blue. Say *blue*."
The children are cleaning up after snack.	On his way to the trash can, Nhan drops his empty cup on the floor.	"Nhan, you dropped your cup. Go back and pick it up, please."

Corrective Feedback Sometimes, children give incorrect responses or engage in behavior that is not appropriate for the setting. Corrective feedback lets a child know when a response or behavior is incorrect or unacceptable and shows the child a more appropriate alternative. Corrective feedback should *never* be punitive. When using corrective feedback, adults do not repeat the child's mistake or describe inappropriate behavior. Corrective feedback offers the child information about the desired behavior, provides guidance on how to improve behavior, and should be delivered in a neutral tone of voice. See Table 7.3 for some examples of corrective feedback.

Peer-Mediated Strategies

Teachers cannot be everywhere at once, so in some inclusive early childhood settings, a teacher may rely on peers to assist other children in learning or practicing some skills. To incorporate peers into an individualized program for a child with identified disabilities or diverse needs, several points are important to remember (Barton & Smith, 2015; Schwartz & McBride, 2014).

- *The peer needs to know how to do the skill.* For example, if the objective for the child with more complex learning needs is to follow the routine of putting on coats and boots and going outside, the peers who are helping should be able to do each step of the routine by themselves.

- *The peers need to know what to do to help the child learn the skill.* The teacher must explain to the peers exactly what they should do to help. For example, the teacher goes over each step of the routine with the peers. Peers should provide help only when the child cannot do a part of the task. For example, the child with complex learning needs may be able to find their cubby when the teacher says, "Time to line up and go outside," but may have difficulty putting on their coat all the way. The peers need to know to *not* provide help in finding the child's cubby but to provide help with the coat.

- *Different peers should be incorporated into the learning process.* The teacher should choose several peers to be helpers for the child with complex learning needs. One peer who is asked to be a helper all the time may grow tired of it.

- *The peers need to know that the teacher values their work.* Teachers can show how much they value the peers' assistance in several ways. They can praise them, give them a hug or pat, or provide a more formal reward, such as getting to do a special activity. Such adult recognition is a critical part of most peer-mediated teaching approaches.

- *The peers should be taught not to treat the child with complex learning needs as the "helpee."* The teacher should point out the things that the child can do independently (i.e., recognize the child's strengths). In fact, sometimes it is appropriate to ask a child with complex learning needs to be the peer helper. Also, when peers are giving too much assistance or assisting with things the child already knows how to do, the teacher needs to step in and suggest that they wait to see whether the child can do the task by themself.

- *Remember that some of the curriculum modifications also involve peers but may require less time teaching the peers.* Examples are the ways that teachers group children for some activities, the use of peer buddies, and other simple modifications. Peer-to-peer support, whether as a simple modification or peer-mediated instruction, helps create a culture of caring and belonging.

The examples in this chapter should guide teachers and their teams in the use of more explicit instruction. The forms in Chapter 4 provide direction for planning. Teachers may want to use the Instruction-at-a-Glance form (see Figure 7.1, Instruction-at-a-Glance for Tina, and the blank form in Appendix K, which is also available as a download) to guide the teaching episodes.

This planning form will help teachers highlight the elements necessary to implement CFIS and help them collect daily data to keep track of how the child is doing. Note that on the second page of the Instruction-at-a-Glance, the number of the trials or opportunities is given. The teacher circles the number if the child is correct and slashes the number if the child is incorrect, and the teacher then uses the data to make instructional decisions. Chapter 8 and the professional development module on ongoing assessment provide more guidance on making instructional decisions.

TIPS FOR USING CHILD-FOCUSED INSTRUCTIONAL STRATEGIES

Consider several issues when using CFIS and implementing the strategies described in this chapter. Additional resources to consult for using CFIS are found in Appendix T (also available as a download). The professional development modules on math and science and for infants and toddlers provide additional examples for using CFIS.

Scheduling

It may seem overwhelming to try to identify times during a busy day when the teacher or other adult can concentrate on a single child and provide specialized instruction. However, it is likely that this child is already demanding adult attention. For example, this may be the child that the teacher always has to help, remind, or have by their side. Why not use the time more productively? Here are some ideas:

- *Identify and use times when the other children are independent and engaged in activities.* This might be in the middle of free-choice time, out on the playground, or at mealtime.

- *Select times that are followed by a fun or preferred activity.* The specially designed instructional time is hard work for a child; make sure it is followed by something fun.

- *Avoid selecting times that are the child's favorite or times when the child is successful in the early learning environment.* No one wants to leave something they enjoy or are good at.

- *Even a few minutes of special time is worth it.* Be consistent and provide this time every day. You and the child may be more successful if you select several short opportunities (e.g., 5 minutes) to work together rather than try to find one extended 30-minute block of time.

APPENDIX K

Instruction-at-a-Glance

Date: 2/11

Child's name: Tina   Teacher's name: Dolores

Objective: With contextual cues, Tina will independently and accurately tell events that occurred on the same day at least 30 minutes after the occurrence of the event.

---

1. Setting for instruction

When? End of work time

Where? Near large-group area

How often? 5 trials; repeat at recall time

Materials needed? Pictures or toys from centers; review work time with Tina

2. Instructional interaction

Antecedent	Child behavior	Consequence
Instruction "What did you do at work time?" Wait 3 seconds.	Contextually accurate 2- to 3- word phrase (e.g., "I paint hearts.")	Positive reinforcement If correct, affirm and expand on response.
Prompt Model, such as "I paint hearts."		Corrective feedback If incorrect or no response, model.

(page 1 of 2)

Figure 7.1. Instruction-at-a-Glance for Tina. *(Blank version available in Appendix K and as a download.)*

Figure 7.1. *(continued)*

APPENDIX K *(continued)*

3. Monitoring progress:

Instructions: For the numbers 5–0 and ND ("No data") in the columns representing number of trials, circle or draw a line through each number, depending on response:

○ = correct, ╱ = incorrect.

		Date												
Current step														
Will tell events that occurred on the same day immediately after work time	⑤	5	5	5	5	5	5	5	5	5	5	5	5	5
	4̸	4	4	4	4	4	4	4	4	4	4	4	4	4
	3̸	3	3	3	3	3	3	3	3	3	3	3	3	3
	②	2	2	2	2	2	2	2	2	2	2	2	2	2
	1̸	1	1	1	1	1	1	1	1	1	1	1	1	1
	0̸	0	0	0	0	0	0	0	0	0	0	0	0	0
Criteria:	ND	ND	ND	ND	ND	ND	ND	ND	ND	ND	ND	ND	ND	ND

4. Comments, questions, or issues to discuss with the team:

____

____

____

____

____

____

____

____

____

____

____

____

____

____

____

(page 2 of 2)

The activity matrix (see Chapter 4) is an indispensable tool for scheduling. The activity matrix helps the teacher and team see the whole schedule and the many planned activities. They can then identify the best available times to provide frequent opportunities using CFIS to address an individual child's high-priority learning objective(s) and to distribute these opportunities throughout the day, whether in the classroom, in child care, or at home.

Selecting Materials

Here are some things to keep in mind when selecting materials for helping the child learn their specific learning objective:

- Use materials that are similar to those the child uses in the classroom or community.
- Use materials that the child finds interesting.
- Use materials that are developmentally appropriate.
- Use materials that are appropriate to the learning objective.
- Vary the materials.

Motivation and Reinforcement

Few people are motivated to work on something that is difficult without some added incentive. Remember that children are working hard to participate, follow the routine, and learn their individualized objectives. Here are some ideas for making CFIS time more enjoyable for children:

- Identify potential motivators. These can be activities, such as getting more playground time, listening to music, or rocking in a rocking chair, or tangible motivators, such as a favorite toy or a sticker. There are also social motivators, such as a smile and a pat on the back. Give the child choices from a set of potential motivators. Keep track of those the child prefers.

- During the teaching time, use a motivator along with the positive feedback you give to the child.

- Make sure the child receives these motivators at a rate that keeps the child trying the activity or working at the skill. For example, if a child likes to make paper chains, give the child a slip of paper as a tangible reinforcer for every correct response. When the child gets 10 (or at the end of the session), let the child make the paper chain. If the child is interested in letters, give the child a magnetic letter every time they make a correct response and spend time at the end of the session spelling words together. Here, the idea is that you take an activity that the child likes (is reinforcing) and give the child "pieces" of the activity to keep working.

- If the special time involves more than one child, make sure the activity is motivating for everyone.

Monitoring Progress

It is important to collect regular data on the child's performance so that the teacher or the team can decide whether to continue the instruction or to change it. It is unfair to the child to continue doing the same thing if the child is not learning. The consulting or itinerant ECSE teacher may help devise a way of collecting these data so that the ECE teacher, child care provider, or assistants can carry out the plan, given the time

Table 7.4. Troubleshooting for child-focused instructional strategies

Challenge	Potential solutions
The child is not progressing at an adequate rate on IFSP/IEP objectives.	Increase the intensity of instruction by providing more opportunities for the child to practice the skill with adult guidance.
	Replace the reinforcer with something you think will be more motivating for the child. Break down the objective into smaller steps; teach each of these intermediate objectives.
The child demonstrates challenging behavior during instructional sessions.	Shorten the sessions. Provide more of these shorter sessions. Provide more positive reinforcement. Alternate the new tasks the child is learning with skills the child already knows how to do; that is, alternate between acquisition tasks and maintenance or practice tasks. Provide choices if possible (e.g., choice of materials, location for teaching)
The child becomes dependent on prompts and waits for the teacher's instructions or assistance before trying to complete the task independently.	Decrease the amount of physical guidance. Increase the amount of time between giving a direction and providing assistance.
The data collected indicate that the child performs inconsistently depending on which teacher is working with the child.	Examine the fidelity with which the intervention is being implemented. Is everyone on the team following the procedure as written and presenting it the same way to the child?
Team members believe that they have "done everything," but the child is still not making progress.	Examine the targeted learning objective and how it was selected. Team members should ask themselves these questions: Did you use a curriculum to select the goal? Are you addressing the correct spot in the scope and sequence for this particular child at this time in their learning history? Do you need to back up and teach some keystone or entry skills?

Key: IEP, individualized educational program; IFSP, individualized family service plan.

and resources available to them. The Instruction-at-a-Glance (Figure 7.1) provides space for regular data collection along with guidance for delivering instruction. It may be the itinerant ECSE teacher's responsibility to do a check or mini-test every few days to make sure that the child is learning the skill or concept.

Troubleshooting

Although many children will start making progress quickly with intensive instruction, some will provide challenges for the teacher and the educational team. See Table 7.4 for some ideas for troubleshooting instructional plans for children who are not making progress at the rate the team expects.

SUMMARY

This chapter describes how and when teachers and teams use more explicit CFIS. The strategies themselves (i.e., using good instructions, prompting, and using appropriate consequences) are similar to the strategies used for ELOs. The primary difference is the intensity with which instruction is provided. Sometimes, children continue to have difficulty with learning despite rich and inviting activities and environments and despite teachers' attempts to provide additional learning opportunities. Some children have very individual learning needs that demand more explicit instruction. In any case, it is the team's responsibility to ensure that sufficient and appropriate teaching occurs.

Chapter 8

Ongoing Assessment and Instructional Decision Making

Assessment is defined as the process of gathering information to make decisions. In early childhood, assessment is done for a variety of reasons, including developmental screening, educational diagnosis or determination of eligibility for special services, program planning and goal setting for the individual child, monitoring the child's progress, and program evaluation. We assess to answer questions and make decisions: Is Mateo eligible for special services? Will Samisha accomplish her social goals faster with peer-mediated instruction or adult modeling? Is Nhan increasing his vocabulary in both his home language and English? What classroom activities are difficult for Drew? What activities are preferred? Are the goals and objectives being addressed in class important to Tina's family?

In this chapter, we focus on gathering information to plan for the individual child as well as for monitoring the child's progress and making instructional decisions. There are many books and resources that cover the more expansive topic of early childhood assessment (e.g., Pretti-Frontczak et al., 2023).

ASSESSMENT AND THE BUILDING BLOCKS FRAMEWORK

One of the first considerations is determining *what to teach*. There are many sources that detail what young children should know and be able to do, such as Head Start's Early Learning Outcomes Framework, state early learning standards or benchmarks, and research-based curricula. For young children with identified disabilities, developmental delays, and diverse abilities, these sources remind us of the importance of ensuring active participation and progress in the general education curriculum.

Within the Building Blocks framework, we add focus on the individual child's learning needs as well as the child's strengths and interests and arrive at a continually evolving set of learning goals and objectives. A child's individual learning goals and objectives come from the following:

- An individual plan such as the IEP, IFSP, behavior support plan, or other individual learning plan

- A curriculum-referenced assessment or checklist used with all the children in the classroom or group

- Observation of the child's current participation and learning

- Input from the family about their priorities, concerns, and goals for their child

The teaching team also completes a routines-based assessment using the Child Assessment Worksheet (available in Appendix C and as a download) to better understand how the child does in their typical learning environments. The team gathers and synthesizes all this information. For more about identifying individual objectives, see Chapter 4 and the professional development module on planning for the individual child.

Then, the teaching team designs and delivers instructional support to help the child make progress toward their learning goals and objectives. This means taking advantage of evidence-based teaching practices as well as teaching practices based on wisdom and experience. It also means taking advantage of the child's interests and preferences.

A challenge of designing effective instruction is making the right match between the child's learning needs and just the right amount of support. In the early years, much of the child's learning happens through active participation with toys, materials, other children, and adults. Sometimes a child will need just a little bit of help to participate, and sometimes a child will need lots of help or a special kind of assistance to participate. In designing instruction for each learning objective, the team needs to figure out if a modification is sufficient (and what type of modification), if more learning opportunities are needed and when and where to embed them, or if specially designed instruction is required.

Once the amount of support is determined and instruction is designed, a plan is created and delivered. Various methods of ongoing assessment are used to find out if the plan actually works, the instruction is making a difference, and the child is progressing. To do this, the teaching team collects data regularly and makes instructional decisions based on the data.

Frequency of Assessment Practices

The assessment practices we use in the Building Blocks framework are consistent with the progress monitoring requirement in a multi-tiered systems of support (MTSS) framework. Our systematic and continuous process of ongoing assessment occurs at each tier or level of the Building Blocks framework as shown in Figure 8.1.

At the foundation (high-quality early childhood program) level, programs collect assessment information on all children two to three times per year often using a curriculum-referenced tool. This information helps identify learning priorities and monitor progress for the group of children as well as individual children. This information helps to identify children for whom more intensive or specific instruction or support is needed. Such tools need to be accurate, reliable, and efficient so that children who are not meeting benchmarks are identified and timely assistance is provided. MTSS refers to this kind of assessment as universal screening.

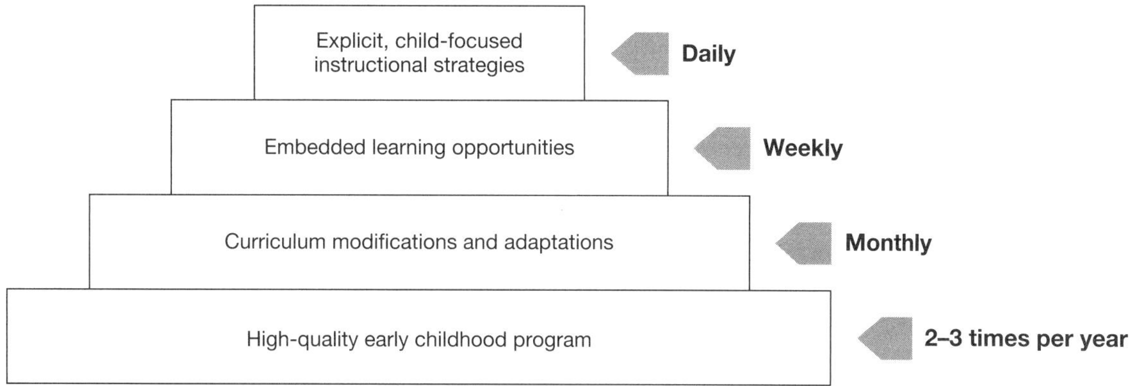

Figure 8.1. Frequency of data collection.

At the next level (curriculum modifications), the teaching team observes the effects of the modification or adaptation for the individual child. Often modifications work almost immediately. If not, the team may want to try another modification or decide to provide more intensive instruction. If observational data show that the modification works, the team will consider whether to remove the modification or keep it in place. At this level of support, assessment data are collected at least monthly.

At the next level of Building Blocks (embedded learning opportunities), the team collects ongoing assessment data for the individual child about once a week and uses the data to make decisions about continuing the instruction or adjusting the current plan.

At the next, most intensive level (child-focused instructional strategies [CFIS]), the team collects ongoing assessment data almost daily and uses the data to make decisions about continuing the instruction or making changes. Note that when instruction is more intensive, data are collected more frequently so that instructional decisions are made in a timely manner.

These are suggestions for the frequency of data collection. The child's individual plan will likely provide guidance. What is important is that ongoing assessment is planned, systematic, continuous, and used to inform teaching and learning.

Benefits of Assessment

A key benefit of assessment is the documentation of the child's progress that can be shared with families, caregivers, and other team members. The assessment information should aid communication by answering the assessment questions initially posed. In addition, systematic and ongoing assessment helps the team make revisions and adjustments to their teaching so that children are gaining the most benefits from their participation in early learning care and education programs.

Research supports the value of ongoing assessment (DEC, 2014; McLeskey et al., 2017). Teachers and teams who gather, summarize, and interpret child data in systematic and frequent ways create higher-quality individual plans. Teachers and teams who regularly collect and use data are better able to revise and adjust their teaching and provide more meaningful instruction for children with disabilities, delays, and diverse abilities. This leads to better rates of learning and enhanced child outcomes. Ongoing assessment helps teachers know children well and deeply understand their learning trajectories across different skill areas. They know the child's strengths, abilities, and interests as well as the child's learning needs. Finally, teachers and teams with solid knowledge of child development and effective teaching practices, as well as individual children, are better able to match or individualize instruction for that child.

Guidance From Law and Policy

Both NAEYC and DEC provide guidance on appropriate assessment practices (DEC, 2014; NAEYC, 2022). Observing, documenting, and reflecting on or analyzing each child's development and learning are necessary to plan and provide effective learning experiences including special instruction. Effective assessment methods are developmentally, culturally, and linguistically responsive, systematic yet authentic, and involve the family. One recommended practice (DEC, 2014) has particular relevance for Building Blocks:

> A9. Practitioners implement systematic ongoing assessment to identify learning targets, plan activities, and monitor the child's progress to revise instruction as needed.

Assessment for young children is also guided by federal and state laws related to the Individuals with Disabilities Education Act (IDEA, 2004). IDEA has clear requirements related to assessment for eligibility, program planning, and procedural safeguards. The school district or lead early intervention agency is responsible for ensuring that requirements are met. Some of the themes described previously (e.g., family participation, multiple methods, unbiased, systematic, and timely) are not just recommended but required. The IEP or IFSP must include a description of how the child's progress will be monitored.

Early childhood programs enroll children with a range of cultural and linguistic backgrounds and abilities. It is critical to take intentional steps to ensure the assessment is done in ways that are equitable. The strengths-based guidance that has been described is part of this intentionality. It is also important to recognize that one's own culture can affect expectations for children, the ways that children are assessed, and the decisions that are made. Such recognition can lead to valuable reflection on assessment practices.

Methods for Ongoing Assessment

Assessment plan   An assessment plan is essential. The plan includes procedures for all the children in the classroom or group as well as for individual children. Figure 8.1 indicates the frequency of assessment. The plan should also include who will assess, what to assess, and how to assess. A data collection matrix (Figure 8.2) is a simple way to keep track of data collection schedules in a classroom or group setting. This example is a weekly plan. Note that data are collected daily for objectives requiring high-intensity instruction (CFIS), whereas data are collected weekly for objectives that are embedded (ELOs). For objectives requiring curriculum modifications, data are collected monthly so only some appear on this weekly matrix. Finally, data are also collected for all children on some goals, and a note shows that, in this case, work samples are collected during the month. Teaching teams make assessment plans that work for them.

Most methods for collecting child information rely on direct observation (i.e., watching and listening) but may also incorporate interviews (e.g., parent report). Methods should be easy to use, meaningful, and practical. Ideally, methods for ongoing assessment are integrated within the typical activities and routines of the learning environment whether it is a classroom, child care setting, or home. We collect and

Data Collection Matrix

Date: Week of 1/8 Teacher's name: Dolores

	Monday	Tuesday	Wednesday	Thursday	Friday	
Arrival	Tyrone — identify name	Tyrone — identify name	Tyrone — identify name	Tyrone — identify name	Tyrone — identify name	
Planning					Ricky — use schedule, all day	
Work time			Tina — sorting		Ricky — picture schedule	All — collect name-writing sample by end of month
Recall			Tina — use words to recall			
Snack time						
Toileting	Tina — fasteners	Tina — fasteners	Tina — fasteners	Tina — fasteners	Tina — fasteners	
Outside				Tyrone — play near peers		
Small-group time		Tina — sorting	Tyrone — descriptive words			
Large-group time						All — collect story recall by end of month
Departure	Tina — fasteners					

Figure 8.2. Data collection matrix.

review data for children with disabilities, delays, or diverse abilities more frequently. However, whenever possible, we use similar methods to collect the data. We highlight three methods: counts, notetaking, and work samples or permanent products.

Counts   Counting refers to watching and listening to the child and tallying or recording the child's demonstration of the target behavior or skill. It requires that the target behavior or skill—the child's learning objective—be carefully defined or described. The behavior must be observable.

It may not be necessary or feasible to record every occurrence of the behavior throughout the day. We can take a sample to gauge whether the child is making progress and learning the new behavior or skill or is no longer demonstrating an unwanted behavior. *Event sampling* refers to counting each time the child does the behavior during a specified time frame. For example, the teacher observes during the first 15 minutes of free-choice time and tallies each time the child talks to a peer. Or, as another example, at arrival time, the teacher watches a young toddler and counts how many steps the child takes independently.

With *event sampling*, the plan is to record every instance of a behavior during a specific observation period. With *time sampling*, the plan is to determine whether a behavior occurred during a specific interval. If a teacher was interested in how much time a child spent actively engaged in a specific center or activity, the teacher could set a timer as an alert at the end of every minute of a 10-minute observation period and the teacher would record whether the child was actively engaged. The teacher would then be able to determine the percentage of intervals over a specified time in which the child was engaged. Time sampling is especially helpful to observe behaviors that are not discrete, such as peer interaction and active engagement.

Sometimes we will want to measure other dimensions of the target behavior or skill. *Rate* is determined by dividing the number of occurrences of the behavior by the time observed. *Duration* is the time between the onset and end of a behavior such as playing cooperatively. *Latency* is the time from the cue or direction to the onset of the behavior, such as the time from the teacher's direction to "clean up" to the child's picking up toys.

Notes   Notetaking refers to observing and listening to the child and then making a written or electronic record of the child's performance of the target behavior or skill. Notes may be written during the observation or shortly after the activity or session. It is important to write notes as soon as possible to improve accuracy. Separate objective information (i.e., what the child says or does) from subjective information (e.g., your interpretations of the child's motivation or preferences). For example, the child care provider observes on the playground and writes down what the child did, the activities selected, and who (if anyone) the child interacted with.

Teachers and child care providers often create forms to keep track of daily routines, such as feedings and meals, diapering and toileting, and naps. Individual objectives can be inserted into these forms to remind caregivers to monitor progress on specific learning objectives. For example, on the toileting chart, the child care provider records the hand-washing steps that a child completes independently.

Products   Products or work samples refer to a collection of samples of the child's work that are related to the child's target behavior or skill. Various artwork (e.g., drawings, paintings, sculptures) and writing or language samples are typical examples of products. They are natural parts of the learning activities. Collect similar samples over time to show progress. For example, in one classroom, children sign in every morning by writing their name on a whiteboard. The teacher takes a photo of the whiteboard each week to assess name writing.

Digital tools can make it easier to collect and store data using any of the three methods. For example, counts can be recorded on a data sheet that is loaded on a tablet or phone. Similarly, notes can be written on a tablet or phone. By making video or audio recordings, you not only have a permanent product but can also review the recording and count behaviors or make additional notes. It is also possible to quickly take a photo of the child's work or interaction either as documentation or as a reminder for recording notes. Products, whether the actual work or a digital record, should be labeled with the date and other relevant information. Of course, the digital tools, like all assessment information, need to be secure, and care must be taken to maintain confidentiality.

Teaching teams select a data collection method that both matches the child's objective and can be implemented in their setting. For example, if Nhan is working on following routine directions in his child care classroom, using counts of the directions he is following within a certain activity or during transition makes the most sense. For Drew's objective related to emotional regulation, the team chooses to take notes on the level of help Drew needs to calm down and how he starts to take breaks more independently over time. Sometimes teams use two data collection methods. Tina's sorting objective is easily tracked by snapping a photo of her work, including a short description noting if she needed help or not, and uploading this to an electronic portfolio.

Using Ongoing Assessment to Inform Teaching

Getting organized   Regardless of the methods, the data need to be both collected and analyzed. The data are used to inform teaching. Teaching teams are sometimes overwhelmed by the data—the accumulation of data sheets and notes, products, and artifacts. The following three steps can help:

- *Organize the information.* Keep the information organized by child, learning objective, and date. Information can be kept in an electronic folder or portfolio. The information can also be kept in binders or boxes if that makes it more accessible.

- *Analyze the information.* Review the data on a regular basis. The teaching team determines how frequently to summarize and analyze each child's information. Generally, the team will summarize and analyze data for a child more frequently when a child needs more specific and intensive instruction. The team asks the question, "Is this child making progress?" Graphing is a useful way to summarize data collected by counting behaviors. The Instruction-at-a-Glance (in Appendix K and also available as a download) form lends itself to graphing. See Nhan's graphed data in Figure 8.3 showing his progress. Rubrics or rating scales can be used with notes and products to look for patterns in those data.

- *Make a decision.* The teaching team will determine whether the child is making good progress and adjust as needed.

Instructional Decision Making

Ongoing child assessment helps the teaching team identify individual learning objectives and provide an appropriate level of instructional support. On a planned and regular basis, the team collects data to see how the child is progressing. Then, the team

3. Monitoring progress:

Instructions: For the numbers 5–0 and ND ("No data") in the columns representing number of trials, circle or draw a line through each number, depending on response:

○ = correct, / = incorrect.

Date

Current step	4/4	4/11	4/18	4/25										
When asked "Where's the _____?" Nhan will say the location using in, on, or under.	5	5	5	5	5	5	5	5	5	5	5	5	5	5
	4	4	4	4	4	4	4	4	4	4	4	4	4	4
	3	3	3	3	3	3	3	3	3	3	3	3	3	3
	2	2	2	2	2	2	2	2	2	2	2	2	2	2
	1	1	1	1	1	1	1	1	1	1	1	1	1	1
	0	0	0	0	0	0	0	0	0	0	0	0	0	0
Criteria: 4/5 2 days	ND	ND	ND	ND	ND	ND	ND	ND	ND	ND	ND	ND	ND	ND

4. Comments, questions, or issues to discuss with the team:

____

____

____

____

____

____

____

____

____

____

____

____

____

____

(page 2 of 2)

Figure 8.3. Nhan's Instruction-at-a-Glance data. *(Blank version available in Appendix K and as a download.)*

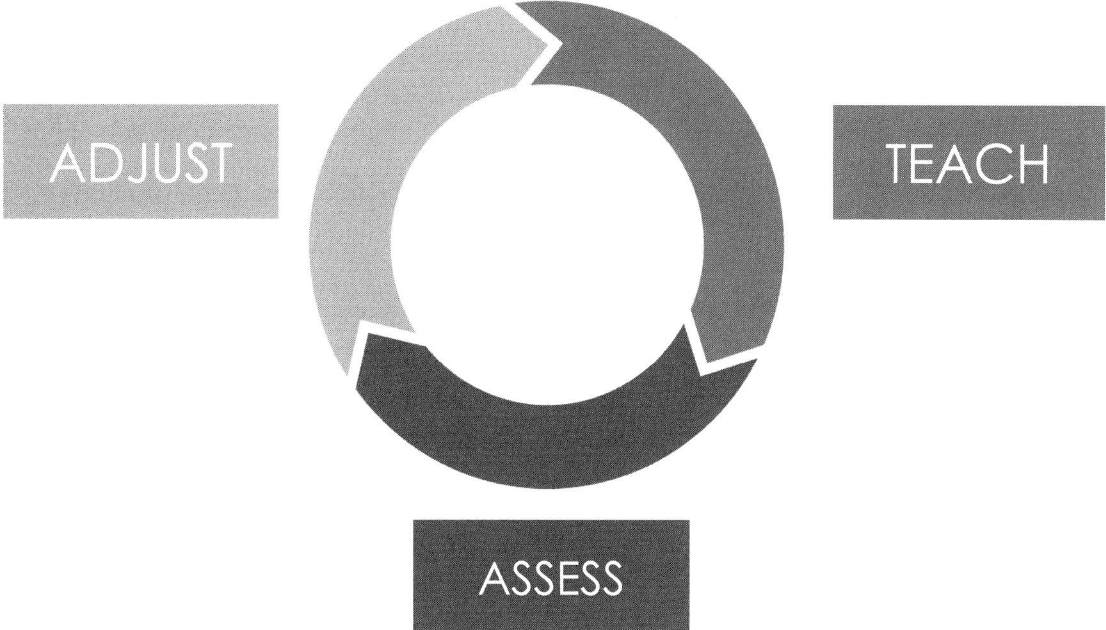

Figure 8.4. Teach, assess, adjust.

adjusts their teaching based on the data. This sequence of teach, assess, and adjust is depicted in Figure 8.4.

What kinds of adjustments or decisions might the team make? It depends on what the data say about the child's progress (or lack of progress). Here are some general guidelines:

- If the child is making progress, keep doing what you are doing.

- If the child has achieved the learning objective, move on to the next step or to a new objective.

- If the child is not making progress, adjust your teaching. Some of the ways that teaching teams adjust teaching include the following:

  - Change the instruction or cue.

  - Change the materials.

  - Change how often you provide opportunities to respond.

  - Change the type of consequence or feedback.

  - Teach a smaller part of the objective.

  - Teach the prerequisites.

For example, Figure 8.5 shows Drew's graphed data. He is not making progress on his objective to share with peers. His team needs to change the instruction perhaps by adjusting the consequence or by changing the prompt.

There are many useful resources on collecting and analyzing child data (e.g., Hojnoski et al., 2009). However, child performance data are not the only important data to collect. The teaching team wants to know if their teaching is making a difference. Thus, it is important to collect data on whether the planned teaching was implemented as intended. This is sometimes called intervention integrity.

3. Monitoring progress:

Instructions: For the numbers 5–0 and ND ("No data") in the columns representing number of trials, circle or draw a line through each number, depending on response:

◯ = correct, ╱ = incorrect.

															Date
Current step	3/6	3/13	3/20												
With verbal prompt, Drew will share or exchange object with peer.	⑤	5̸	5̸	5	5	5	5	5	5	5	5	5	5	5
	4̸	4̸	4̸	4	4	4	4	4	4	4	4	4	4	4
	③	③	3̸	3	3	3	3	3	3	3	3	3	3	3
	2̸	②	②	2	2	2	2	2	2	2	2	2	2	2
	1̸	1̸	1̸	1	1	1	1	1	1	1	1	1	1	1
	0	0	0	0	0	0	0	0	0	0	0	0	0	0
Criteria: 4/5 3 days	ND	ND	ND	ND	ND	ND	ND	ND	ND	ND	ND	ND	ND	ND

4. Comments, questions, or issues to discuss with the team:

____

____

____

____

____

____

____

____

____

____

____

____

____

(page 2 of 2)

Figure 8.5.　Drew's Instruction-at-a-Glance data. *(Blank version available in Appendix K and as a download.)*

SUMMARY

Assessment is essential to providing quality learning experiences and effective, efficient, and meaningful instruction for young children. This chapter described assessment as used in the Building Blocks framework with specific attention to levels of frequency and different methods for collecting information. A key principle of ongoing assessment is using the information to guide instructional decisions to improve child outcomes. For more about ongoing assessment and examples, see the professional development module.

More About the Building Blocks Framework

The Building Blocks framework can be used to teach new concepts and skills across all curriculum domains, including early literacy and numeracy, communication, fine and gross motor, adaptive, and social-emotional learning. The framework can be applied in a variety of community-based classrooms, child care, and early learning programs that include children with identified disabilities, developmental delays, and diverse abilities.

In this section, we begin with a brief discussion of implementation. To assist in the implementation of the Building Blocks framework, we provide additional forms, tools, and checklists that can facilitate use of each component of the framework. Later in this section, we show how the Building Blocks framework can be applied to teaching independence, friendship skills, and social behavior in groups. These skill areas are usually not separate curricular domains. However, they represent important developmental skills for children to learn in early childhood, are important topics of focus in inclusive programs, and serve as a solid foundation for future learning.

Chapter 9

Implementing the Building Blocks Framework
Putting It All Together

Effective implementation refers to how well teams carry out a specific program, intervention, or teaching approach with the intended outcomes in mind. *Implementation science* refers to understanding the processes and procedures that promote or impede the transfer, adoption, and use of evidence-based practices in real-world contexts (Fixsen et al., 2005). Key principles gleaned from implementation science can support the application of the Building Blocks framework in classrooms, in child care, when learning to read, and in other early settings. However, discussion of the many systemic components necessary to support inclusive early childhood education is beyond the scope of this chapter. Rather, we focus on Building Blocks implementation at the classroom level.

Implementing the Building Blocks framework means that teams and supporting personnel (e.g., supervisors, coaches, managers) collaborate to carry out each block: 1) a high-quality early childhood education, 2) curriculum modifications, 3) embedded learning opportunities (ELOs), and 4) child-focused instructional strategies (CFIS), as well as ongoing assessment for monitoring children's progress. In lively, active early childhood settings, this can be challenging.

This chapter builds on Chapter 4, Getting Started. In this chapter, we provide additional forms and checklists that supervisors or coaches can use to observe and offer focused feedback on use of the Building Blocks practices (for more on coaching, see Snyder et al., 2022). These same forms and checklists can be used by teaching teams as self-assessment tools. In this way, team members can reflect on their own use of the practice. Regardless of who uses these tools, the goal is utilizing Building Blocks practices with increased fidelity, leading to inclusive early learning programs where every child thrives. Note that all blank forms and checklists are found in the Appendix (and are available as downloads).

TOOLS FOR COLLABORATION

Collaboration is often difficult and complex, especially in busy early learning settings where there is consistently limited time. We offer resources, focused on the teaching team, for making this easier: 1) the Inclusion Collaboration Checklist (Figure 9.1 and Appendix L), 2) a Classroom Zoning Map (Figure 3.2), and 3) the Staff Matrix (Appendix H). As discussed in Chapter 3, collaboration sets the context for inclusion and is a critical component of inclusive teams.

The Inclusion Collaboration Checklist (Figure 9.1) helps teams identify practices that are already in place and prioritize practices that may not be fully implemented, with the goal of more effective, efficient collaboration. Of course, teams vary in size and membership. Regardless of who is a part of the team, collaboration practices are essential to the Buildings Blocks framework.

Drew's team completed the Inclusion Collaboration Checklist (Figure 9.1). As we can see here, this team has some great collaboration practices but is not able to meet consistently and struggles to take notes while multitasking as they set up or clean up the classroom. So, they plan to switch to using voice memos. We also see that they have prioritized conversations about implicit bias and plan to ask for support from a supervisor.

Other tools for collaboration, including the Staff Matrix and Classroom Zoning Map are discussed in detail in Chapter 3. The matrix helps everyone know where they are supposed to be and what they are supposed to be doing across the day and aids in clarifying roles and responsibilities. The Classroom Zoning Map is a valuable tool for organizing teachers across the classroom environment and planning for individual children's instruction.

BUILDING BLOCKS BLUEPRINT

Chapter 4 described the steps for getting started with the Building Blocks framework. Figure 9.2 lists the tools, checklists, and resources that help guide implementation of each step.

The Learning Environment and Clarifying the Schedule

The importance of the learning environment and ways to assess it are described in Chapter 4. A consistent and predictable schedule provides a necessary sense of comfort and stability for children and helps teaching teams plan for instruction. Not following a schedule, avoiding certain routines on the schedule, or limiting and/or extending the time for certain routines can contribute to children's challenging behaviors. The Clarifying the Schedule Checklist (Figure 9.3 and Appendix M) is designed to help teams ensure their schedule is part of a high-quality early learning environment. This checklist can be used by a supervisor, coach, or the team to check that the basic elements of an effective, meaningful schedule are in place. Figure 9.3 shows an example of this checklist completed by Chris, the principal at Drew's preschool.

Planning for the Individual Child

Methods for planning for the individual child are described in Chapter 4 and in the professional development module. To help teams as they make plans for an individual child, the supervisor, coach, or team can respond to a set of questions related to this step: Was the Child Assessment Worksheet completed? Were other assessments and/or individual child plans gathered and reviewed? Were the Child and IEP/IFSP Planning Worksheets completed? Does the "IEP Today" portion of the IEP/IFSP Planning Worksheet show current learning objectives aligned with the child's IEP, IFSP, or other individual plan?

APPENDIX L

Inclusion Collaboration Checklist

Classroom: _Room 134_

Team members: _Jennie, Marlene, Erin, Tara, and Anthony_

Date: _7/23/2023_

Collaboration practice	Implemented?			Notes
	Yes	No	Sometimes	
Our team creates opportunities to get to know one another.	✔			
Our team has developed our shared goals and classroom expectations.	✔			
Our team has regular, protected meeting times.			✔	It's hard to find regular meeting times!
Our team has a way to share documentation and meeting notes.			✔	It can be hard to take notes when we are also prepping the classroom, so we are going to use voice memos instead of written notes.
Our team has clearly defined roles and responsibilities.	✔			Started our staff matrix this year, and just filled out a zoning map.
Our team supports each other to reflect on behavior and have difficult conversations about equity and implicit bias.			✔	We would like to prioritize this and talk to our supervisor to get support.

(page 1 of 1)

Figure 9.1.   Inclusion Collaboration Checklist for Drew's team. *(A blank version is available as Appendix L and as a download.)*

Building Blocks step	Tool or resource
Step 1: Assessing the quality of the learning environment.	Quality Classroom Assessment Form (or another assessment of the environment; Chapter 4 and Appendix A) Classroom Action Worksheet (Chapter 4 and Appendix B)
Step 2: Planning the classroom schedule	Clarifying the Schedule Checklist (Appendix M)
Step 3: Planning for the individual child	Child Assessment Worksheet (as well as individualized education program [IEP], individualized family service plan [IFSP], behavior or individual plan, other assessment information; Chapter 4 and Appendix C)
Step 4: Clarify the problem, issue, or concern	IEP/IFSP Worksheet (Chapter 4 and Appendix D) Child Planning Worksheet (Chapter 4 and Appendix E) Clarifying the Child's Objective (Appendix N)
Step 5: Create plans	ELO-at-a-Glance (Chapter 6 and Appendix J) Instruction-at-a-Glance (Chapter 7 and Appendix K) Curriculum Modifications Checklist (Appendix P)
Step 6: Construct an activity matrix	Child Activity Matrix (Chapter 4 and Appendix F) Classroom Activity Matrix (Chapter 4 and Appendix G)
Step 7: Implement and evaluate plan	Embedded Learning Opportunities Checklist (Appendix R) Child-Focused Instruction Strategies Checklist (Appendix S) Teaching Episode Checklist (Appendix Q) Ongoing assessment forms developed by team Evaluation Worksheet (Chapter 4 and Appendix I)

Figure 9.2. Building Blocks blueprint.

To clarify a child's individual learning objectives, use the Clarifying the Child's Objective form (Figure 9.4). This form includes a series of questions to help closely examine the bigger or annual goal and define the specific objectives to guide instructional plans and help the child make progress. Usually, this includes breaking the goal into smaller parts (see Chapter 8) or making the objective more functional. As with other forms in this chapter, this can be used by the teaching team, supervisor, or coach to focus discussions on clarifying objectives so that they are specific, measurable, achievable, relevant, and time bound (SMART). This form can be used to inform individual curriculum modifications and ELO and CFIS plans. In Figure 9.4, we see how Drew's team has clarified his annual IEP.

CREATING AND IMPLEMENTING INSTRUCTIONAL PLANS: CURRICULUM MODIFICATIONS, EMBEDDED LEARNING OPPORTUNITIES, AND CHILD-FOCUSED INSTRUCTIONAL STRATEGIES

This section includes resources for reflection on how instructional plans are developed and used. We include tools related to curriculum modifications, ELOs, and CFIS. These tools can be used in at least two ways: a program supervisor or coach may use these tools to guide their observations in the early learning setting, or teachers and teams may use these tools as self-assessments. The tools help to pinpoint specific practices that support Building Blocks implementation.

Activity Matrix

Once plans are created for children's individual learning objectives, the team creates a Classroom Activity Matrix and a Child Activity Matrix, as described in Chapter 4. As part of the implementation process, the supervisor or coach and/or the team can ask themselves the following questions: Did we create matrices as needed? Have we created a Classroom Activity Matrix with all individual objectives needing a curriculum modification, ELO, or CFIS appearing on the matrix? Have we posted the Classroom Activity Matrix so that all who need to use it have access? Is the matrix up to date with all children's current objectives?

Clarifying the Schedule Checklist

Classroom: Room 134

Team members: Jennie, Marlene, Erin, Tara, and Anthony

Observer: Chris, principal

Date: 7/27/23

Effective schedule practice	Yes	No	Sometimes	Notes
The team uses a visual schedule that is posted at children's eye level and includes visual information about each activity.	✔			
The team references the schedule throughout the day and before each transition.			✔	It would be good to focus on this more. Transitions are hard for several children, and you should use your visual schedule when giving children a warning so they know what is coming next. The team did this sometimes but not all the time today.
There is a balance of active and quiet times.	✔			
There are times for smaller group and whole-group instruction and/or play.	✔			
There is outdoor time every day.	✔			

(page 1 of 2)

Figure 9.3. Clarifying the Schedule Checklist. *(A blank version is available as Appendix M and as a download.)*

Figure 9.3. *(continued)*

APPENDIX M *(continued)*

Effective schedule practice	Yes	No	Sometimes	Notes
There is a balance of child- and adult-directed activities.	✔			
Children are actively participating in activities and play during the majority of the day.	✔			
There is adequate time for routines and activities, including transitions.	✔			
We minimize children's waiting time between activities and during transitions.		✔		Sometimes, toileting and transitioning outside take a very long time. The team could have children transition in two groups to minimize waiting, starting next week.
The schedule is used to create an activity matrix.			✔	Matrix hasn't been created just yet. Can I do anything to support this?

Next Steps for Clarifying the Schedule

What will you do? Who is responsible? What is our timeline?

The team will work on our activity matrix next week during the team meeting on Tuesday. Erin will make smaller visuals for each activity in the schedule and put these on an O-ring, so we can easily show these to children during transitions. Chris will come back to check in next Friday.

(page 2 of 2)

APPENDIX N

Clarifying the Child's Objective

Team members: _Jennie, Marlene, Erin, Tara, and Anthony_

Observer: _Chris, principal_

Child: _Drew_   Date: _8/3/2023_

Overarching goal (What is the main point of this goal?): Drew will communicate with his friends and teachers.
What is the IEP or IFSP goal? Drew will maintain conversation with a peer or adult on topic for 2–3 turns.
What is the main point of this goal? What does the child need to learn? Is this goal developmentally and culturally appropriate? We want Drew to have conversations with his friends, teachers, and family. He needs to learn how to respond to certain questions, listen when someone else is talking, and make comments or ask questions. This is a priority for Drew's family and is developmentally and culturally appropriate.
What is the child's baseline? (e.g., What are they currently doing in relation to this skill?) Drew can respond to other people when they initiate a topic (such as, "What did everyone do at free choice?" or "What do you like to play outside?") with verbal prompts.
Do we need to break this down into smaller components? Step 1:   Drew will answer common questions with a prompt (verbal or pictorial).
Step 2:   Drew will answer common questions without a prompt.
Step 3:   Drew will ask a question or make a comment with a prompt.
Step 4:   Drew will ask questions or make comments without a prompt.
Step 5:   Drew will take 2–3 conversational turns.
How will we know when the child has learned this skill? (e.g., What assessment strategy will we use to measure the child's learning?) We will know Drew has learned this when he can ask and answer questions with peers or adults and take at least two turns in a conversation. We will use counts and notes to measure this skill. We know Drew will be able to talk more about his favorite things (e.g., trains, Disney characters) and want to have info on the topics of his conversations, too.

(page 1 of 1)

Figure 9.4. Clarifying the Child's Objective form for Drew. *(A blank version is available as Appendix N and as a download.)*

Curriculum Modifications

As part of the process of planning for the individual child, the team may decide that curriculum modifications could be sufficient for some learning objectives. The Curriculum Modification Planning Form (Figure 9.5) can be used by the team for both planning when and where the modifications will occur and to review if these are in place across the day. It can also be used by another observer, such as a coach or director, to see if the modifications remain in place. Figure 9.6 shows the form Drew's team used to plan for his curriculum modifications across the day, with Chris's (the principal's) observation notes.

The process of planning for the individual child may also lead to selection of ELOs or CFISs as the best match for an individual child and their learning objective. Two intervention plans are provided, and examples of ELO-at-a-Glance and Instruction-at-a-Glance forms are shown in Chapters 6 and 7. To guide implementation, supervisors, coaches, or teams using a self-assessment format may ask a series of questions: Have we selected an intervention practice for each individual objective? Have we created the appropriate intervention plan with all sections completed? Is intervention information posted on the activity matrix?

Whether using ELOs or CFIS, both involve an instructional interaction or teaching episode. Accurate use of these planned teaching episodes is important. A simple observation form like the one in Figure 9.7 can be used to check on the adult's use of the planned elements of the teaching episode. The observer or teacher fills in the details about the teaching episode prior to the observation: the plan for the cue, prompt, response, and feedback. During the observation, the observer collects data on each component of the teaching episode using a checkmark or "x." A teacher can use this form in a self-assessment format by making a mark after each episode (trial) (see Figure 9.7).

Embedded Learning Opportunities

In our practice, the challenge with implementing ELOs is intentionally planning for them to occur across activities. This checklist is designed to help supervisors, teachers, and teams reflect on ELOs. Notice that this form has a space for the children in the classroom who need embedded instruction. This may be for one child, or as we see in Drew's example (Figure 9.8), or for multiple children. The observer, in this example the school's principal, uses this form and also has access to the activity matrix and the child's ELO-at-a-Glance planning forms. The observer records what they see and hear. Later when providing feedback and discussing the completed form, the conversation focuses on the observation and these objective data. Similarly, teachers can use the form at the end of the activity or routine to reflect on their use of ELOs.

Child-Focused Instructional Strategies

CFIS involve specific, intensive instruction. Use of CFIS can feel complicated because they involve specific prompting and consequence strategies that may be new to the early childhood teacher or child care provider. Use of CFIS may be necessary for a few children or for a few of their learning objectives. Fortunately, a consulting or itinerant teacher, therapist, or behavior specialist will often be available to help create and implement the plan. Because a child who needs this level of instruction requires instruction every day, the teaching team needs to implement the plan in between visits from the specialist. The Child-Focused Instruction Strategies Checklist is designed to help supervisors or coaches provide support to teachers or for teachers to self-assess their use of CFIS. Data will tell us if the CFIS is working, but we must examine this on a regular basis. See the Child-Focused Instruction Strategies Checklist for Tina in Figure 9.9.

Curriculum Modification Planning Form

Team members: _Jennie, Marlene, Erin, Tara, and Anthony_

Child: _Drew_

Observer: _Chris, principal_   Date: _8/10/2023_

Routine	Curriculum modification	In place?
Arrival	Visual schedule	✔
Circle Time	Picture on his carpet square to help him find his spot for circle time Invisible support: Seated next to Arjun as peer model	✔
Outdoor Time	Special equipment: Trike with block pedals so he can reach	Trike wasn't outside today; check with the occupational therapist about this.
Hand Washing/Toileting	Visual schedule for hand washing and toileting routines Soap bottle firmly attached to sink	✔
Free Play	Calm Down Kit with visuals Picture schedule with preferred activity as final choice	✔
Snack	Picture on his name tag	✔
Circle	Picture on his carpet square to help him find his spot for circle time Invisible support: Seated next to Arjun as peer model	✔

(page 1 of 1)

Figure 9.5. Curriculum Modification Planning Form for Drew. *(A blank version is available as Appendix O and as a download.)*

APPENDIX P

Curriculum Modifications Checklist

Team members: _Jennie, Marlene, Erin, Tara, and Anthony_

Observer: _Chris, principal_

Child: _Drew_   Date: _8/5/2023_

Curriculum modification(s) (CM): _Picture schedule with the final choice of trains (his favorite activity)_

Routine(s): _Free Play_

CM practice	Yes	No	Sometimes	Notes
Is the CM enabling the child to participate in the learning environment?	✔			
Is the CM enabling the child to be more independent?			✔	Today, Drew needed some help transitioning between activities and getting started in a new area.
Is the CM implemented intentionally and consistently?	✔			Team did a great job using this the whole time. Nice work!
Is the CM ready to be faded in some way, to promote independence?		✔		Let's plan to keep this visual schedule in place for a few more weeks and reassess.
Is the CM included and up to date in the activity matrix?	✔			

Next Steps for CM Implementation
What will you do? Who is responsible? What is our timeline? I wonder how we can help Drew transition more independently between areas. Today, he needed teacher help to move from sensory table to dramatic play and from the book area to art. We may need to plan for an ELO related to transitions. Let's talk more in our next team meeting and make a plan.

(page 1 of 1)

Figure 9.6. Curriculum Modifications Checklist for Drew. *(A blank version is available as Appendix P and as a download.)*

Teaching Episode Checklist

Team members: _Gia, David_

Observer: _Susan, Manager_

Routine or activity: _Free play, game table center_

Child: _Samisha_   Date: _8/5/2023_

Objective: _During playtime, Samisha will join her peers in play and maintain play with them for 3 minutes or more in cooperative play activities. She will do this in four different play areas._

Directions: Place a checkmark in the cells for each component of the teaching episode that was implemented correctly and an "x" in the cells for each component that was not implemented.

Complete this row prior to the observation.	Cue	Prompt	Response	Feedback
	"Samisha, take a turn" or "Samisha, it's your turn."	Gestural: Point to the game and game piece.	Samisha takes a turn in the game.	**Correct:** Praise and emphasize how she is playing together. **Incorrect:** Hand her the game piece and repeat the cue.
Trial 1	✔		X	✔ – Samisha did not take her turn; Gia handed her the Candy Land card.
Trial 2	✔	✔	✔	✔
Trial 3	X	X	✔	X – Gia was distracted answering Olivia's question, but Samisha played that round and took her turn after Rohan said, "Go Samisha."
Trial 4	✔	✔	✔	✔

Figure 9.7. Teaching Episode Checklist for Gia and Samisha. *(A blank version is available as Appendix Q and as a download.)*

Figure 9.7. (continued)

APPENDIX Q (continued)

	Cue	Prompt	Response	Feedback
Trial 5	✔	✔	✔	✔
Trial 6				Game ended, and children made different choices.
Trial 7				
Trial 8				
Trial 9				
Trial 10				

Next Steps for Teaching Episodes

Great work with this, Gia! You did a really nice job balancing this instruction while tending to the needs of other children. Your cues were very clear and helped Samisha understand the expectation. I think we should talk about fading back the prompt. Let's look at her data together and plan for this during our meeting tomorrow!

Embedded Learning Opportunities Checklist

Team members: _Jennie, Marlene, Erin, Tara, and Anthony_

Completed by: _Chris, principal_

Child's objective: _Drew will follow routine classroom directions using a picture prompt._

Routine or activity: _Arrival, Circle, Snack_

Child(ren): _Drew_   Date: _8/20/23_

ELO practice	Yes	No	Sometimes	Notes
The classroom/environment has an activity matrix with planned ELOs across the day.	✔			Matrix is posted on the staff board and in each area of the classroom. Great work!
ELOs are taught within natural routines that make sense for the objective (e.g., working on a child identifying their name during circle when name tags are out or working on zipping a coat before going outside).	✔			Erin used the pictures on an O-ring to instruct Drew to put his backpack away, wash hands, and join circle. Anthony used the O-ring to show Drew pictures for lining up, washing hands, and sitting at the snack table.
ELOs involve materials and activities the child is interested in.			✔	While Drew was interested in some of these activities, getting to circle was more difficult for him. Maybe we need to add in child preference and have a train waiting for him on the carpet square?

(page 1 of 2)

Figure 9.8. Example Embedded Learning Opportunities Checklist for Drew. *(A blank version is available as Appendix R and as a download.)*

Figure 9.8. *(continued)*

APPENDIX R *(continued)*

ELO practice	Yes	No	Sometimes	Notes
ELOs include a clear teaching episode: 1. Clear directions 2. Enough time for the child to respond 3. Immediate feedback			✔	In some instances, teacher gave Drew a direction several times and did not give him enough time to respond. Let's talk about how to be intentional with wait time.
ELOs are provided often enough for the child to make progress on their goals.	✔			Today, the team did a great job embedding instruction in routine classroom directions. Excellent work!
The team checks each week to make decisions about the next steps.		✔		I know this team has wondered about meeting times and how to document the notes. Let's have one person be in charge of reviewing Drew's data on Friday. I can make sure there is protected time for this.
Next Steps for ELO Implementation				

What will you do? Who is responsible? What is our timeline?

Let's talk about how to plan for giving Drew more time and how we can modify the curriculum to help him transition to circle time.

Child-Focused Instruction Strategies Checklist

Team member: Dolores

Completed by: Lisa, Head Start coach

Child: Tina

Child's objective: With contextual cues, Tina will independently and accurately tell events that occurred on the same day at least 30 minutes after the occurrence of the event.

Setting for instruction:

When: At the end of the day

Where: Classroom

How often: Everyday

Materials needed: iPad with photos from the day

Date: 9/3/23

CFIS component: Teacher behavior	Yes	No	Sometimes	Notes
The classroom has an activity matrix with planned CFIS across the day.	✔			Matrix posted on the staff board and on Dolores's clipboard.
The teacher sets the environment up for instruction (has the necessary materials and has arranged the environment).	✔			Dolores intentionally stayed in the classroom with Tina and a few other children so they could talk about their day. Dolores had photos on the iPad to show Tina close by.
Teacher gives a clear, discrete cue.	✔			Really nice, clear direction: "Tina, what did you play outside today?" Then "What did you have at snack?" and "What did you do at free choice?"
Teacher provides enough wait time.	✔			Dolores waited 3 seconds; nice work! I know this can seem like a long time!

(page 1 of 2)

Figure 9.9. Child-Focused Instruction Strategies Checklist for Tina's team. *(A blank version is available as Appendix S and as a download.)*

Figure 9.9. *(continued)*

APPENDIX S *(continued)*

CFIS component: Teacher behavior	Yes	No	Sometimes	Notes
The teacher provides immediate feedback that matches the child's response (within 1–2 seconds of the child's response).			✔	During busy routines, Tina did not consistently get immediate feedback.
If the child is correct, the teacher provides positive reinforcement aligned with the Instruction-at-a-Glance (e.g., "You stood up! Well done!").			✔	The first time, you responded, "That's right! I saw you and Amal playing in the sand box!" but you were not able to provide this affirmation and expansion with the other two responses. Instead, you replied, "Uh huh," and as time ran out, you had to hurry children to the bus.
If the child is incorrect or does not respond, the teacher provides corrective feedback when the child makes an error, and the teacher models the correct response.			✔	Tina did not respond to the question about free choice, and you did not reply to her. Let's talk about how to make sure you have ample time to engage in this instruction with her at the end of the day!
Teacher collects data.			✔	How can we have a data collection system that is easy for this goal. Since you already have the iPad, maybe we could use a voice memo or make tallies in an electronic note?
Number of CFIS trials observed	3			
Did the number of trials match with the Instruction-at-a-Glance?	Planned for 5 trials but ran out of time.			
Next Steps for CFIS Implementation				

What changes need to be made with this CFIS?

Let's talk about how we can be more intentional with ensuring there is enough time to provide this instruction. I know the end of the day is busy! Perhaps you could walk with the rest of the class and then do this instruction with Tina in the lobby and then walk her up to the bus. Or, leave the classroom a bit early and have another teacher help with getting other children on the bus. Let's talk more in our meeting tomorrow!

(page 2 of 2)

SUMMARY

The resources and tools in this chapter are designed to provide sustained and practical implementation support and help teachers feel confident and empowered to use the Building Blocks framework to meet the needs of young children in inclusive settings. Effective implementation of the Building Blocks framework involves a combination of planning, assessment, instruction, and reflection based on observation to ensure that children receive the best possible instruction and opportunities to grow and thrive. This work involves the child's team and takes place over time. Effective implementation requires not just the teaching team but also other support personnel including supervisors and coaches. We encourage use of the guiding questions and checklists to promote application of the practices contained in the Building Blocks framework. Although the steps and tools may seem overwhelming, a couple of key questions are as follows: Are we doing what we intended to do? Is this helping the child learn their objectives and goals? And, if it's not working, are we making data-based adjustments?

Chapter 10

Becoming More Independent

Tina attends Head Start at the community center in her neighborhood. Her teachers and her mother are pleased with her progress. She participates in the classroom activities and plays with the other children in the classroom. She has learned many new skills and concepts this year. As part of her kindergarten transition plan, the consulting ECSE teacher, Tamika, observed Tina in her classroom. Tamika was concerned by Tina's lack of independence in the classroom. She observed that a teacher or another child was always available to help Tina make transitions, complete tasks, and manage her materials. Tamika wondered what the team could do to help Tina learn some independence skills (e.g., hang up her backpack in her cubby, clean up after a task) that will help her succeed in kindergarten.

Mateo is one of the young toddlers at Dara's family child care home. Dara notices that he enjoys their group music time but often gets very excited, especially when the older children sing loudly and do active physical movements. He bounces, waves his arms, and makes noises. Dara is happy that Mateo is participating, but she also notices that he has difficulty calming down when the song stops or when they change to another activity. Sometimes, he is so agitated that he bursts into tears. Dara shares her concerns with Mateo's family and the rest of the team.

Independence includes being able to rely on oneself and one's own ability, being self-confident, and being self-reliant. These valued characteristics appear to be related to school and work success. The U.S. Office of Special Education Programs and the Office of Head Start identified those characteristics as important outcomes for young children who participate in federally funded early learning programs. Independent behavior is related to how children take care of themselves, fulfill their basic needs, and interact with the world around them in general. Although it is premature to talk about children's taking care of themselves, living on their own, or making vocational choices during the early years, some of the foundational skills and behaviors taught in preschool serve children throughout their lifetimes. Independence skills are foremost among these important and functional skills. Independent behavior in early childhood settings includes but is not limited to the following:

- Making independent transitions within the classroom and school or child care (e.g., walking from the classroom to the playground without holding the teacher's hand)

- Managing personal possessions and classroom materials appropriately (e.g., hanging up coat and backpack in cubby)

- Asking for help when needed, and completing tasks without help when able

- Completing developmentally appropriate tasks without adult assistance

- Staying engaged in a play activity for increasing amounts of time

- Actively participating in a developmentally appropriate group activity

- Appropriately completing self-care tasks, such as those involved in toileting, dressing, eating, and personal hygiene (e.g., nose care)

- Assuming developmentally appropriate responsibility (e.g., child has a classroom job)

The ability to stick to a task and complete it independently is highly valued by kindergarten and elementary school teachers, yet these skills are often not explicitly taught in preschool classrooms. In fact, children's opportunities to be independent or to practice doing things by themselves are often preempted. This chapter suggests strategies that can be used in inclusive early childhood settings to help children develop and practice appropriate independent behavior. (For further reading about helping children become more independent, see Baker & Brightman, 2004; Kroeger & Sorensen-Burnworth, 2009; Schwartz et al., 2017.)

EXECUTIVE FUNCTION

Executive function plays an important role in helping children learn several valued skills, including independence skills (Diamond & Lee, 2011; McClelland & Cameron, 2018). Executive function includes those skills that "make it possible to sustain attention, keep goals and information in mind, refrain from responding immediately, resist distraction, tolerate frustration, consider the consequences of different behaviors, reflect on past experiences, and plan for the future" (Zelazo et al., 2016, p. 1). Three specific skills that fall under the umbrella term of executive function are cognitive flexibility, working memory, and inhibitory control. Young children, especially those with disabilities, delays, or diverse abilities, may need specially designed instruction to acquire these important skills. Teachers can assist children in acquiring the skills associated with executive function by:

- Ensuring that children have opportunities to engage in physical activity every day

- Incorporating music, dance, and activity in the classroom

- Supporting pretend play where children take on different roles

- Scaffolding new learning with visual supports

- Teaching children to take turns

- Helping children learn to label and recognize their feelings

- Providing opportunities for choice, expression, and autonomy

- Assisting children to persist with challenging and multistep activities

- Systematically increasing demands so that children can practice executive function skills

TEACHING INDEPENDENCE SKILLS

One of the first steps in teaching children to be more independent is to determine which skills to focus on. It is very important to remember that children cannot and should not be expected to complete a skill or behavior independently until they can complete it accurately and fluently with adult supervision. Once children have shown mastery of skills, it is time to help them become more independent with those skills. Therefore, independent performance can be thought of as another level of skill acquisition; teachers must begin to plan for independence in the same way they plan for generalization and maintenance. Although it may not be necessary for children to demonstrate some skills independently in early childhood, it is important for teachers and families to consider the expectations that children will encounter in their next setting (e.g., a playgroup, preschool, or kindergarten classroom), especially in the few months before children make the transition to that setting.

Next, team members need to determine when and how they are going to teach independence. Like any new skill, independence must be taught. This includes providing multiple opportunities across the day to be independent and systematically decreasing the amount of support the child receives while maintaining appropriate child behavior. The steps outlined in Chapter 4 may help a teacher or the team identify the child's learning needs and plan how to teach the identified skills.

Once the team has decided which skill to target for independence, the team needs to assess how much support the child is currently receiving to complete the task. When teaching independence, select tasks that have steps the child can complete independently. For example, if a teacher wants to teach the child to hang up their coat and backpack on arrival in the classroom, the teacher needs to be sure that the child can currently complete all the steps of that task with adult supervision. Then, the teacher needs to determine how much teacher and peer support is currently provided to complete the task. For example, can the child do it if a teacher is standing right next to them? Does the teacher need to talk the child through the task and provide constant encouragement to keep going?

When describing the amount of support or prompting a child currently receives, consider three categories of prompting: physical support, instructional support, and environmental support. Physical support includes proximity, any touching of the child (e.g., holding their hand during transitions), and physically helping a child complete a step of the task (e.g., turning on the water during hand washing). Instructional support includes teacher directions, comments, praise, and encouragement. Environmental support includes any type of pictures, process charts, or other visual supports that the teacher has displayed to facilitate child performance (e.g., steps to washing hands posted over the sink). Understanding the amount of support children currently receive helps teachers determine which tasks are good candidates for independence training and how to change their own behaviors to facilitate children's independence.

The next step is to determine when to teach the identified skills. Using the activity matrix, the team can plan times of the day when all the children will work on independent tasks or schedule times to provide specially designed instruction on identified skills for individual children. For some teachers, one of the most difficult parts of teaching independence skills is providing children with opportunities to be independent. It is easy to fall into the habit of offering help rather than giving children a little extra time and opportunity to complete the task independently. To avoid this, teachers can schedule their own activities on the activity matrix. If a child can already put their things in the cubby but always waits for help, then the teacher can welcome the child at the first activity of the day rather than while standing at the cubbies. If the child needs instruction in the steps involved in becoming independent, the teacher can plan to be nearby.

The next step is to begin the independence training. When planning the intervention, teams should consider what they expect the child to do and what the adults will do while the child is working independently. Do any special materials need to be prepared or organized in a particular way to facilitate child independence? Remember that as the amount of support provided for the child decreases, praise and encouragement are still necessary. In planning this part of the intervention, it may be helpful to spend a day observing a classroom that represents the child's next school environment or next age group (e.g., kindergarten) to see the level of independence demonstrated by the children in that classroom. It is most helpful to observe early in the year to get an idea of what children are doing at the beginning of the school year.

It is also important to remember that cultural traditions and beliefs about children influence notions about developmentally appropriate independence. For example, the norms for independent eating vary from one culture to another. Teachers and their team members should learn about the beliefs of families in their programs and reflect on their own beliefs regarding independence.

Finally, to teach children independence, teachers need to provide children with multiple opportunities to practice independence throughout the day and across different activities. Begin with small steps. If children are learning to walk in the halls without holding the teacher's hand, it does not mean that the teacher can never hold children's hands; it simply means that the teacher does not *need* to hold their hands. Children can also learn to complete work independently early in preschool. When children are working on tabletop activities (e.g., puzzles, manipulatives, visual discrimination tasks such as matching parquetry blocks), they should be encouraged to complete the activity independently. Often, in an attempt to be helpful, adults preempt children's opportunities to develop the ability to do things by themselves. Children, however, need these opportunities to develop self-reliance and self-confidence, so perhaps the most important part of teaching independent classroom behavior is to provide opportunities for children to be independent and to support their accomplishments.

Tina's teachers asked the consulting ECSE teacher to help them pinpoint Tina's learning needs in the area of independence. Together they decided to begin working on greater independence at the learning centers using ELOs. Their observations told them that although Tina's picture schedule helped her move from activity to activity, she was often slow to begin the transition. Consequently, a peer was often asked to hold her hand to help her get to the next activity. The teachers planned a new intervention that they used for all the children. Everyone was told to make the transition "all by yourself," and a highly preferred event followed for those who got to the next activity by themselves. Tina received a selected reinforcer if she was one of the first to make the transition. After a week, the new plan appeared to be working.

To help Mateo practice self-regulation and manage his excitement, Dara and the team decide to add some "start and stop" games, "freeze dance," and similar activities during music time and outdoor time. Mateo is not walking yet, but he participates with his arms and whole body. These sorts of games help him practice shifting his attention and regulating his activity level in a fun way.

Table 10.1 provides additional examples of instructional support at each level of the Building Blocks framework. Use the information presented in the table to spark your own ideas about providing the level of support a child needs.

Table 10.1. Examples of instructional strategies supporting independent classroom behavior using the Building Blocks framework

	Building Block strategies
Child-focused instructional strategies (CFIS)	Teach children the play skills needed to participate in classroom activities.
	Teach children the self-help skills needed to perform and participate in routine events; gradually decrease the adult's support to encourage independence.
	Teach children the steps involved in completing classroom routines, such as putting materials in their cubby, getting ready to go outside or come back inside, getting ready for snack time, or cleaning up after playtime; gradually decrease the adult's support to encourage independence.
	Use behavior-specific praise and tangible reinforcers as necessary to teach children to persist with difficult and multistep activities.
Embedded learning opportunities (ELOs)	Provide opportunities for children to practice the steps in classroom routines.
	Incorporate independence skills within relevant classroom themes or projects (e.g., practice brushing teeth to a special song, do a project on shoes to offer practice putting on shoes).
	Add a "finished box" to appropriate activities (e.g., when children are finished writing in their journal, they can put the journal in the "finished box").
	Use visual supports to teach children to take on different roles during pretend play.
Curriculum modifications (CMs)	Use process charts for hand washing and other tasks to help children remember all the steps.
	Place materials at children's level so that they can get them by themselves.
	Allow extra time for children to complete a task without adult assistance.
	Use pictures or objects to help children remember where they are going during a transition.
	Use pictures, labels, or special containers to help children be more independent during cleanup time.
	Use preferred materials and rotate materials in the learning centers to encourage engagement.
High-quality early childhood environment	Have developmentally and chronologically age-appropriate expectations for all children.
	Provide opportunities for children to experiment with new tasks, materials, and activities.
	Include opportunities for children to do things independently, and have adults available when children request assistance.
	Provide a predictable schedule, routines, and staff.
	Provide facilities and equipment that are the appropriate size for young children.
	Provide opportunities for group physical activities, such as dance or yoga.

SUMMARY

Independence does not appear as a separate domain in most early childhood curricula, yet independent behavior is highly valued and implicit in many aspects of a curriculum. For children, *independence* refers to managing one's personal needs and adapting one's behaviors to the social expectations of the teachers and the other children in the group. Learning these kinds of skills is often a factor in a child's successful participation in community-based classrooms and other activities.

All young children are provided with learning opportunities to be more independent. For example, their teachers help them learn to put on their shoes and coats, follow classroom routines, and persist in solving problems. Children with disabilities, delays, or diverse abilities may need modifications to the materials or the skills, extra practice, or more deliberate teaching to learn independence, however. This chapter reminds teachers to evaluate their own behaviors so that they do not provide too much help. The Building Blocks framework can guide teachers in offering the right amount of help.

Chapter 11

Friendships and Peer Relationships

Although Nhan is interested in his peers, he is not sure how to initiate interactions with them. He does not demonstrate strong preferences for certain children, and other children do not seek him out as a play partner. Nhan's teachers are concerned that he is spending more and more time playing alone, and they want to help him develop friendships with his peers.

Tina's teacher, Dolores, has recently completed training on the Pyramid Model (Hemmeter et al., 2016) and is excited to foster a sense of community, friendship, and belonging in her Head Start classroom. She has been teaching Head Start for many years but has several children with complex social-emotional needs and two children with IEPs, including Tina. These children appear to need more specific instruction to develop social relationships than what was covered in her training. What can she do to support friendship skills for a range of diverse learners?

Developing meaningful, positive, and reciprocal peer relationships is one of the most important parts of early childhood. Within these relationships, children develop important communication, social, play, and cognitive skills, and they gain emotional support. Friendships are a protective factor for all children and are associated with positive health, academic, and vocational outcomes in postsecondary settings (Goldstein et al., 2014; Hemmeter et al., 2020, Kasari et al., 2011). Simply put, having friends in preschool leads to great things for adults! Playful social interactions with peers are an essential part of the early childhood years and "positive social-emotional skills (including social relationships)" have been identified as one of the child outcomes for young children with special needs by the Office of Special Education Programs (OSEP) of the U.S. Department of Education (Early Childhood Technical Assistance Center, n.d., p. 1). Further, the Head Start Early Learning Outcome Framework (U.S. Department of Health and Human Services, 2015) also identifies social and emotional learning, and specifically developing relationships with peers, as an important outcome for toddlers and preschoolers.

Many early childhood curricula such as the Creative Curriculum (Teaching Strategies, 2022) and HighScope (HighScope, 2021) provide guidance on how to teach friendship and social skills. The Pyramid Model (Hemmeter at al., 2016) is a very useful framework for social-emotional learning (SEL), as well. We can use the Building Blocks framework to plan for instruction when children need additional support with friendship and/or SEL skills.

Children who establish reciprocal friendships during early childhood often have better social and academic outcomes (Hartup, 2017), whereas children who are socially rejected tend to have poorer mental health and academic outcomes. (To read more about children's friendships, see Strain et al. [2013].) As early learning providers, there is so much we can do to foster friendships and sense of belonging for all children in inclusive settings using the Building Blocks framework.

DEVELOPING FRIENDSHIPS AND SOCIAL RELATIONSHIPS

To develop friendships, children need repeated opportunities to have meaningful, positive interactions with their peers. These interactions can be simple, such as passing materials to the child sitting next to them during a meal, or more complex and extended, such as working together to create a large, winding train track. Teachers play an important role in planning and supporting these activities. Instruction to develop social relationships should occur every day, across all classroom areas and activities. We can easily embed sharing materials by passing things out at circle time or serving food family style during meals. The teacher's role in supporting positive social relationships is often a delicate balance between helping and stepping back. The teacher should facilitate children's interaction but not interfere or take over the situation.

Not only can teachers arrange the classroom environment to support positive social interactions, but they can also teach their students skills that are key to positive relationships. These skills include but are not limited to the following:

- Being aware of others in the environment
- Sharing
- Demonstrating empathy
- Helping others
- Being able to enter play situations
- Persisting or making efforts to maintain social interactions
- Organizing play with others
- Giving compliments
- Negotiating
- Solving conflicts

As with all skills, friendship skills can be incorporated into the general curriculum, and teachers should identify friendship learning objectives for children who are struggling with peer interaction.

USING THE BUILDING BLOCKS FRAMEWORK TO PROMOTE FRIENDSHIPS AND SOCIAL RELATIONSHIPS

The teacher or the team may use the steps outlined in Chapter 4 to identify friendship learning objectives, plan the level of intervention, determine when and where to intervene, and evaluate the effects of intervention. As always, teams need to select the appropriate level of support, whether it is a curriculum modification, an embedded learning opportunity (ELO), or more explicit instruction, such as a child-focused instructional strategy (CFIS). Table 11.1 provides more ideas for facilitating friendships and social relationships using the Building Blocks framework. Teaching and supporting positive peer interactions often feels more abstract than teaching other concepts, but we encourage teachers to think about it the same way we teach any other skill. Good instruction requires planning, teaching, and assessment. Teams should be mindful to target the outcomes that are important to children and families. For example, if the families value participating in group activities, then teach that skill directly in the classroom. Of course, the most meaningful instruction takes place in the environment where children will need to use the specific skills, so social skill instruction should take place in the classroom, on the playground, in the community, and any other place where children interact (rather than in a "pull out" setting).

When we consider social skills and a high-quality early childhood environment, our bottom block, there are so many things we can do to promote friendships, community, and a sense of belonging! There should be multiple opportunities every day for meaningful social interaction, by creating engaging activities and providing interesting, culturally relevant materials that require more than one child to participate. Certainly, some materials lend themselves to more social interaction than others (e.g., playing games, dramatic play), but even seemingly solitary activities (e.g., puzzles, art) can be arranged to encourage social interaction. Planned classroom activities can also incorporate social opportunities. For example, pairs or small groups of children can complete class jobs, be dismissed for outdoor play, make art projects, build collaborative sculptures, or explore books together. We can easily change our routine classroom activities to embed social skills instruction, such as lining up with a peer, putting away nap cots as a small group, or even altering common songs, games, or rhymes to include these concepts. For example, we might make a book inspired by Eric Carle's *Brown Bear, Brown Bear* that includes photos of all the children in the classroom or switch the lyrics in common songs such as "give a friend a high five" in "If You're Happy and You Know It." A number of frameworks and interventions have been shown to be successful in teaching the skills that are related to developing friendships and engaging in positive social relationships (for reviews, see Brown & Conroy, 2011; Hemmeter et al., 2016; Wong et al., 2015).

CURRICULUM MODIFICATIONS AND FRIENDSHIP SKILLS

We know that even with these strategies in place, some children will need additional support and special instruction to make friends and maintain positive social relationships. Open-ended activity and social interactions can be especially tricky for children with disabilities and suspected delays, and curriculum modifications provide more support (though we can anticipate that *all* young children will benefit from social-emotional support at one time or another). This might include visual supports to simplify the activity, a "problem-solving kit" with pictures of different solutions, or a "stay-play-and-talk" visual in the dramatic play or block area (Milam et al., 2021). Visuals are especially helpful with social-emotional skills (see Appendix T for a list of easily downloadable,

Table 11.1. Examples of strategies for facilitating friendships and social relationships using the Building Blocks framework

Building block	Strategies
Child-focused instructional strategies (CFIS)	Systematically teach children to take turns with peers during a highly preferred activity.
	Teach children to compliment a child before attempting to join an ongoing activity (e.g., "I like your tower!").
	Use direct instruction methods to teach children to answer questions from their peers during play activities.
	Teach specific play routines that include peers, such as playing with figurines, blocks, or dramatic play.
	Teach children to take turns with their favorite toys so they understand that they will get the toy back after their peer has a turn.
Embedded learning opportunities (ELOs)	Plan dramatic play activities with specific roles (e.g., grocer, shopper, shelf stocker) and assign the roles.
	Include actions of friendship, such as exchanging high fives or fist bumps during songs, circle time, or other planned activities.
	"Sabotage" a small-group activity by putting out an insufficient amount of materials; encourage the children to problem solve how to share the materials and take turns.
	Set up a special buddy center during free-choice time; have children play with special toys and games that require working with a partner or a buddy.
	Assign two children to complete a classroom job together, such as "buddy plant waterers" or "buddy line leaders."
	Assign a "greeter" job and have the child greet each child as they enter the classroom. Have them ask each child if they would like a high five or a fist bump.
	Assign a child to hand out the props or instruments at circle time, providing multiple opportunities to interact with peers by asking which color, shape, instrument, etc., that they would like.
Curriculum modifications (CMs)	Intentionally pair children together for a buddy activity, ensuring that a child who needs a higher level of support is with a peer with strong social-emotional learning skills.
	Use a visual conversation board to encourage children to interact during mealtimes.
	Use visual supports to help children solve conflicts, such as creating a "solution box" with images of different solutions.
	Create visual play ideas that include more than one child, such as "Step 1: Cut Food. Step 2: Put in a Bowl. Step 3: Give to a Friend."
	Have children share or pass materials at circle time and mealtime.
	Use preferred activities (e.q., art, bubbles, vehicles) to teach new friendship skills.
High-quality early childhood environment	Provide opportunities for children to observe and interact with peers during all activities across the day.
	Plan cooperative activities that require more than one child.
	Assign classroom jobs in pairs.
	Use behavior-specific praise to comment on children who demonstrate friendly behaviors, such as playing or interacting together.
	Use behavior-specific praise to comment on children who are working out a conflict in a positive manner.
	Incorporate toys that require two people to use together (e.g., rocking boats, teeter-totters).
	Set up the environment to encourage two or more children to work together on projects and activities.
	Provide both structured and unstructured play times, with engaging, developmentally appropriate, and culturally relevant materials.
	Read books and have class discussions about friendship, problem solving, and conflict resolution.

free visual supports). Incorporating child preference is another very useful curriculum modification. Social skills instruction should be incorporated within activities that build on children's interests and experiences. In other words, if a child who is socially isolated enjoys playing in the block area and really dislikes sensory play activities, teachers will be more successful in helping that child play with friends during block play than at the sensory table. Finally, teachers can also enlist other children to provide peer support to help children learn how to play a gross motor game or participate in a dramatic play activity.

EMBEDDED LEARNING OPPORTUNITIES AND FRIENDSHIP SKILLS

Some children need extended and repeated interactions with peers to develop friendships and social relationships. Although we encourage all teams to include social skills instruction across the day during all activities, some children need intentionally planned ELOs to make progress on these goals. This could include making a child who needs more practice initiating with peers the "classroom greeter" or intentionally planning for a specific child to be "in charge" of the animal crackers at snack, so they get many opportunities to practice responding. Remember, ELOs help take advantage of friendship or social skill opportunities within existing routines and activities but must be thoughtfully planned.

CHILD-FOCUSED INSTRUCTIONAL STRATEGIES AND FRIENDSHIP SKILLS

Some children will need CFIS to make progress on their goals. With friendship or positive social behavior, this might include systematic instruction on how to say hello to a peer using augmentative or alternative communication (AAC), signing, or using a picture card to ask for a turn with an item, identifying emotions in others, or individual help to resolve a conflict with a peer while remaining calm.

Nhan's team took another look at his current performance in the classroom and decided to do two things. First, when planning his special language instruction sessions, whether using ELOs or CFIS, the team decided to have peers participate in the session or learning opportunity. Second, they planned more social opportunities for Nhan by seating him next to preferred peers at snack time and circle time and by adding a preferred social activity during outdoor time. Since implementing these interventions, the team has noticed that Nhan is spending more time with some of his pals.

Dolores decided to implement group friendship activities in her classroom. She created a "classroom greeter" job, where a child is in charge of warmly greeting everyone each day, and used the curriculum modification of a visual with different ideas for saying hello to peers, such as a wave, high five, words in families' home languages, or a gentle tap with a stuffed animal to support Tina with this routine. Every day at circle time, she does one activity in which children shake hands, give high fives, or pass a toy around the circle. After she implemented these group friendship activities, she observed that more children were playing together at free-choice time, and no one was being rejected anymore. Dolores was pleased by these results and impressed with how easy it was to implement this strategy. By being more intentional in her teaching, she helped the children develop more meaningful social relationships and created a culture of inclusion in the classroom.

SUMMARY

Teaching children friendship skills and how to be in good relationships with the people in their environment is one of the most meaningful things we do as teachers. In inclusive classrooms, friendship should always be emphasized and teams should intentionally create ways for children to play, learn, and interact with each other. The Building Blocks framework helps to provide children with the right amount of support; some may need curriculum modifications, others may need more opportunities to practice friendship skills, and a few children may need individual instruction.

Chapter 12

Inclusive Interactions
Teaching Group Behaviors

Marta and Mao are preschool teachers in a full-day program and started the school year with high hopes. Over the summer, they participated in a weeklong workshop on school-wide positive behavioral interventions and support (SWPBIS) at a local university. What they learned made sense, but they were not sure how this approach would work for a large class of 19, with five children with identified disabilities and four dual language learners. Now, it is November, and they are frustrated; the strategies they talked about in the workshop seem impossible to implement in their classroom, and they feel like all they do is put out fires! Children frequently have conflicts and play with each other too roughly, and the classroom feels chaotic and overwhelming. They are not sure where to start or who to turn to for help.

Drew, who has autism, enjoys school—once he is there. He seems to enjoy every activity at school once he is engaged in the activity. In fact, he does not like to stop any activity in which he is engaged, whether it is at home, school, or child care. When he is asked to stop one activity and move to another, he usually begins to have a tantrum. Often, his teachers and parents let him continue doing what he is doing, but when they require him to move on to the next activity, he often cries during the entire transition. Once he is settled at the new activity, he calms down and begins to participate and, after a few minutes, seems to be happy. Drew's transition behavior is stressful for the children and adults in the classroom, and many children are beginning to avoid Drew because of it. His parents also report that this behavior is becoming more difficult to deal with at home and in the community. What strategies can help Drew, his parents, and his teachers to have more successful transitions?

At one point or another, most young children demonstrate some sort of behavior that is challenging for their teachers, parents, and other caregivers or interferes with their participation in group activities. Experimentation with rules, boundaries, and consequences is a part of child development and something we can expect from almost all children at some point in time. For some young children, however, learning how to use materials, participate in a routine, and interact with peers and adults in group settings can be difficult. It is essential that we teach children these common classroom behaviors because they affect success in a range of settings including community activities (e.g., swim lessons, participating at places of worship, playing on the neighborhood playground, standing in line to buy ice cream) and in settings with family (e.g., gatherings, celebrations, other family events). It is easy to assume that children will figure out the group skills they need to be successful at their own pace, but in many cases, this does not happen. Children end up engaging in behaviors that are challenging and interfere with their participation in school and community settings. The Building Blocks framework helps teams plan for and teach the social and emotional skills children need to participate in group learning settings and to help prevent challenging and interfering behaviors.

The chapter provides some practical suggestions for teaching appropriate group behaviors and supporting children's participation, inclusion, and feelings of belonging in classroom and community settings. We use the term *challenging behavior* to refer to behavior that is persistent; that interferes with a child's participation in the classroom, community, or home activities; that impacts the learning of other children (e.g., aggression, property destruction); and that is perceived by caregivers and teachers to be a problem. The strategies are based on many years of work with young children and the research literature on SWPBIS. Our focus is to use the Building Blocks framework to teach the skills and behaviors children need to demonstrate in early childhood settings. Learning these important social-emotional skills helps to prevent challenging or interfering behaviors. (For more information on preventing and responding to challenging behavior, see Dunlap and colleagues [2022].)

WHAT GROUP BEHAVIORS DO WE NEED TO TEACH?

The Head Start Early Learning Outcome Framework (U.S. Department of Health and Human Services [DHHS], 2015), under the domain of Approaches to Learning, notes that by age 5, children should be able to follow a classroom routine, ask for assistance when necessary, and manage materials in the classroom. Designing engaging classrooms and instruction to support children's on-task and appropriate behavior is fundamental. The belief that "every child is unique and can succeed" (U.S. DHHS, 2015, p. 3) reminds us that student failure is instructional failure, and it is the responsibility of the adults in the environment to make any necessary changes to ensure the success of every child.

A beginning step in any early learning classroom should involve *directly teaching* children what to do and how to engage with the toys and materials in our space. Child care, play groups, and preschool classrooms are often the first experience young children have being in a group and in a setting away from their immediate family. In many cases, children must learn the specific behaviors and skills necessary for being in a group with other children. These include but are not limited to the following:

- Following simple directions given to an individual.

- Following simple directions given to the group.

- Making classroom transitions, including putting materials away.

- Following basic classroom rules or expectations.

- Regulating and expressing emotions in a relevant manner.

- Using effective strategies to resolve conflicts with peers.

- Stopping an inappropriate behavior when asked by an adult.

Intentionally teaching children these skills goes a long way in preventing challenging behavior. By taking a proactive approach, we help children succeed and learn that school is a place where they can confidently succeed and are supported to learn new things. Waiting for children to struggle, be off task, or demonstrate challenging behavior requires that teachers must react, redirect, and respond to this misbehavior in some way. This may also lead to potentially negative consequences, such as a child being unofficially suspended or a family being told that a program is unable to meet their child's needs. Conversely, preemptively teaching children how to engage in certain routines and have meaningful, positive interactions with peers ensures they experience success and feelings of belonging in their early childhood setting. This is a large part of our bottom block in the Building Blocks framework—a high-quality early childhood environment.

THE IMPACT OF IMPLICIT BIAS ON TEACHERS' PERCEPTION OF CHALLENGING BEHAVIOR

Whenever we talk about behavior that is challenging for adults, we must talk about implicit bias and how it impacts both the overrepresentation in special education and high suspension and expulsion rates for children of color. Implicit bias refers to the attitudes or stereotypes that affect our understanding, actions, and decisions in an unconscious way. These biases can influence how we perceive and treat others, including young children in educational settings. Suspension and expulsion in early childhood education can have serious consequences for children's social, emotional, and academic development. Preschoolers who are suspended or expelled are more likely to experience negative outcomes, such as disengagement from school, lack of friendships, increased risk of dropping out later in life, and involvement with the juvenile justice system. Studies have consistently highlighted the disproportionate rates of suspension and expulsion for preschoolers of color, especially black, Hispanic, and Native children, when compared to their white peers (Gilliam et al., 2016; Hemmeter et al., 2021). The reasons for these disparities are multifaceted, but implicit bias on the part of educators and school or child care personnel is one significant factor. Preschoolers of color are more likely to experience harsher discipline due to stereotypes and assumptions about their behavior. This can lead to a cycle where young children are unfairly labeled as "problematic" or "difficult" when their behavior is developmentally typical.

To counteract implicit bias, teams must reflect on their interpretation of children's behavior and strive to be comfortable having potentially difficult conversations. Educators must create a culturally relevant classroom, where children and families are authentically represented. Adults need to spend positive time with each child each day, especially those who engage in behaviors that are challenging. Assessment methods need to be developed and used that do not perpetuate the systemic racism in education, but rather help teachers view behavior objectively and identify the function that behavior serves for the child. Finally, we must reach out to our supervisors, families, coaches, managers, and colleagues and ask for feedback about our teaching practices and environment to help identify biases and aim for improvement. Although increasing our awareness of bias is ongoing, difficult work, it is vital as we seek to create inclusive, welcoming, culturally responsive classrooms.

SCHOOL-WIDE POSITIVE BEHAVIORAL INTERVENTION AND SUPPORT

SWPBIS is a comprehensive approach focusing on teaching appropriate behaviors while preventing and reducing challenging and stigmatizing behaviors (www.pbis.org). A major goal of SWPBIS is to facilitate participation in meaningful activities and inclusive settings. A fundamental tenet of SWPBIS is that challenging behaviors have a communicative function. In other words, when children demonstrate these behaviors, they are trying to tell us something. They may be asking for attention or asking to be left alone; they may be trying to obtain some materials or trying to tell someone they do not want to share the materials. The Pyramid Model is one commonly used conceptual framework aligned with SWPBIS that is designed to prevent challenging behaviors while promoting social-emotional development and health for all children (Hemmeter et al., 2021).

Determine the Function: What Is the Child Trying to Tell Us With This Behavior?

All behavior is communication. When adults accept that challenging behaviors have a communicative function, the approach to preventing these behaviors changes. Rather than attempt to eliminate the behaviors immediately, teachers should try to understand what the child is attempting to communicate by engaging in the behavior. Are they telling us they are hungry? Do they need help with a new activity? Do they need the music turned down because it seems too loud? Do they need a break from an adult-directed activity? Once we have a clear idea of what a child is trying to tell us by engaging in the behavior, we can teach the child a better way to accomplish their goal that can be understood by everyone in their environment.

Teaching Alternative Behaviors: What Is a Better Way to Get a Need or Want Met?

When planning interventions around challenging behaviors, we always start by identifying an alternative behavior. An alternative behavior is one that helps the child express the same want or need as the challenging behavior but is universally understood and considered to be appropriate by the adults in their environment. We want all children to have the skills to get their needs and wants met in a way that is understood by the children and adults around them and to regulate their emotions when they feel upset, anxious, frustrated, or sad. For example, if a child throws a puzzle because they become frustrated and cannot get the pieces to fit, they need to learn three things: 1) how to ask a teacher for help, 2) how to regulate their emotions when frustrated or upset, and 3) that it is not okay to throw a puzzle. If we take a punitive approach and "punish" the child by putting them in time out or making them clean up the pieces, we are missing an opportunity to teach the child what they really need to learn—how to ask for help when frustrated. Consider the following example. A child hits a teacher to get the teacher's attention. The child needs to learn how to tap the teacher gently on the arm, raise their hand, or call the teacher's name to get their attention. They also need to learn that hitting is not acceptable. Again, if the child was punished or ignored for hitting, they would miss out on the instruction they need to get an adult's attention in a better way. See Table 12.1 for examples of challenging behaviors, functions, and alternative behaviors.

Drew's challenging behavior during transitions may be because he is trying to tell his teachers and family that he does not want to stop a fun activity or because he does not understand what is going to happen next. Drew's teachers and family could help him achieve this need for information by providing him with visual cues (e.g., pictures or

Table 12.1. Examples of functionally equivalent alternative behaviors

Challenging behavior	Function	Alternative behaviors to teach
Crawling around the middle of the circle area while the group is reading a book or singing a song	Getting peers' attention Getting a teacher's attention Needing more sensory input	Teach the child to get attention in better ways by raising their hand to share with the group or commenting to a peer. Teach the child to hold a fidget toy so they have something to do with their body. Teach the child to sit on a wobble seat so they have more input during the circle time routine.
Hitting a peer who came very close to the child	Trying to get away from a peer or get more personal space	Ask for more space. Ask for a teacher's help. Move away from the peer.
Running away from the group when it is time to line up and come inside from outdoor time	Getting a teacher's attention Wanting more time outside	Teach the child to ask for a teacher's attention. Teach the child to ask for more time to play. Teach the child to follow a schedule so they know what is coming next.
Biting a peer who took a toy away from the child	Access to the toy Needing sensory input	Teach the child to ask for a teacher's help. Teach the child to say, "No, that's mine." Teach the child to ask for the toy back. Teach the child other ways to get sensory input (e.g., an oral motor toy) if biting seems to feel good to them.

symbols) for the transition so he knows what to expect. They could teach him to ask for more time, using words or a picture card, so he could communicate the need to stay and play with a highly preferred activity for a bit longer.

THE BUILDING BLOCKS APPROACH TO PREVENTING CHALLENGING BEHAVIOR

The Building Blocks framework offers ways to approach challenging behaviors that meet the needs of an individual child. The framework encourages teachers to work with the team, including the family, to provide the right amount of support and instruction (e.g., Lucyshyn et al., 2015). When addressing challenging behaviors, teachers should begin by looking at the environment, whether classroom, child care setting, or play group (see the Quality Classroom Assessment Form in Appendix A and also available as a download), to ensure the bottom block (high-quality early childhood program) is in place. The classroom must provide appropriate activities, including a mix of active and quiet activities; an engaging environment, including enough space and materials in good working order; and an appropriate level of structure, including a schedule, simple classroom rules, and a room with clearly defined centers. There should be intentional teaching around social and emotional skills, in addition to other content and curricular topics. Perhaps most important are the meaningful and authentic relationships teachers have with children and their families.

Some children may need curriculum modifications to the physical or temporal environment and to the activities in the classroom. Many children, especially those who have difficulty with communication, may benefit from picture schedules or other visual cues to learn skills for successful transitions and free-choice time. Other children may need additional visual reminders to help them participate more fully, such as work mats during art projects, carpet squares during circle time, or labels or symbols on containers to facilitate cleanup. Other children may need more explicit instruction with ELOs or CFIS to acquire new skills in place of more interfering behaviors. For example, Drew needs explicit instruction to learn how to use the picture schedule and other visual supports, but once he learns the new routine, the visual supports will function like simple curriculum modifications. A child who demonstrates aggressive behavior may need repeated ELOs to learn how to share preferred materials without hitting. This type of intervention is not easy, but spending time with a child *before* the challenging behavior occurs will make teaching more effective and improve the entire classroom climate because the disruptive behavior is prevented. See Table 12.2 and the resources in Appendix T for additional information.

When the team is deciding what type of intervention to use with a child, it is helpful to systematically collect information about the child and the behavior (see Chapter 8). The problem-solving framework provides a series of steps for collecting information that will lead to a potential solution (e.g., Dunlap et al., 2022). Once you begin to use this framework to address challenging behaviors, you will realize that although many of the behaviors that occur in group settings are quickly resolved through intervention, others are not. It is important to monitor (i.e., collect data about) the child's behavior to make sure that the challenging behavior is decreasing. If it is not, you may need to reassess the behavior and try a different intervention.

All the strategies described in this chapter can be used across settings and by different adults (e.g., Dunlap et al., 2022). For example, a visual schedule used to provide information to the child during transitions could also be used at home, child care, or Sunday school. Consistency across settings and adults is a crucial characteristic of any plan to teach children new behaviors. When working with families to implement these strategies outside of the classroom, we must ensure that the behaviors being addressed are just as important to the family. Teachers should always ask for caregivers' feedback and input on behavior support plans and potential alternative behaviors. For example, families may have a specific word they use for "help" or "I'm finished" in their home language or have specific ways they help their child to calm down. In some cases, caregivers and other adults will also need training and coaching to help feel confident implementing these strategies. Regardless of the plan and whether coaching is necessary for caregivers, teachers should check in frequently with the family, share positive news and updates from school, and offer support.

PROBLEM-SOLVING FRAMEWORK FOR CHALLENGING BEHAVIORS

The following list outlines a system of addressing challenging behaviors in the classroom. This system includes the careful assessment, planning, and implementation of teaching plans that are used throughout the Building Blocks framework.

1. Define the challenging behavior.
2. Assess where and when the behavior is and is not a problem.
3. Assess what happens before and after the challenging behavior.
4. Determine what the child is attempting to communicate with the behavior.
5. Determine if the child needs to learn a better way to get their needs met.
6. Assess classroom supports (e.g., adults, instructional, environmental).
7. Assess classroom barriers.
8. Select an intervention (e.g., curriculum modification, ELO, or CFIS) and make a plan.
9. Implement the intervention.
10. Monitor the child's behavior to ensure change.
11. Monitor the implementation to make sure that the adults are doing what they planned to do.

Table 12.2. Examples of strategies for supporting developmentally appropriate group behavior using the Building Blocks framework

Building block	Strategies
Child-focused instructional strategies (CFIS)	If children do not have an effective communication system, teach them how to request and protest in ways that are understood by others in the environment.
	Teach children specific vocabulary to use in problem solving.
	Teach children to label their emotional states and be able to provide solutions to potential problems.
	Teach children how to say "Stop," "No, thank you," or "I don't like that," or some other way to protest in an appropriate manner.
	If a child is aggressive toward peers and the result of a functional behavioral assessment (FBA) suggests that they are attempting to gain their peers' attention, teach the child a more appropriate way to get their attention (e.g., tapping the person on the shoulder or saying their name).
	Teach children to use a solution chart or kit, a visual support strategy that provides alternative ways to solve common problems.
Embedded learning opportunities (ELOs)	Systematically teach calm-down strategies, such as taking deep breaths ("sniffing a flower and blowing out a candle"), counting to 10, or asking for a hug to help children manage and regulate emotions.
	Systematically teach children how to request toys from peers to decrease grabbing and aggression.
	Systematically teach children problem-solving skills for times when peer conflicts can occur.
	Teach children to use words to label their emotional states when they are experiencing the emotion (e.g., happy, sad, mad, frustrated, anxious).
	Provide positive, behavior specific feedback for children who are participating in classroom activities and following classroom rules.
Curriculum modifications (CMs)	Create a break area in the classroom where any child can take a break away from the group.
	Use picture schedules and other visual support strategies, including process charts that outline complex play activities.
	Use work mats and other strategies to help children define their own space.
	Limit the number of children in a center at one time to avoid crowding; use a check-in/check-out chart.
	Provide activities and materials in every center that appeal to the interest and abilities of the entire range of children in your classroom.
High-quality early childhood environment	Provide a clear and consistent classroom schedule, and teach children how to engage in each routine or activity.
	Establish a few simple classroom rules and/or expectations.
	Offer a well-designed environment, including clearly marked activity centers.
	Provide interesting, developmentally appropriate, and well-maintained materials.
	Include a variety and balance of activities, including activities for both active and quiet play.
	Develop meaningful, authentic relationships with children and their families and spend positive time with them each day.
	Ensure all aspects of a child's and family's identities are represented in the classroom.
	Create a break area or calm-down corner in the classroom where any child can take a break away from the group when necessary.

The system described here is similar to a *functional behavioral assessment* (FBA), which was first required by the Individuals with Disabilities Education Act Amendments of 1997 (PL 105-17) for children with challenging behaviors. The purpose of an FBA is to determine what function the behavior is serving for the child (Dunlap et al., 2022). In other words, an FBA attempts to determine what is motivating the behavior and what the child is communicating when they demonstrate the behavior. If the child has an IFSP or an IEP and demonstrates challenging behavior, you should conduct an FBA before you begin intervention or reach out to the child's IEP/IFSP case manager. In these cases, the representative from the school district is a key member of the team. This individual knows the district's procedures and can provide specific forms and assist with designing the FBA and behavior support plan.

Marta and Mao decided that they were trying to do too many different things at once and felt that they may be ignoring the basics of good planning and classroom arrangement. During nap time one afternoon, they used the Quality Classroom Assessment Form to assess their bottom block. Based on this form, they made plans for changing three simple things:

1. They developed a regular daily schedule and stuck to it. They also made a copy of the schedule with pictures and taught the children how to determine what the next activity would be.

2. They taught specific friendship skills at large-group time, such as sharing, problem solving, and emotional regulation. They used curriculum modifications (visuals, peer support) to ensure this instruction was accessible for everyone.

3. They increased the number of positive statements they made to children every day.

Making these changes was hard at first, but Marta and Mao are very pleased with the changes. After only 2 weeks, the children knew the routine and everyone in the classroom seemed happier and calmer. Children were starting to navigate conflicts on their own, and they recently introduced a "Problem-Solving Box" that was a great help. Their next step is developing specific plans for three children who need additional help with physical behaviors, but they are proud of themselves and the children.

After reflecting on the function of Drew's behavior, the team thought the best way to proceed was to create a curriculum modification and make Drew his own visual schedule of the daily activities. They thought that he may be communicating his need for more information about changes to the schedule and wanted to make sure he knew what was coming next. After trying this for 2 weeks with no change in behavior, the team decided that Drew needed more instruction. They made Drew a series of transition cards using picture symbols the teacher downloaded from www.challengingbehavior.org and created an ELO plan to focus on teaching these transitions using each card. When it was time for a transition, the teacher simply put the appropriate symbol in Drew's hand and said, "Drew, it is time to go to circle/snack/free play/outside." It worked! After only 1 week, Drew was making transitions with no problem. His teacher has made a set of these cards for home and the child care center to see if they help with his transition problems in those settings. They are so happy to see him appearing more calm, regulated, and happy in the classroom.

SUMMARY

Teaching children the skills they need to be in a group with others is a huge part of creating inclusive environments. As part of the bottom block, high-quality early childhood program, all children must be taught the routines and expectations and teachers must intentionally develop meaningful relationships with every child. Even with this foundation in place, many children will need extra help and instruction to participate with their peers. This instruction often includes teaching children how to get their needs and wants met, without engaging in challenging behaviors. The Building Blocks framework helps teams plan for the right amount of support: curriculum modifications, more practice with ELOs, or individualized instruction with CFIS.

Chapter **13**

Final Thoughts

Inclusion is about belonging and participating in a diverse society. Inclusive early learning environments—classrooms, child care, play groups, and homes—reflect the cultures, values, and beliefs of the communities in which they are located. The inclusion of young children with identified disabilities, developmental delays, and diverse abilities in early childhood classrooms is not only supported by federal law and research but also a reality for many children and families and an aspiration for others. A substantial number of research studies report positive outcomes for children with and without disabilities in inclusive settings (e.g., Odom et al., 2011). Although inclusion is supported by law, science, and civil rights, too many children and families still do not have access to inclusive early learning settings. Research identifies some of the challenges and complexities of inclusion. One of the challenges is how to provide needed specialized instruction without interfering with the social ecology or curricular integrity of the inclusive classroom or early learning program.

The Building Blocks framework offers practical suggestions to help teachers accomplish this task. This book offers early childhood teachers and teaching teams practical and evidence-based strategies for including and teaching each child in their early learning settings. Our aim is to help teachers and teams make good, data-based decisions when selecting and using appropriate levels of assistance, work collaboratively, and use effective teaching strategies to help children attain important and worthwhile objectives.

Specialized instruction is an important component of inclusion. It is the cornerstone of special education. Instruction is intentional and evaluated. In fact, if the instruction being provided in any program is not helping the children learn, it is the responsibility of the educational team to make changes to that instruction. Effective instruction yields child success. At the same time, in the effort to enhance children's development and learning, teaching teams should remember that the early childhood curriculum is broad and that there are many important things for young children to learn during the early years. For example, children expand their communication skills and begin to learn about reading and writing. They learn to get along with others and make friends. They refine their physical abilities. They learn to solve problems. They learn all sorts of new concepts and ideas about the world. They become more capable and independent. Always, the goal is to promote curiosity and a positive attitude toward learning and life. Thus, teaching efforts in inclusive classrooms must focus on the whole child and demonstrate appreciation for all these important areas of learning.

Inclusion is not simply about children's social experiences. One of the repeated findings of inclusion research is that just being in the general education classroom is not sufficient. There are critical features that are necessary for any child's early learning experiences. Their development must be nurtured. Experiences must be developmentally appropriate, engaging, culturally sustaining, and individually planned. The child must be supported so that the child may take advantage of the full complement of learning experiences. Instruction must be tailored to address individual needs, and the effects of the instruction must be evaluated to ensure that every child is making meaningful progress.

The Building Blocks framework recognizes that providing individualized, specialized instruction in busy, action-packed classrooms and early learning programs is difficult. It takes planning, attention, evaluation, and teamwork. The framework provides teachers with differing levels of instructional supports—modifications, embedded teaching, and more intensive teaching—that build on a high-quality program for all. The goal is to make inclusion successful and rewarding for everyone. Successful teaching results in children learning the valuable skills and concepts identified for them and being able to use them in meaningful ways. Successful teaching means that children will participate, learn, and thrive in the classroom, in child care programs, in their homes, and in their communities.

Appendices

Quality Classroom Assessment Form

Date: _________________________   Classroom: _________________________________

Team members: ____

____

Goal: ____

Indicator	Yes	No	Not sure	Examples
1. Do children spend most of their time playing and working with materials or with other children?				
2. Do children have access to various activities throughout the day?				
3. Do teachers work with individual children, small groups, and the whole group at different times during the day?				
4. Is the classroom decorated with children's original artwork, their own writing, and stories they've dictated?				
5. Do children learn within meaningful (i.e., relevant to their home cultures, interests, and experiences) contexts?				
6. Do children work on projects and have periods of time to play and explore?				
7. Do children have an opportunity to play and explore outside every day?				

(page 1 of 2)

Indicator	Yes	No	Not sure	Examples
8. Do the literacy materials used in the classroom reflect the diversity of the children and families in the program?				
9. Is the curriculum adapted for those who are ahead as well as those who need additional help?				
10. Do the children and their families from all cultures, languages, and backgrounds feel welcome, safe, and secure within their early childhood program?				

Notes: ____

____

____

____

____

____

(page 2 of 2)

Classroom Action Worksheet

Date: _______________________

Team members: _______________________

Indicator*	What's the problem?	What can we do?	Who will do it?	By when?

* Abbreviated from Quality Classroom Assessment Form.

Child Assessment Worksheet

Date: _______________________

Teacher's name: ____   Child's name: ____

Classroom activities	Classroom expectations	Child's level of performance
		Strength _________ Average _________ Area of concern _________
		Strength _________ Average _________ Area of concern _________
		Strength _________ Average _________ Area of concern _________
		Strength _________ Average _________ Area of concern _________

APPENDIX C *(continued)*

Classroom activities	Classroom expectations	Child's level of performance
		Strength __________ Average __________ Area of concern __________
		Strength __________ Average __________ Area of concern __________
		Strength __________ Average __________ Area of concern __________
		Strength __________ Average __________ Area of concern __________

(page 2 of 2)

IEP/IFSP Planning Worksheet

IEP Today

Date: _______________________

Teacher's name: _______________________   Child's name: _______________________

The "IEP Today" is based on the child's complete individualized education program (IEP) and tells the team the child's individual goals and the associated objectives that are the current focus of instruction.

Goal/domain	Current objective(s)

Child Planning Worksheet

Date: _______________________

Teacher's name: ____ Child's name: _______________________

This planning guide will help you collect more specific information for areas of concern for specific children. Using the Child Assessment Worksheet, identify three activities on which you would like to focus your attention. Once you identify the problem, collecting information is the next step for instructional planning for children in inclusive settings.

Key: CM = curriculum modification; ELO = embedded learning opportunity; CFIS = child-focused instructional strategy.

Activities	Define concern	What are you currently doing?	Ideas for instruction
			CM _________ ELO _________ CFIS _________ Describe:
			CM _________ ELO _________ CFIS _________ Describe:
			CM _________ ELO _________ CFIS _________ Describe:

Child Activity Matrix

Date: ___________________

Teacher's name: _________________________________   Child's name: _________________________________

Write the classroom schedule in the left-hand column. Write the child's current learning objectives across the top row. Fill in the appropriate cells with brief versions of the selected teaching strategy.

Key: CM = curriculum modification; ELO = embedded learning opportunity; CFIS = child-focused instructional strategy.

(page 1 of 1)

Classroom Activity Matrix

Date: _____________________ Teacher's name: ____

Write the children's names across the top row. Write the c assroom schedule in the left-hand column, starting with the second row. Fill in the appropriate cells with brief versions of the selected teaching strategy.

Key: CM = curriculum modification; ELO = embedded learning opportunity; CFIS = child-focused instructional strategy.

Staff Matrix

Classroom: ____

	Teacher 1	Teacher 2	Teacher 3
Routines and activities			

(page 1 of 1)

Evaluation Worksheet

Date: _______________________

Teacher's name: _______________________________________   Child's name: _______________________

Concern	Plan	Evaluation information		
		Counts _________________ Notes _________________ Products _________________ Did the plan work? Yes No What will you do next week?		
		Counts _________________ Notes _________________ Products _________________ Did the plan work? Yes No What will you do next week?		
		Counts _________________ Notes _________________ Products _________________ Did the plan work? Yes No What will you do next week?		

ELO-at-a-Glance

Date: _______________________

Team members: ____

____

Child's name: ____

Routines: ____

Objective: ____

____

What are you going to do?
What are you going to say?
How will you respond?
What materials do you need?
How many opportunities will you provide each day?

Monday	Tuesday	Wednesday	Thursday	Friday

Instruction-at-a-Glance

Date: _______________________

Child's name: ___________________________________ Teacher's name: ___________________________________

Objective: ____

____

1. Setting for instruction

When? ____

Where? ____

How often? ____

Materials needed? ____

2. Instructional interaction

Antecedent	Child behavior	Consequence
Instruction		Positive reinforcement
Prompt		Corrective feedback

(page 1 of 2)

3. Monitoring progress:

Instructions: For the numbers 5–0 and ND ("No data") in the columns representing number of trials, circle or draw a line through each number, depending on response:

◯ = correct, ╱ = incorrect.

Date

Current step														
	5	5	5	5	5	5	5	5	5	5	5	5	5	5
	4	4	4	4	4	4	4	4	4	4	4	4	4	4
	3	3	3	3	3	3	3	3	3	3	3	3	3	3
	2	2	2	2	2	2	2	2	2	2	2	2	2	2
	1	1	1	1	1	1	1	1	1	1	1	1	1	1
	0	0	0	0	0	0	0	0	0	0	0	0	0	0
Criteria:	ND	ND	ND	ND	ND	ND	ND	ND	ND	ND	ND	ND	ND	ND

4. Comments, questions, or issues to discuss with the team:

____

____

____

____

____

____

____

____

____

____

____

(page 2 of 2)

Inclusion Collaboration Checklist

Classroom: ____

Team members: ____

Date: _______________________________

Collaboration practice	Implemented?			Notes
	Yes	No	Sometimes	
Our team creates opportunities to get to know one another.				
Our team has developed our shared goals and classroom expectations.				
Our team has regular, protected meeting times.				
Our team has a way to share documentation and meeting notes.				
Our team has clearly defined roles and responsibilities.				
Our team supports each other to reflect on behavior and have difficult conversations about equity and implicit bias.				

(page 1 of 1)

Clarifying the Schedule Checklist

Classroom: ____

Team members: ____

Observer: ____

Date: ___________________________

Effective schedule practice	Yes	No	Sometimes	Notes
The team uses a visual schedule that is posted at children's eye level and includes visual information about each activity.				
The team references the schedule throughout the day and before each transition.				
There is a balance of active and quiet times.				
There are times for smaller group and whole-group instruction and/or play.				
There is outdoor time every day.				

Effective schedule practice	Yes	No	Sometimes	Notes
There is a balance of child- and adult-directed activities.				
Children are actively participating in activities and play during the majority of the day.				
There is adequate time for routines and activities, including transitions.				
We minimize children's waiting time between activities and during transitions.				
The schedule is used to create an activity matrix.				
Next Steps for Clarifying the Schedule				
What will you do? Who is responsible? What is our timeline?				

(page 2 of 2)

Clarifying the Child's Objective

Team members: ____

Observer: ____

Child: ____ Date: ____________________

Overarching goal (What is the main point of this goal?):
What is the IEP or IFSP goal?
What is the main point of this goal? What does the child need to learn? Is this goal developmentally and culturally appropriate?
What is the child's baseline? (e.g., What are they currently doing in relation to this skill?)
Do we need to break this down into smaller components? Step 1:
Step 2:
Step 3:
Step 4:
Step 5:
How will we know when the child has learned this skill? (e.g., What assessment strategy will we use to measure the child's learning?)

Curriculum Modification Planning Form

Team members: ____

Child: ____

Observer: ____ Date: _______________

Routine	Curriculum modification	In place?

(page 1 of 1)

Curriculum Modifications Checklist

Team members: ____

Observer: ____

Child: ____ Date: _____________

Curriculum modification(s) (CM): ____

Routine(s): ____

CM practice	Yes	No	Sometimes	Notes
Is the CM enabling the child to participate in the learning environment?				
Is the CM enabling the child to be more independent?				
Is the CM implemented intentionally and consistently?				
Is the CM ready to be faded in some way, to promote independence?				
Is the CM included and up to date in the activity matrix?				
Next Steps for CM Implementation				
What will you do? Who is responsible? What is our timeline?				

(page 1 of 1)

Teaching Episode Checklist

Team members: ____

Observer: ____

Routine or activity: ____

Child: ____ Date: __________________

Objective: ____

Directions: Place a checkmark in the cells for each component of the teaching episode that was implemented correctly and an "x" in the cells for each component that was not implemented.

	Cue	Prompt	Response	Feedback
Complete this row prior to the observation.				Correct: Incorrect:
Trial 1				
Trial 2				
Trial 3				
Trial 4				

APPENDIX Q *(continued)*

	Cue	Prompt	Response	Feedback
Trial 5				
Trial 6				
Trial 7				
Trial 8				
Trial 9				
Trial 10				

Next Steps for Teaching Episodes

(page 2 of 2)

Embedded Learning Opportunities Checklist

Team members: ____

Completed by: ____

Child's objective: ____

Routine or activity: ____

Child(ren): _____________________________________ Date: __________

ELO practice	Yes	No	Sometimes	Notes
The classroom/environment has an activity matrix with planned ELOs across the day.				
ELOs are taught within natural routines that make sense for the objective (e.g., working on a child identifying their name during circle when name tags are out or working on zipping a coat before going outside).				
ELOs involve materials and activities the child is interested in.				

ELO practice	Yes	No	Sometimes	Notes
ELOs include a clear teaching episode: 1. Clear directions 2. Enough time for the child to respond 3. Immediate feedback				
ELOs are provided often enough for the child to make progress on their goals.				
The team checks each week to make decisions about the next steps.				
Next Steps for ELO Implementation				
What will you do? Who is responsible? What is our timeline?				

(page 2 of 2)

Child-Focused Instruction Strategies Checklist

Team member: _______________________________________

Completed by: _______________________________________

Child: _______________________________________

Child's objective: _______________________________________

____

Setting for instruction:

When: _______________________________________

Where: _______________________________________

How often: _______________________________________

Materials needed: _______________________________________

Date: _______________________________________

CFIS component: Teacher behavior	Yes	No	Sometimes	Notes
The classroom has an activity matrix with planned CFIS across the day.				
The teacher sets the environment up for instruction (has the necessary materials and has arranged the environment).				
Teacher gives a clear, discrete cue.				
Teacher provides enough wait time.				

(page 1 of 2)

CFIS component: Teacher behavior	Yes	No	Sometimes	Notes
The teacher provides immediate feedback that matches the child's response (within 1–2 seconds of the child's response).				
If the child is correct, the teacher provides positive reinforcement aligned with the Instruction-at-a-Glance (e.g., "You stood up! Well done!").				
If the child is incorrect or does not respond, the teacher provides corrective feedback when the child makes an error, and the teacher models the correct response.				
Teacher collects data.				
Number of CFIS trials observed				
Did the number of trials match with the Instruction-at-a-Glance?				
Next Steps for CFIS Implementation				
What changes need to be made with this CFIS?				

Online Resources

Cultivate Learning

https://cultivatelearning.uw.edu/
Cultivate Learning is a professional learning, research, and evaluation center at the University of Washington with a focus on early childhood and expanded learning opportunities. The center produces professional development resources and provides training for early childhood teachers, child care and after-school providers, and leaders through institutes, workshops, and coaching. An important focus is building systems of quality early care and education. The website offers a multitude of professional development modules, tip sheets, and other resources. Many are aligned with the Building Blocks framework.

The Division for Early Childhood

https://www.dec-sped.org/
The Division for Early Childhood (DEC) is the largest international professional organization dedicated to supporting families and young children who have or are at risk for developmental delays and disabilities. DEC is one of 17 divisions of the Council for Exceptional Children (CEC), the largest professional organization dedicated to improving the educational success of individuals with disabilities and/or gifts and talents. This site includes position statements, professional development opportunities, and information on the DEC Recommended Practices.

Early Childhood Technical Assistance Center

https://ectacenter.org/
The Early Childhood Technical Assistance (ECTA) Center supports state IDEA Part C and Part B, Section 619 programs in developing more equitable, effective, and sustainable state and local systems that support access and full participation for each and every young child with a disability and their family. The ECTA Center's website includes many resources for providers to implement evidence-based practices.

Early Childhood Learning and Knowledge Center

https://eclkc.ohs.acf.hhs.gov/
The Early Childhood Learning and Knowledge Center (ECLKC) provides high-quality, practical resources and approaches that build early childhood education program capacity. ECLKC is a primary resource for Head Start. The National Training and Technical Assistance section of the website also supports consistent practices across communities, states, tribes, and territories via a range of modules, tip sheets, resources, and information for families.

Harvard Center on the Developing Child

https://developingchild.harvard.edu/
The Harvard Center on the Developing Child includes many resources related to key scientific concepts that impact child development. Videos on brain architecture, executive functioning, toxic stress, serve and return interactions, and resilience are fantastic resources for better understanding how children's brain development is influenced by high-quality early childhood environments and interactions.

Head Start Center for Inclusion

https://headstartinclusion.org/
Housed within the ECLKC site, the Head Start Center for Inclusion provides resources and guidance for organizing and planning instruction for the inclusive Head Start classroom. This site contains numerous training materials, tip sheets, visuals, social stories, and more to support all children's learning and growth in the classroom.

IRIS Center

https://iris.peabody.vanderbilt.edu/
The IRIS Center develops and disseminates free, engaging online resources about evidence-based instructional and behavioral practices to support the education of all students, particularly struggling learners and those with disabilities.

National Association for the Education of Young Children

https://www.naeyc.org/
The National Association for the Education of Young Children (NAEYC) is a professional membership organization that works to promote high-quality early learning for all young children, birth through age 8, by connecting early childhood practice, policy, and research. NAEYC provides articles, books, professional learning, and a range of useful resources for early childhood educators.

National Center for Pyramid Model Innovations

https://challengingbehavior.org/
The National Center for Pyramid Model Innovations (NCPMI) provides resources, training materials, and tools to implement, scale up, and sustain effective practices and policies to equitably support the social, emotional, and behavioral outcomes of young children with, and at risk for, developmental delays or disabilities. The goal of the center is assisting states and programs in developing sustainable systems for the equitable implementation of the Pyramid Model for Promoting Social-Emotional Competence in Infants and Young Children (Pyramid Model) within early intervention and early education programs. The Resource Library contains a wealth of visual and classroom supports and related materials translated into multiple languages.

The Haring Center

https://haringcenter.org/
The Haring Center for Inclusive Education at the University of Washington provides early childhood education to children with and without disabilities, conducts leading-edge research to advance inclusive learning, and provides innovative professional development to educators and providers worldwide. The Professional Development and Training Team page includes tip sheets, recorded webinars, and current professional development opportunities. Many of these resources align with the Building Blocks framework.

References

Allen, K. E., Hart, B., Buell, J. S., Harris, F. T., & Wolf, M. M. (1964). Effects of social reinforcement on isolate behavior of a nursery school child. *Child Development, 35*(2), 511–518.

Americans with Disabilities Act (ADA) of 1990, PL 101-336, 42 U.S.C. §§ 12101 *et seq.*

Baker, B. L., & Brightman, A. J. (2004). *Steps to independence: Teaching everyday skills to children with special needs* (4th ed.). Paul H. Brookes Publishing Co.

Barnett, W. S., Jung, K., Wong, V., Cook, T., & Lamy, C. (2007). *Effects of five state prekindergarten programs on early learning.* National Institute for Early Education Research.

Barton, E. E., & Smith, B. J. (2015a). Advancing high-quality preschool inclusion: A discussion and recommendations for the field. *Topics in Early Childhood Special Education, 35,* 69–78.

Barton, E. E., & Smith, B. J. (2015b). *The preschool inclusion toolbox: How to build and lead a high-quality program.* Paul H. Brookes Publishing Co.

Berrueta-Clement, J. R., Barnett, S. J., & Weikart, D. P. (1984). Changed lives: The effects of the Perry Preschool Program on youths through age 19: Reviewing and interpreting study outcomes over time. In L. H. Aiken & B. H. Kehrer (Eds.), *Evaluation studies review annual* (Vol. 10). Sage Publications.

Boyes-Watson, C., & Pranis, K. (2015). *Circle forward: Building a restorative school community.* Living Justice Press.

Bredekamp, S., & Joseph, G. E. (2024). *Effective practices in early childhood education: Building a foundation* (5th ed.). Pearson.

Bricker, D., Dionne, C., Grisham, J., Johnson, J., Macy, M., Slentz, K., & Waddell, M. (2022a). *Assessment, Evaluation, and Programming System for Infants and Children (AEPS-3)* (3rd ed.). Paul H. Brookes Publishing Co.

Bricker, D. D., Felimban, H. S., Lin, F. Y., Stegenga, S. M., & Storie, S. O. M. (2022b). A proposed framework for enhancing collaboration in early intervention/early childhood special education. *Topics in Early Childhood Special Education, 41*(4), 240–252.

Brillante, P., Chen, J. J., Cuevas, S., Dundorf, C., Brown Hoffman, E., Meier, D. R., Mindes, G., & Roy, L. R. (2023). *Casebook developmentally appropriate practice in early childhood programs.* National Association for the Education of Young Children.

Brown, W. H., & Conroy, M. A. (2011). Social-emotional competence in young children with developmental delays: Our reflection and vision for the future. *Journal of Early Intervention, 33*(4), 310–320.

Build Initiative: Strong Foundations for Our Youngest Children. (2024). https://buildinitiative.org/

Burchinal, M. (2018). Measuring early care and education quality. *Child Development Perspectives, 12,* 3–9.

Buysse, V., & Peisner-Feinberg, E. S. (Eds.). (2013). *Handbook of response to intervention in early childhood.* Paul H. Brookes Publishing Co.

Carle, E. (1967). *Brown bear, brown bear, what do you see?* Henry Holt.

Carle, E. (1969). *The very hungry caterpillar.* Philomel.

Catalino, T., & Meyer, L. E. (Eds.). (2016). *DEC Recommended Practices Series No. 2: Environment.* Division for Early Childhood.

Center for Applied Special Technology (CAST). (2018). *Universal design for learning guidelines* (Version 2.2). http://udlguidelines.cast.org

Collins, B. C. (2021). *Systematic instruction for students with moderate and severe disabilities* (2nd ed.). Paul H. Brookes Publishing Co.

Cost, Quality, and Child Outcomes Study Team. (1995). *The study of cost, quality, and child outcomes in child care centers.* Department of Economics, University of Colorado at Denver.

Daugherty, S., Grisham-Brown, J., & Hemmeter, M. L. (2001). The effects of embedded skill instruction on the acquisition of target and nontarget skills in preschoolers with developmental delays. *Topics in Early Childhood Special Education, 21,* 214–221.

Diamond, A., & Lee, K. (2011). Interventions shown to aid executive function development in children 4 to 12 years old. *Science, 333*(6045), 959–964.

Division for Early Childhood. (2014). *DEC recommended practices in early intervention/early childhood special education 2014.* http://www.dec-sped.org/recommendedpractices

Division for Early Childhood. (2021). *Position statement on multitiered system of support framework in early childhood.* https://www.decdocs.org/position-statement-mtss

Division for Early Childhood & National Association for the Education of Young Children. (2009). *Early childhood inclusion: A joint position statement of the Division for Early Childhood (DEC) and the National Association for the Education of Young Children (NAEYC)*. The University of North Carolina, FPG Child Development Institute.

Dunlap, G., Fox, L., Lee, J. K., Strain, P. S., Vatland, C., Joseph, J. D., & Turnbull, A. (2016). *Prevent-teach-reinforce for families: A model of individualized positive behavior support for home and community*. Paul H. Brookes Publishing Co.

Dunlap, G., Wilson, K., Strain, P., & Lee J. K. (2022). *Prevent-teach-reinforce for young children*. Paul H. Brookes Publishing Co.

Early Childhood Technical Assistance Center. (n.d.). *Outcomes*. http://ectacenter.org/outcomes.asp

Elementary and Secondary Education Act of 1965, PL 89-10, 20 U.S.C. §§ 241 *et seq.*

Eastman, P. D. (1961). *Go, dog, go*. Random House.

Emberley, E. (1992). *Go away, big green monster!* Little, Brown, and Company.

Epstein, A., Hohmann, M., & High/Scope Educational Research Foundation. (2012). *The HighScope preschool curriculum*. High/Scope Press.

Every Student Succeeds Act of 2015, PL 114-95, 20. U.S.C.

Fixsen, D. L., Naoom, F. F., Blasé, K. A., Friedman, R. M., & Wallace, F. (2005). *Implementation research: A synthesis of the literature*. University of South Florida, Louis de la Parte Florida Mental Health Institute, The National Implementation Research Network (FMHI Publication #231). https://nirn.fpg.unc.edu/resources/implementation-research-synthesis-literature

Fowler, S. A., Dougherty, B. S., Kirby, K. C., & Kohler, F. W. (1986). Role reversals: An analysis of therapeutic effects achieved with disruptive boys during their appointments as peer monitors. *Journal of Applied Behavior Analysis, 19*(4), 437–444.

Friend, M., & Cook, L. (2013). *Interactions: Collaboration skills for school professionals* (7th ed.). Pearson.

Fritsch, K., & McGuire, A. (2021). *We move together*. AK Press.

Fuson, K. C., Clements, D. H., & Sarama, J. (2015). Making early math education work for all children. *Phi Delta Kappan, 97*(3), 63–68.

Gauvreau, A., & Sandall, S. R. (2018). Activity matrices: Tools for planning, organizing and implementing instruction in early childhood settings. In P. A. Snyder & M. L. Hemmeter (Eds.), *Instruction: Effective strategies to support engagement, learning, and outcomes*. DEC Recommended Practices Monograph Series No. 4. Division for Early Childhood.

Gauvreau, A. N., & Schwartz, I. S. (2013). Using visual supports to promote appropriate behavior in young children with Autism and related disorders. *Young Exceptional Children Monograph Series, 15*, 29–44.

Gay, G. (2010). *Culturally responsive teaching* (2nd ed.). Teachers College Press.

Giangreco, M., Dennis, R., Edelman, S., & Cloninger, C. (1994). Dressing your IEPs for the general education climate: Analysis of IEP goals and objectives for students with multiple disabilities. *Remedial and Special Education, 15*, 288–326.

Gilliam, W. S., Maupin, A. N., Reyes, C. R., Accavitti, M., & Shic, F. (2016). Do early educators' implicit biases regarding sex and race relate to behavior expectations and recommendations of preschool expulsions and suspensions. *Yale University Child Study Center, 9*(28), 1–16.

Goldstein, H., Lackey, K. C., & Schneider, N. J. (2014). A new framework for systematic reviews: Application to social skills interventions for preschoolers with autism. *Exceptional Children, 80*(3), 262–286.

Grisham-Brown, J., & Hemmeter, M. L. (2017). *Blended practices for teaching young children in inclusive settings*. Paul H. Brookes Publishing Co.

Gulbou, E., Yucesoy-Ozkan, S., & Rakap, S. (2023). Embedded instruction for young children with disabilities: A systematic review and meta-analysis of single-case experimental research studies. *Early Childhood Research Quarterly, 63*, 181–193.

Guralnick, M. J., & Bruder, M. B. (2016). Early childhood inclusion in the United States: Goals, current status and future directions. *Infants and Young Children, 29*, 166–177.

Hamre, B. K., LaParo, K., Pianta, R. C., & LoCasale-Crouch, J. (2014). *Classroom Assessment Scoring System (CLASS) manual, infant*. Paul H. Brookes Publishing Co.

Hamre, B. K., & Pianta, R. C. (2005). Can instructional and emotional support in the first-grade classroom make a difference for children at risk of school failure? *Child Development, 76*(5), 949–967.

Harms, T., Clifford, R. M., & Cryer, D. (2015). *Early Childhood Environment Rating Scale* (3rd ed.). Teachers College Press.

Harms, T., Cryer, D., & Clifford, R. M. (2007). *Family Child Care Environment Rating Scale* (Rev. ed.). Teachers College Press.

Harms, T., Cryer, D., Clifford, R. M., & Yazejian, N. M. (2017). *Infant/Toddler Environment Rating Scale* (3rd ed.). Teachers College Press.

Hart, B., & Risley, T. R. (1975). Incidental teaching of language in the preschool. *Journal of Applied Behavior Analysis, 8*, 411–420.

Hart, B., & Risley, T. R. (1995). *Meaningful differences in the everyday experience of young American children*. Paul H. Brookes Publishing Co.

Hartup, W. W. (2017). Children and their friends 1. In *Issues in childhood social development* (pp. 130–170). Routledge.

Hemmeter, M. L., Ostrosky, M. M., & Fox, L. (2020). *Unpacking the Pyramid Model*. Paul H. Brookes Publishing Co.

Hemmeter, M. L., Ostrosky, M. M., & Fox, L. (2021). *Unpacking the Pyramid Model: A practical guide for preschool teachers.* Paul H. Brookes Publishing Co.

Hemmeter, M. L., Snyder, P. A., Fox, L., & Algina, J. (2016). Evaluating the implementation of the Pyramid Model for promoting social-emotional competence in early childhood classrooms. *Topics in Early Childhood Special Education, 36*(3), 133–146.

Hepting, N. H., & Goldstein, H. (1996). What's natural about naturalistic language intervention? *Journal of Early Intervention, 20,* 249–265.

Heroman, C., Tabors, P. O., & Teaching Strategies, Inc. (2010). *Teaching Strategies GOLD: Birth through kindergarten: Assessment toolkit.* Teaching Strategies.

HighScope Educational Research Foundation. (2015). *Child Observation Record (COR) advantage.* High/Scope Press.

HighScope. (2021). *Essentials of active learning in preschool* (2nd ed.). HighScope Educational Research Foundation.

Hintz, A., & Smith, A. T. (2013). Mathematizing read-alouds in three easy steps. *The Reading Teacher, 67*(2), 103–108.

Hojnoski, R. L., Gischlar, K., & Missall, K. N. (2009). Improving child outcomes with data-based decision-making: Graphing data. *Young Exceptional Children, 12*(4), 15–30.

Horn, E., & Banerjee, R. (2009). Understanding curriculum modifications and embedded learning opportunities in the context of supporting all children's success. *Language, Speech, and Hearing Services in Schools, 40,* 406–415.

Horn, E., Lieber, J., Li, S. M., Sandall, S. R., & Schwartz, I. (2000). Supporting young children's IEP goals in inclusive settings through embedded learning opportunities. *Topics in Early Childhood Special Education, 20,* 208–223.

Individuals with Disabilities Education Act Amendments of 1997, PL 105-17, 20 U.S.C. §§ 1400 *et seq.*

Individuals with Disabilities Education Improvement Act of 2004, PL 108-446, 20 U.S.C. §§ 1400 *et seq.*

Kasari, C., Locke, J., Gulsrud, A., & Rotheram-Fuller, E. (2011). Social networks and friendships at school: Comparing children with and without ASD. *Journal of Autism and Developmental Disorders, 41,* 533–544.

Kroeger, K. A., & Sorensen-Burnworth, R. (2009). Toilet training individuals with autism and other developmental disabilities: A critical review. *Research in Autism Spectrum Disorders, 3*(3), 607–618.

La Paro, K. M., Hamre, B. K., & Pianta, R. C. (2012). *Classroom Assessment Scoring System (CLASS) manual, toddler.* Paul H. Brookes Publishing Co.

Ledford, J. R., Lane, J. D., Elam, K. L., & Wolery, M. (2012). Using response-prompting procedures during small group direct instruction: Outcomes and procedural variables. *American Journal on Intellectual and Developmental Disabilities, 117*(5), 413–434.

Lee, S. H., Wehmeyer, M. L., Soukup, J. H., & Palmer, S. B. (2010). Impact of curriculum modifications on access to the general education curriculum for students with disabilities. *Exceptional Children, 76*(2), 213–233.

Lieber, J., Beckman, P. J., Hanson, M. J., Sando, S., Marquart, J. M., Horn, E. M., & Odom, S. L. (1997). The impact of changing roles on relationships between professionals in inclusive programs for young children. *Early Education and Development, 8,* 67–83.

Lieber, J., Horn, E., Palmer, S., & Fleming, K. (2008). Access to the general education curriculum for preschoolers with disabilities: Children's school success. *Exceptionality, 16*(1), 18–32.

Lucyshyn, J., Fossett, B., Bakeman, R., Cheremshynski, C., Miller, L., Lohrmann, S., Binnendyk, L., Khan, S., Chinn, S., Kwon, S., & Irvin, L. (2015). Transforming parent–child interaction in family routines: Longitudinal analysis with families of children with developmental disabilities. *Journal of Child and Family Studies, 24*(12), 3526–3541.

McBride, B. J., & Schwartz, I. S. (2003). Effects of teaching early interventionists to use discrete trials during ongoing classroom activities. *Topics in Early Childhood Special Education, 23,* 5–17.

McClelland, M. M., & Cameron, C. E. (2018). Developing together: The role of executive function and motor skills in children's early academic lives. *Early Childhood Research Quarterly, 46,* 142–151.

McCormick, L., & Feeney, S. (1995). Modifying and expanding activities for children with disabilities. *Young Children, 50*(4), 10–17.

McLean, M., Banerjee, R., Squires, J., & Hebbeler, K. (Eds.). (2020). *Assessment: Recommended practices for young children and families.* DEC Recommended Practices Monograph No. 7. Division for Early Childhood.

McLeskey, J., Barringer, M. D., Billingsley, B., Brownell, M., Jackson, D., Kennedy, M., Lewis, T., Maheady, L., Rodriquez, J., Scheeler, M. C., Winn, J., & Ziegler, D. (2017). *High-leverage practices in special education.* Council for Exceptional Children and CEEDAR Center.

Milam, M. E., Hemmeter, M. L., & Barton, E. E. (2021). The effects of systematic instruction on preschoolers' use of Stay-Play-Talk with their peers with social delays. *Journal of Early Intervention, 43*(1), 80–96.

Milam, M. E., Velez, M. S., Hemmeter, M. L., & Barton, E. E. (2018). Implementing peer-mediated interventions in early childhood classrooms (pp. 77–90). In P. A. Snyder & M. L. Hemmeter (Eds.), *Instruction: Effective strategies to support engagement, learning, and outcomes.* DEC Recommended Practices Monograph Series No. 4. Division for Early Childhood.

National Association for the Education of Young Children. (2019). Advancing equity in early childhood education https://www.naeyc.org/sites/default/files/globally-shared/downloads/PDFs/resources/position-statements/advancingequitypositionstatement.pdf

National Association for the Education of Young Children. (2022). *Developmentally appropriate practice in early childhood programs* (4th ed.). NAEYC.

National Professional Development Center on Inclusion. (2009). *Research synthesis points on quality inclusive practices.* https://npdci.fpg.unc.edu/sites/npdci.fpg.unc.edu/files/resources/NPDCI-Research-SynthesisPointsInclusivePractices-2011_0.pdf

No Child Left Behind Act of 2001, PL 107-110, 115 Stat. 1425, 20 U.S.C. §§ 6301 *et seq.*

Odom, S. L. (Ed.). (2001). *Widening the circle: Including children with disabilities in preschool programs.* Teachers College Press.

Odom, S. L., Buysse, V., & Soukakou, E. (2011). Inclusion for young children with disabilities: A quarter century of research perspectives. *Journal of Early Intervention, 33,* 344–356.

Paris, D., & Alim, H. S. (Eds.). (2017). *Culturally sustaining pedagogies.* Teachers College Press.

Peisner-Feinberg, E. S., Burchinal, M. R., Clifford, R. M., Culkin, M. L., Howes, C., Kagain, S. L., & Yazejian, N. (1999). *The children of the cost, quality and outcomes study go to school: Technical report.* University of North Carolina at Chapel Hill, Frank Porter Graham Child Development Center.

Phillips, B., & Halle, J. (2004). The effects of a teacher-training intervention on student interns' use of naturalistic language teaching strategies. *Teacher Education and Special Education, 27,* 81–96.

Pianta, R. C., La Paro, K. M., & Hamre, B. K. (2008). *Classroom Assessment Scoring System™ (CLASS).* Paul H. Brookes Publishing Co.

Pretti-Frontczak, K., Grisham, J., & Sullivan, L. (2023). *Assessing young children in inclusive settings.* Paul H. Brookes Publishing Co.

Ramey, C. T., Campbell, F. A., Burchinal, M., Skinner, M. L., Gardner, D. M., & Ramey, S. L. (2000). Persistent effects of early intervention on high-risk children and their mothers. *Applied Developmental Science, 4,* 2–14.

Razzetti, G. (2022). *Remote not distant: Design a company culture that will help you thrive in a hybrid workplace.* Liberationist Press.

Rehabilitation Act of 1973, PL 93-112, 29 U.S.C. §§ 701 *et seq.*

Sadao, K. C., & Robinson, N. B. (2010). *Assistive technology for young children: Creating inclusive learning environments.* Paul H. Brookes Publishing Co.

Sandall, S. R., Hemmeter, M. L., Smith, B. J., & McLean, M. (2005). *DEC recommended practices: A comprehensive guide for practical application in early intervention/early childhood special education.* Sopris West Educational Services.

Sandall, S. R., & Schwartz, I. S. (2013). Building Blocks: A framework for meeting the needs of all children. In V. Buysse & E. S. Peisner-Feinberg (Eds.), *Handbook of response to intervention in early childhood* (pp. 103–120). Paul H. Brookes Publishing Co.

Sandall, S. R., Schwartz, I. S., & Gauvreau, A. (2016). Using modifications and accommodations to enhance learning of young children with disabilities: Little changes that yield big impacts. In B. Reichow, B. A. Boyd, E. E. Barton, & S. L. Odom (Eds.), *Handbook of Early Childhood Special Education.* Springer.

Schreibman, L., Dawson, G., Stahmer, A. C., Landa, R., Rogers, S. J., McGee, G. G., Kasari, C., Ingersoll, B., Kaiser, A. P., Bruinsma, Y., McNerney, E., Wetherby, A., & Halladay, A. (2015). Naturalistic developmental behavioral interventions: Empirically validated treatments for autism spectrum disorder. *Journal of Autism and Developmental Disorders, 45*(8), 2411–2428.

Schwartz, I. S., Ashmun, J., McBride, B. J., Scott, C., & Sandall, S. R. (2017). *The Project DATA model for teaching preschoolers with autism.* Paul H. Brookes Publishing Co.

Schwartz, I. S., Garfinkle, A., & Davis, C. (2002). Arranging preschool environments to facilitate valued social and educational outcomes. In M. Shinn, H. Walker, & G. Stoner (Eds.), *Interventions for academic and behavior problems II: Preventive and remedial approaches.* National Association of School Psychologists.

Schwartz, I. S., & Kelly, E. M. (2021). Quality of life for people with disabilities: Why applied behavior analysts should consider this as a primary dependent variable. *Research and Practice for Persons with Severe Disabilities, 46*(3), 159–172.

Schwartz, I. S., & McBride, B. (2014). Getting a good start: Effective practices in early intervention. In K. D. Burton & P. Wolfberg (Eds.), *Educating learners on the autism spectrum: Preparing highly qualified educators and related practitioners* (2nd ed., pp. 82–105). Autism Asperger Publishing Company.

Schweinhart, L. J., Barnes, H. V., & Weikart, D. P. (1993). *Significant benefits: The High Scope Perry preschool study through age 27.* HighScope Press.

Snyder, P. A., & Hemmeter, M. L. (Eds.). (2018). *Instruction: Effective strategies to support engagement, learning, and outcomes.* In P. A. Snyder & M. L. Hemmeter (Eds.), *Instruction: Effective strategies to support engagement, learning, and outcomes.* DEC Recommended Practices Monograph Series No. 4. Division for Early Childhood.

Snyder, P., Hemmeter, M. L., & Fox, L. (2022). *Essentials of practice-based coaching.* Paul H. Brookes Publishing Co.

Snyder, P., Hemmeter, M. L., McLean, M. E., Sandall, S. R., McLaughlin, T., & Algina, J. (2018). Impact of professional development in preschool teachers' use of embedded instructional practices. *Exceptional Children, 84*(2), 213–232.

Snyder, P. A., Rakap, S., Hemmeter, M. L., McLaughlin, T. W., Sandall, S., & McLean, M. E. (2015). Naturalistic instructional approaches in early learning: A systematic review. *Journal of Early Intervention, 37*(1), 69–97.

Soanes, C. (Ed.). (2006). *Oxford dictionary of current English* (4th ed.). Oxford University Press.

Soukakou, E. (2016). *The Inclusive Classroom Profile.* Paul H. Brookes Publishing Co.

Strain, P. S., & Bovey, E. H. (2011). Randomized, controlled trial of the LEAP model of early intervention for young children with autism spectrum disorders. *Topics in Early Childhood Special Education, 31*(3), 133–154.

Strain, P. S., Guralnick, M. J., & Walker, H. M. (Eds.). (2013). *Children's social behavior: Development, assessment, and modification.* Elsevier.

Strain, P. S., & Hoyson, M. (2000). The need for longitudinal, intensive social skill intervention: LEAP follow-up outcomes for children with autism. *Topics in Early Childhood Special Education, 20,* 116–122.

Style, E. (1996). Curriculum as window and mirror. *Social Science Record, 33*(2), 21–28.

Teaching Strategies. (2022). *Creative curriculum for preschool* (6th ed.). Teaching Strategies.

Trivette, C. M., Dunst, C. J., Hamby, D. W., & O'Herin, C. E. (2010). Effects of different types of adaptations on the behavior of young children with disabilities. *Research Brief, 4*(1). Tots-n-Tech Institute.

U.S. Department of Health and Human Services, Administration for Children and Families, Office of Head Start. (2015). *Head Start early learning outcomes framework.* https://eclkc.ohs.acf.hhs.gov/sites/default/files/pdf/elof-ohs-framework.pdf

Weikart, D. P., Bond, J. T., & McNeil, J. T. (1978). The Ypsilanti Perry Preschool Project: Preschool years and longitudinal results through fourth grade. *Monographs of the High/Scope Educational Research Foundation* (Vol. 3). High/Scope Press.

Willems, M. (2003). *Don't let the pigeon drive the bus.* Hyperion.

Winton, P. J., Guillen, C., & Schnitz, A. (Eds.). (2019). *Teaming and collaboration building and sustaining relationships.* DEC Recommended Practices Monograph Series No. 6. Division for Early Childhood.

Wolery, M., Anthony, L., Caldwell, N. K., Snyder, E. D., & Morgante, J. D. (2002). Embedding and distributing constant time delay in circle time and transitions. *Topics in Early Childhood Special Education, 22,* 14–25.

Wong, C., Odom, S. L., Hume, K. A., Cox, A. W., Fettig, A., Kucharczyk, S., Brock, M. E., Plavnick, J. B., Fleury, V. P., & Schultz, T. R. (2015). Evidence-based practices for children, youth, and young adults with autism spectrum disorder: A comprehensive review. *Journal of Autism and Developmental Disorders, 45*(7), 1951–1966.

Wood, A. (2000). *The napping house.* HMH Books for Young Readers.

Yazejian, N., Bryant, D. M., Kuhn, L. J., Burchinal, M., Horm, D., Hans, S., File, N., & Jackson, B. (2020). The Educare intervention: Outcomes at age 3. *Early Childhood Research Quarterly, 53,* 425–440.

Yoshikawa, H., Weiland, C., Brooks-Gunn, J., Burchinal, M., Espinosa, L., Gormley, W. T., Ludwig, J., Magnuson, K., Phillips, D., & Zaslow, M. (2013). *Investing in our future: The evidence base on preschool.* Society for Research in Child Development. https://www.fcd-us.org/the-evidence-base-on-preschool/

Zelazo, P. D., Blair, C. B., & Willoughby, M. T. (2016). *Executive function: Implications for education* (NCER 2017-2000). National Center for Education Research, Institute of Education Sciences, U.S. Department of Education. http://ies.ed.gov/